INCOME BOOSTER
100+ Businesses you can start from home & ditch the 9-5

Large Print Edition

By: Andrew Borst
Consult A Blind Guy

ISBN: 979-8-9885221-2-6

Table Of Contents

Introduction

In this book, you're going to see a lot of ways you can work from home or online, to be your own boss, as well as be remote worker if you want to be an entrepreneur. This book was created to help you decide on what path you want to take for making an income that you will be happy with instead of being stuck in the typical day job or career everyone is used to today. Many people dream of the day they can have a liveable income and lifestyle that they desire, and this book covers many different ways for you to accomplish that. So I hope you find this information helpful in your journey to making an income and reaching your desired lifestyle. Some of these opportunities require further learning to comply with state and federal regulations, and others only require you to have the desire to do them. Others require personal experience, and some require no skill at all. I have created this book for you to see your options that most people don't consider or may not even know exist because they are not something you hear about like most jobs everyone is used to doing. I hope you enjoy this book filled with tons of opportunities, and there are also some worksheets included to help you figure out exactly how to go about moving forward with some of these options that you can make an income. If you're interested, feel free to watch my YouTube channel, where I also cover these options and answer questions from the audience. If you have questions, feel free to ask because if it already hasn't been answered, I may just make a video to answer it for you. Happy reading and good luck on your journey ahead, giving your income a boost. YouTube Channel: https://youtube.com/c/consultablindguy Website: https://consultablindguy.com Blog: https://consultablindguy.com/blog   By Andrew Borst

My disability is only part of who I am.

Yes. I have a disability. However, it is only one part of my life. I firmly believe that only the strongest are given these kind of challenges, such as the ones I face. My life would certainly be more accessible without such a demanding matter. However, I manage to nurture my health every day and still maintain a normal life.

I experience days that my blindness gets the best of me. On those days, I choose to take it easy and give my body the rest that it needs. Nevertheless, there are seven days in a week & 24 hours in a day. I can honestly say that much of that time is spent living my life according to my standards. I keep a positive mindset. This allows me to remain strong and feed my passion for life.

Unlike many others with similar conditions. I consider my vision challenge to be one of many responsibilities of life rather than a constriction. I maintain a perspective of hope & stick to a healthy lifestyle and follow a regimen that my doctor has prescribed. However, once I have done so, the rest of the day is mine to live as I choose. I refuse to throw in the towel on life simplyHome because I have been diagnosed with X-Linked Retinitis Pigmentosa. Instead,

I live life to the fullest & know that I deserve success. Today, I am grateful for all of the beautiful aspects of my life. I have a loving family, a cozy home, & a fun lifestyle. I truly live a good life.

Self-Reflection Questions:
1. Do I surround myself with supportive & positive people?
2. What can I do to boost my confidence?
3. Do I often dampen my mood by asking "why me"
Consider these questions and what they say about your perspective. You have the power to change your life by changing your mind. I, too dealt with these thoughts myself for the longest time, BUT I started looking at ways to make myself happier. One of those ways is helping others in similar situations.

Now ask yourself this question, What is my Superpower?

I bet you have a skill or joy in life that many of the disabled community has. Maybe it's music, perhaps it's writing, maybe it's singing or dancing. These are all things that can be shared and help you make new friends, achieve your dreams, or help find a career. The possibilities are endless.

Is Working From Home
a Good Choice for You?

Do you fantasize about waking up in the morning, walking sleepily down the hall to your home office with a steaming Cup of Joe, and plopping down in your chair to start working? Imagine the amount of money you'll save on gas, clothing, and childcare working from home. With today's technology, it's possible to make your fantasy of working at Consider the following as you decide whether you're a good candidate for working from home:

1. Do you work for a national or international company? The larger the company, often the more flexibility you'll have to work from home.
2. Is your company progressive? If the owners and management think out of the box and embrace change, you're in a great position to inquire about working at home.
3. Do you have a computer-oriented job? If most of your work is on the computer, present a good argument for how you can remain productive working from home. As long as you have a computer at home, you can get the proper software to perform your job at home.
- You'll have fewer co-worker interruptions when you work at home. If your house is quieter than working in a buzzing, lively office setting, you might be able to get more work done each day.

4. Can you obtain the special supplies your job requires? For example, a design architect will need a drafting table and various drawing tools, plus a computer to work from home. The nature of your work is a huge determinant as to whether you can work from home.
5. You'll need a designated workspace. Nothing fancy, a desk and chair devoted to work will suffice, along with a computer and internet connection.
6. How flexible is your boss? Supervisors and managers who demonstrate more flexibility in the work setting are more likely to agree to a trial period where you work at home. If your supervisor knows you well and understands your work, then they might be more willing to allow a trial work at home situation.

- During the trial period, you have an opportunity to demonstrate how well you can perform in your own home setting.
- When speaking with your supervisor, remember to mention that companies that promote more flexible work schedules benefit from less absenteeism and have reduced turnover.

7. Can you motivate yourself to get your work done? If you want to work from home, it's crucial for you to possess specific personal and professional characteristics. Are you a self-starter? Can you diligently follow a work schedule?

- If you're self-motivated and super-responsible, you'll likely be able to work from home with great success.

8. Can you prevent distractions at home? Think about everything that could interrupt or disturb your work efforts

at home. It will be necessary for you to take steps to ensure your work won't be disrupted.

- However, if you live alone or with a partner that works away from home full-time during the same time you'll be doing your job, you're already ahead of the game in terms of creating a productive work environment.

Depending on your company, the type of work you do, and your motivation, working from home might be a perfect solution. Think through these considerations to help you determine whether working in a home office setting is right for you. In the end, it just may pay off foryou and employer in terms of productivity and employee satisfaction.

6 Mistakes That Can Bring Disaster to Your New Business

Starting and running your own business can be very lucrative and fulfilling. It's also very challenging. Most small businesses fail. It's necessary to avoid the common pitfalls of small business ownership if you want to experience success. Most small businesses face considerable financial challenges at first. There's little room for mistakes in the early days. Ensure that you're not making avoidable errors. Educate yourself before taking the plunge. Small business owners can avoid many of the mistakes that lead to disaster:

1. **Failing to listen to customers**. Find out why customers buy your product or service and why they don't. Customer

feedback is imperative. Too many small business owners are so in love with a particular idea that they refuse to change to accommodate the market. Your customers are your best source of information. Conduct surveys or ask informal questions. Be flexible and change your approach when the feedback dictates it.

Weak leadership. It isn't necessary to be Attila the Hun, but small businesses require strong leadership. The typical employee in a small business often isn't considered qualified by larger firms. You'll frequently be faced with employees with limitations. Your leadership is necessary to drive and inspire them.

2. .Hiring the wrong people. Every company is disgruntled regarding the availability of good help. Even the most popular companies are plagued by hiring mistakes. However, big companies can absorb poor hiring decisions and keep on running.

- A small business owner can be severely harmed by a poor hire. Think about the lost time and headaches one bad employee can cause.

- If you don't have a human resources department, you're on your own. Take the time to ensure that you're hiring people that are effective in their job. Consider the job requirements and the temperament and background of any potential employees. It's much easier to avoid a mistake than to fix it.

3. **Undercapitalization**. When you barely have enough money to keep your business afloat, any small mishap can

be disastrous. You're also forced to do anything you can in the short-term to pay your bills. That's a poor way to run and grow a business. Ensure you have the funds you need to get your idea off the ground.

Not understanding the importance of marketing. New business owners are often convinced that their idea is so amazing that marketing is secondary. Nothing could be further from the truth. Most businesses need to spend around 15% of their annual revenue on marketing to survive. This amount can drop as the company gains traction. In many cases, you can do marketing for $1 a day.

- Small businesses need a marketing budget. When planning your business, ensure you have the funds necessary to let the world know that you exist.
4. Failing to recognize your competition. There might not be someone nearby competing with other restaurants of all types within your price point. Consider the other alternatives your customers have for their money. Your customers can always spend their money somewhere else. This is significant.
- Make a list of your closest competitors. How can you provide your product or service in a way that causes customers to favor your business?

Running a small business requires a wide range of skills. With so many hats to wear, mistakes are common. It's not necessary to be perfect, but the biggest mistakes can be avoided. Making a critical mistake can spell the end for your company. Learn about doing this early on before your start your business can save you plenty of time the critical errors business owners make and make plans to avoid them. And mistakes as you launch and grow your business. If you already have a business, it's not too late to learn these things now to save yourself more hassle down the road. The one mistake that you always need to keep in mind "DON'T GIVE UP.". Mindset is a big part of running a business. Every bit of effort put in will pay off in time.

5 Legitimate Ways to Make Money Online

The internet offers numerous opportunities for you to make money online. Unfortunately, the internet can also be a minefield of scammers. Because of this, many who have dreamed of earning a part-time or full-time income from home have given up. If you're dreaming of a way to supplement or replace your income at home, you can do so if you know where to look.

Try one or more of these ways to make money online:
1. **Freelance your expertise**. If your specialty lends itself to freelancing remotely, take advantage of your scheduling flexibility and begin seeking paid work online. If possible, ask your current employer or existing clients if they'd be comfortable allowing you to work from home.
  * Careers that often work well with freelancing include writing and editing, consulting, marketing, transcription,

medical coding, web/graphic designing, voiceover work, and programming, and much much more.

- Find clients by optimizing your website for the search engines, contacting local businesses, applying for gigs on Craigslist, and applying for freelance job openings on bidding sites.
- Some of the most popular bidding sites for freelancers are Upwork.com, Fiverr.com, Rev.com.

2. **Affiliate marketing.** Affiliate marketing is selling the products of others online for a commission If you're inconsistent and sporadic with your efforts, you'll be lucky to make $100 in a year. But if you're consistent and diligent with your efforts, the sky's the limit on your earnings.

- Affiliate marketing is all about doing your research before you begin trying to make money, and most of your money will come by planting seeds. In this industry, "seeds" are affiliate links. The more affiliate links you have on the net, the more money you'll make.
- It can take months to see serious income as an affiliate marketer. It's common to earn just $10 for the first few months of your affiliate marketing career, and then all of a sudden to start earning $2,000, $4,000, or more per month.

3. Virtual assistant. A virtual assistant is essentially an office or personal assistant that serves their clients from home rather than a traditional office setting. You'll likely answer emails, set appointments, and spend time making various types of spreadsheets or being a moderator for social media pages or live streams, depending on the business needs.

- Essentially, being a virtual assistant is like being a freelancer. You can have multiple clients at once. Generally, the pay rate ranges from $10 per hour as an entry-level assistant to about $40 per hour for highly experienced ones.
- Like most freelancers, you can also find virtual assistant jobs on freelance websites and Craigslist.

4. Blogging. As a blogger, you're your own boss. But with this freedom also comes great responsibility. You're in charge of creating daily blog posts, driving traffic to your blog, and sourcing advertisers for your blog. For greater success, you'll also want to build a list of targeted subscribers.

- The income for a blogger varies widely. You're paid by advertising revenue rather than on a per-project basis. Plus, you can make money from selling your products or the products of others for a commission through your blog and newsletter. Your income is directly correlated with your skills, efforts, and likeability.
- Keep your day job for at least a year. It takes a while to build up income in a blog. Some blogs can take two years or more to build up revenue that's equivalent to your current salary.

5. Selling your own product. The classic method of making money online is selling manufactured cell phone accessories, and there's a place for your business on the internet.

- To make money online by selling products, you must market your business diligently. Employ search engine optimization tactics, start a blog for your business, ensure that your website is easy to navigate, and embark on an advertising campaign to attract buyers.

While there are still many scams on the internet, a bit of legwork can help you find legitimate ways to make money from home. Seek forums for like-minded people online that can guide you in the right direction and help you steer clear of scams. Remember that no legitimate work at home opportunity asks you to pay in advance to work for them. Above all, use discretion and proceed with caution. Give the above opportunities a try for a legitimate way to put more cash in your pocket and more freedom into your schedule! These are just a few ways to make money from the comfort of your home or in your local cafe while you drink your favorite kind of coffee. Want to know more? Then you can check the website. https://consultablindguy.com or check out the social media pages and YouTube at Consult A Blind Guy.

5 Ways To Make Money While You Sleep

Who doesn't want to make money while they sleep? If you want to really make a lot of money, it's easier if you can do it 24/7. Any stream of income you can create that doesn't require your regular attention will take you a long way towards your goal. **Here are just a few ideas to get you thinking**:
1. **Hire an assistant.** The idea here is to get the contract for some work that pays reasonably well and then simply hire someone else to do the job. You pay them less than what

you're getting paid and keep the rest. If you can get enough work, you won't have to do much, and you can make some money, all while you sleep.

- For contracts involving offline work, bookkeeping, landscaping, and many other service businesses work well with this concept. Your job would be meeting current clients and getting new clients while your assistant does all the service work. Picking up ongoing, monthly contracts is where you make the most money.

- For contracts involving online work, such as programming, design, or graphics for websites, the least expensive virtual assistants are typically found in foreign countries where a day's pay is considerably less than it is here. Many qualified and skilled people all over the world would love to help you out.

- Online contracts. There are also marketplaces specifically for Look at marketplaces like upwork.com, fiverr.com, and others to obtain your workers in foreign countries. An Internet search will lead you to all the marketplaces you could use.

2. **Create a blog**. If you can get readers, you can make money. With a high-traffic site, you can earn a lot of money from advertising revenue. Pay-per-click ads can amount to a significant income on a popular site.

- With that regular audience, you can also sell products and services to them. The products and services don't even have to be your own! There are probably products related to your blog content that you could sell and take a cut of the proceeds.

3. **Buy a small business**. Most people focus on the Internet when trying to make money while they sleep. Any small business where you can hire other people to run it will work. Do you think the owner of 10 McDonald's franchises is in there flipping burgers? Your own bricks-and-mortar business might be the answer.

4. **Create affiliate websites**. This is similar to the blog idea, but an affiliate website is commonly dedicated to selling a single product. Maybe it's for a diet product or a dating strategy product. By creating a website with worthwhile content, you can attract people looking to spend money on the type of product that you're offering.

- You can find products on websites like clickbank.com and commissionjunction.com. There is no shortage of products, and you're sure to find something that you can sell.

5. **Write a book**. Specifically, write an eBook and sell it online. Amazon.com or barnesandnoble.com makes it extremely easy to sell your eBook, and they take care of everything. It's not likely that you'll make a ton unless you strike a chord with people, but you might be surprised.

- Create a mini-empire. If you have an eBook on raising chickens, why not have a website and a blog about raising chickens? You can establish yourself as an expert and have a lot of cross-advertising going on. Sometimes 1+1+1= 5.

- Pick something that a lot of people are willing to spend money on. Things like money, love, and health are goldmines. Who isn't interested in these things? There's more competition for sure, but that's where big money is located.
- Choose a topic you're passionate about. If you love it, then it's not really work.

Can you come up with some more ideas? Making money while you sleep can create the additional income you crave. Imagine if you spent your spare time creating passive income instead of watching TV every night. You'd be wealthy before you know it! It is a lot easier than most people think to get started and can make a ton of money in just a few simple steps and a short amount of time. There are plenty of influencers out there who can tell you this first hand. Pat Flynn, KarmaCashFlow, Sean Cannell, Dan Currier, Nick Nimmin, Dee Nimmin, Roberto Blake, just to name a few. So get out there and start creating the income you want and make your dreams a reality.

6 Tips for Becoming an Entrepreneur Later in Life

Entrepreneurs aren't limited by age, and you can start a successful business at any stage of your life. However, becoming an entrepreneur later in life has its own unique challenges.

Consider these tips for starting a business as an older individual:

- Avoid allowing others to limit your goals. As you get older, you may have more people in your life who try to persuade you away from the entrepreneur lifestyle.
- Your family and friends may have good intentions, but they can also limit your dreams.
- They may remind you that it's more challenging to start a new business as you get older because you have other responsibilities. Children, aging parents, and others can take up a lot of your time and present challenges when starting a business. However, knowing that these challenges exist can also help you make contingency plans for when time is tight.
- Ignore your age. Dreams don't have expiration dates, and entrepreneurs don't have age limits. As they say, "you're only as old as you feel." So if you feel like taking on the rigors of starting a new business, let your age be the last thing on your mind as you move forward with your business plans.
- Be open to learning from others. The most successful entrepreneurs are open to learning new ideas.
- Stay up to date on new advancements in your field, either by keeping in the loop yourself or by hiring employees or contractors that incorporate this into their tasks.
- Finding a mentor with successful business experience in your field can help your new business see profits quickly and plan for successful growth.

- Get your family involved. Successful entrepreneurs often have their family members involved in the business.
- Do your children want to help you build a business? Does your spouse have interesting ideas and want to collaborate with you? Your family can help you make your dream come true.
- Consider the impact of the business on your personal life. How will the business affect your family and ability to continue working your regular day job?
- A new business venture may be exciting, but it has consequences.
- It's important to consider the full impact of the new business on your personal life. Will you be able to spend time with your children and spouse as you launch the business?
- Your personal finances are another area that can be deeply affected by a new business. How do you plan to pay for the business? If your plan involves draining personal finances or getting new loans, then this can affect your entire family. It's important to discuss the changes with them before you take action.
- Consider the impact of your parents on the business. As your parents age, they may become dependent on you. Can you handle the complexities of being an entrepreneur and caring for your parents?
- Younger entrepreneurs may have decades before they have to worry about caring for their aging parents.

However, as an older entrepreneur, you don't have this luxury.

- You may have to handle multiple roles at the same time. How will you balance your lifestyle and finances to manage everything? Can you afford to start a new business if your parents need your help?
- Your parents can have a serious accident or health issue that makes you responsible for taking care of them. The expense of this situation can be detrimental to your efforts with your new business.

You can become a successful entrepreneur and build a strong business at any age. However, it's important to stay aware of the challenges that come with being an entrepreneur and make plans that will help you overcome these challenges. There can be any number of things that will spring up on you. If you're on disability at any age, it becomes more of a challenge, BUT it is still possible. There are all kinds of restrictions from the SSA. However, will you let that stop you from your success? NO! Because you want to achieve your dream. If you want to be successful as an entrepreneur, you will have to make difficult decisions and weigh many different risks versus rewards. There are several options you can make. I cannot tell you what the correct answer is for you. You can seek out the help of a professional you may know or find a freelancer, contact an attorney to ask questions about your specific situation and the legal side of any regulations for your area and limits you have on licensing, etc. Talk to friends and family who may know someone you can talk to or maybe join groups on Facebook, or

LinkedIn, or something like that to connect with someone. You would be surprised who you might find that may be able to help you. Just be wise on the multitude of scammers out there around the world. This applies to all people. Don't just automatically trust that they can. Check them out make sure they are who they say they are. A good way is to search for info on them on the other platforms. Most of them who know what they're doing or have a team established already for employees are on multiple platforms to connect with potential clients or other business-minded people. You will likely be able to figure it out in a short amount of time. When you're looking, be sure to look around. Some people may be very costly, and some can be reasonably priced. Do what you think is best and go for it. If you have the free time, then you can succeed in no time. There are plenty of options out there, and you can do it on your schedule and not have to spend a dime in some cases to get things started. In others, there can be some minor investment that needs to be made. They can range in price from cents a day to a few dollars a month or an annual fee, as one of my mentors likes to say. "You have skin in the game"-Pat Flynn. No risk, no reward is how I look at it. This pushes you to be successful. It may not succeed right off the bat, depending on what you choose to do. But after a few weeks, few months, you can have a successful beginning.

7 Ways to Make Money
With Your Computer

You can use your computer and free time for more than just surfing the internet and shopping. It's possible to make extra money with your computer in your spare time. There is a wide variety of opportunities to turn your skills and free time into a second income. In some cases, you might be able to create a full-time income.

Avoid just jumping into the first idea that looks good. Take a little time and investigate all the opportunities. The seven suggestions below are merely a good starting point. Investigate other options, too.

Commit to one or more of these tasks to boost your income:

1. **Perform microwork**. You might be familiar with Mechanical Turk on Amazon.com, which is one example of a microwork platform. Micro-tasks are small jobs that can be completed very quickly. A typical task might be to complete a questionnaire or perform a quick online search to find a specific piece of information.

   - Many websites have similar tasks available for pay, such as answering questions. You could be paid a fee or receive a portion of any revenue generation from traffic that reads your post.

   - Many micro-jobs only pay a few cents, so it's essential to work quickly. It's possible to earn as much as $25/hour even with these small jobs.

- Be sure to check the payment details. Some pay weekly while others pay monthly. In most cases, you must reach a payment threshold before you can collect your money.
2. **Become a blogger**. Half the world is trying to make money at blogging, and many people are actually successful. There is nearly unlimited potential, and it's easy to get started. A free Blogger.com account and Google Adsense can get you started without any money coming out of your pocket.
- The only real challenge is bringing enough people to your blog.
- Half the battle is writing well enough to keep people coming back. Covering an interesting topic helps, but you must also develop some writing skills.
- The other half of the battle is marketing. If 10% of the people that land on your site love it, it's just a matter of getting enough eyeballs to your website.
- Unless you can write like Hemingway or have a life that rivals the excitement of James Bond's escapades, writing exclusively about your own life is a challenging blog topic. Find something that interests you that will also appeal to a broad audience.
3. **Be a mock juror**. There are websites that provide mock juries to attorneys. Attorneys can test their cases and see what type of outcome and issues they can expect. Instead of using a mere 12 jurors, these mock juries consist of 50+ people. The attorneys receive a lot of valuable feedback, and you receive a paycheck.

- A couple of these websites include www.ejury.com and www.onlineverdict.com. Your review of the case will be online from the comfort of your home.

In most cases, the pay varies from $5 to $60 for 20-60 minutes of work. Some websites pay more than others, so look around. A few companies require you to attend in person. It can take all day, but the pay increases to $150.

- In most cases, the only requirements are the same as those for being a "real" juror. If you're over 18 years of age and a US citizen, you're probably eligible.
- Some companies pay via check, while others only use PayPal. Be sure that the payment method will work for you.
4. **Monetize your hobby**. Whether you collect baseball cards, create crafts, write romance novels, or like to y kites, there's likely a way you can turn your hobby into a second income.
- Sell your items or related items. If your hobby includes building or creating something, sell your own product. If you love golf, you could sell golf clothing, golf balls, or golf calendars. You could even sell golf vacation packages.
- Sell services. You could act as a consultant and provide your advice and expertise to others. You could also sell the services of others for a commission.

Use local classifieds for free, take advantage of online marketplaces, or set up your own website. It's easy and free when you use the WordPress software from Wordpress.org. All you need is hosting.

5. **Become a peer-to-peer lender.** It's possible to lend your money on one of the peer-to-peer lending websites, like prosper.com, lendingclub.com, and many more. The average return is quite good, and the risks can be small.

- Some websites distribute your loan to multiple borrowers. If one person defaults, it has very little impact on your loan.
- Other websites will allow you to choose a single person or company to loan your money to. It's riskier, but the returns can average over 20% versus the 8% in the previous example.
- Different companies have different requirements. Additionally, some prefer the loans to be business-related, while others are open to nearly anyone. Borrowers are typically well screened.

6. **Try your hand at affiliate marketing**. If you don't have your own product or service to sell, don't fret. There are thousands and thousands of companies that will pay you a commission for selling their product.

- JVZoo.com and ClickBank.com are two of the more popular platforms for having electronic products to sell. These sites provide sales pages with your own unique tracking ID. Just get people to the sales page, and you'll be credited with any sales from that traffic. Some affiliate programs pay 100%. A more typical commission is 50-65% Amazon.com has an affiliate program and will reward you for selling nearly anything from books to televisions. Electronic products tend to have much higher commissions, though.

- There are many affiliate programs available online. Take a look at the bottom of many websites, and you'll nd an affiliate button. All you need to do is sign up.
7. **Flip websites.** You've heard of flipping houses. This is the same idea, only with websites. Many website owners are looking to sell their websites. These websites can be purchased and 'flipped' to another buyer. Or you can build your own website to sell.
- The most popular platform for this activity is Flippa.com. As a general rule, websites sell for around 12 times their monthly income. Traffic is also essential. If you can show that you're getting decent traffic, someone is likely to believe they can monetize that traffic.

There are many ways to earn money with your computer. These are just seven diverse examples. There are many other opportunities, like freelancing, writing Kindle books, paid blog commenting, and installing Word Press themes.

Think about the things you can do better than the average person. This is usually a great starting point. Even if you're lacking in skills, there's still work available. Work that is easy to nd will usually pay less. Be willing to spend the time to dig around. A little work upfront can significantly increase your pay rate.

Use your computer to boost your income. You never know what you can do until you try. This is just a small list of the many ways you can use your computer to make money. If you really want to know the vast number of opportunities,

check out consultablindguy.com for different ways you can make money from home and online. They can all be done with little to no investment at all.

10 Ideas For Boosting Your Income

There are plenty of opportunities to boost your income if you're willing to hustle. A few hours each week can add significantly to your discretionary income. You'll find a few ideas listed below, but come up with a list of your own ideas. With enough creativity, you might discover an untapped source of secondary income.

Boost your income starting tomorrow:

1. **Be a part-time personal assistant**. You can make phone calls, run errands, mow the grass, have the car washed, or pick up the kids. Think of all the things you wish you had help with. You can provide that to someone else. While there aren't too many people that can use an assistant full-time, there are many people that could use an hour or two of help.

2. **Rent your car**. How much time do you actually spend driving it? The rest of the time, it's just sitting in the driveway dripping oil and serving as a target for birds. There are apps that will allow you to list and rent your car. Parkingspotter and Relayrides are two examples.

3. **Knock on doors**. A variety of organizations are looking for people to canvas neighborhoods and solicit donations or

spread information. You can brush up on your social skills, too.

4. **Bartender**. With the right position, you can make a lot of money quickly. Take a class and learn how to mix your favorite drinks.

5. **Clean houses**. Some people actually like to clean. If you're one of them, you're in luck! Some people are too busy to clean and have the financial resources to pay someone else to do it. All you have to do is find each other. A few basic cleaning supplies are enough to get started.

6. **Housesit**. If you spend your evenings in front of the TV or playing on your computer anyway, do it at someone else's house and get paid for it. There's not much to do besides getting the mail.

7. **Teach**. Do you know yoga, algebra, or how to play the violin? Share your knowledge for a price. Use online classifieds or hand out a few fliers. Just a couple of students can provide a nice boost to your income.

8. **Get a roommate.** Split the rent and utilities. That can easily be upwards of $1,000 per month. All you have to do is give up some privacy and half the refrigerator. Be sure to take a shower before the hot water is gone.

9. **Pet-sitter or dog walker.** Pet sitters make around $25 per day. If you're lucky enough to get a good dog, it's an easy job. Dog walkers earn around $15 per 30-minute walk. A few clients can add to your income nicely. Look at rover.com.

10. **Buy and sell things on Craigslist**. People have traded their way from a used cell phone to a Porsche without spending a dime. Look for items selling at a low price. Purchase it and resell at a higher, more reasonable price.

- There are always good deals to be found. You must be knowledgeable of the item, however. Do you know the typical price for a 1988 USA Peavey Predator guitar? Know the market value of what you're buying and look for someone willing to do something silly.

A little extra income never hurt anyone. Think of other ways to boost your income. If you're willing to work, you can create a second income that makes a big difference in your life. Find something that interests you, and you'll enjoy yourself more. Many of these tips can be put into action immediately. The possibilities are endless. There is over 80 ways for you to make a living from the comfort of your home with little to no investment at all and, in many cases, without any experience at all. If you have time to kill and want to make money, then you can create multiple income streams and have a nice cash flow going in a matter of minutes. Want to know more than check out consultablindguy.com or the YouTube channel for all the different ways you can make money from home. You will be surprised by how quick and straightforward it is for you to get started.

10 Sideline Sources of Income
That You Can Earn From Home

Do you have some extra time to kill and need another source of income? There are several ways to generate a secondary source of income without leaving the comfort of your own home. It's surprising how many home employment opportunities exist. Anyone with a few hours to spare can earn extra money.

Check out these ways to stay at home and earn money in your free time:

1. **Crafting**. With the capabilities of the internet and associated technologies, working from home is a snap. Whether your talent is painting, sewing, drawing, there's no end to the amount of work available for someone who likes to share their skills.

- No matter what your skills might be, there's someone out there looking for you. Check out one of the many websites to get started.

2. **Telemarketing**. Any place with a telephone is suitable for your telemarketing headquarters. It's a job that few enjoy, so there are usually employers looking for callers. If you have a pleasant voice and can deal with rejection, telemarketing can be an easy and flexible way to earn some money.

3. **Grow and sell vegetables**. Okay, you might have to leave home to do this. On the other hand, you might be able to convince someone else to sell them for you at the local farmer's market. Seeds are very inexpensive. Mother Nature will take care of the rest, minus weeding.

4. **Make scrapbooks**. Not everyone has the skill to make a custom scrapbook. Create scrapbooks for those who are unable or unwilling to do it themselves. A few supplies are all you need to get started.

- Begin with offering your scrapbooking service to family, friends, and neighbors. You might be able to generate enough referrals to stay busy without additional advertising.

5. **Data Entry**. Most jobs pay for each entry rather than by the hour. It's a great job if you have a few spare minutes here and there. It's super flexible and can work around any schedule. With focus and fast fingers, you can generate a reasonable income.

6. **Tutoring**. Part-time tutors can make $30 or more per hour. You might have to brush up on your geometry or Latin, but tutoring can be a lucrative way to spend your free time.

7. Translate. Are you skilled in a second language? There are many opportunities to translate conversations and documents. While certifications are required to translate for large companies and government agencies, they're totally unnecessary for translating a love letter or a chat on Skype.

8. **Rent out a room**. If you have the space to spare, rent out a room. A good roommate can be a blessing and help you cover the bills. It might help your social life, too.

9. **Host a party**. There are parties for Tupperware, candles, and numerous other types of products. While these parties are typically held in the homes of others, host the parties yourself.

- You could also allow your friends to use your home as a party location and then keep a percentage of the profits.

10. **Sell ad space on a personal blog**. Create a blog and then sell ads on your website. You can sell the ad space directly or sign up with Google Adsense. With Google, they'll post relevant ads for you, and you'll receive money whenever someone clicks on the ad.

Whether you're in financial pain or just need an activity to fill your spare time, a secondary or part-time source of income could be the solution. Someone almost certainly has a need that fits your skillset perfectly. Find them and provide your services. It might be the most enjoyable money you'll ever earn. Another way to do this is to use your affiliate links as an ad. Get a relevant picture or ask the affiliate if they have one you can use and then link the image with the affiliate link on your blog as a freestanding ad and when someone purchases that item or service you make the commission. Just another way for you to use the ad space to your advantage. Be sure to mention on your website that some of the links are affiliate links to meet the FTC guidelines. Want to learn more? Check out www.consultablindguy.com or social media for more resources and information on ways you can work from home and make money. Don't want to read a lot, no problem. Check out the YouTube channel.

10 Online Methods
To Boost Your Income

When it comes to living your best life financially, knowing when you need to bring in more money is smart. If you haven't considered how much extra income you can bring in using online resources, now is your time to do so. Take a look at the following strategies to earn extra income online. Perhaps you'll get inspired and start a new income stream (or two) using your computer from home.

1. Complete online surveys. The internet is filled with websites where you can get paid for simply completing surveys.

- Before signing up at such websites, do a thorough investigation of the website and decide for yourself whether you can earn good, honest dough for completing questionnaires.

- One way to determine the legitimacy of such survey sites is to notice how you'll be paid. Those sites paying through PayPal are usually reputable.

- At any rate, consider spending an hour a day completing online surveys to get more money rolling in.

2. **Write articles**. Submit articles at sites where you earn page view revenue and/or upfront payment for articles. Such sites can be gold mines for someone with writing skills, talent, and gumption.

- Various websites such as Triond, Medium, Helium, HubPages, Constant Content will pay you for your articles based on the page views they receive.
- Some of these sites also offer upfront payment for articles and opportunities to sell full rights to your writing products.
- The internet world for writers is vast and varied. Regardless of the type of writing you do, fiction, poetry, non-fiction, or technical, you'll be able to find several websites where you can sell your work.
- The sites listed above also pay using PayPal and are reputable places to earn some cash.
- If you've been known to turn a phrase or two, navigate to these websites, open your accounts, and write.
3. **Write ebooks and sell them online**. As the electronic books industry grows, so do websites where anyone can write and place their ebooks for sale.
- Amazon Kindle and Pubit (Barnes and Nobles' ebook website) are just 2 of many reputable companies where you can submit and sell your e-books.
- However, be cautious and do your homework on any sites where you're considering selling your ebooks. Some of them will charge you to post your ebooks for sale, while others won't.
- If you love to write and have lots of stories to tell or facts to share, you just might get a cottage industry going by writing and selling your e-books online.

4. **Apply for jobs at online sites**. No matter what type of office work you do, you can most likely find a way to do it online.

- The number and array of websites offering jobs and projects for pay are virtually unlimited.
- Sites such as Upwork and Fiverr are considered reputable and will put you in touch with website owners who will pay you for completing projects.
- Be cautious, however, of websites that charge you to join or gain access to job listings.

5. **Translate documents.** If you're bilingual, check out job sites looking for translators to translate documents from one language to another. Two of the job websites mentioned above, Fiverr and Upwork, do offer opportunities to translate documents for pay.

- Also, TranslatorsCafe.com allows you to join and put your translation skills up for hire. At TranslatorsCafe, you can also browse available translation and interpreter jobs and apply for them.

Examine options to boost your income on the internet. Regardless of your training and education, if you can type and own a computer with a net connection, you'll surely discover some fascinating strategies for increasing your income online. Always be sure to research the sites as terms and conditions are always subject to change, sometimes for the better and others not so much. This is where having your own website comes in extra handy to generate income from your own products, affiliate products, Ads, etc. Never solely rely on one site or platform to generate your income, as the changes in policy can always affect you negatively.

There is truly money to be made on the internet. Whether it's mystery shopping, selling on eBay, or creating a blog, there are plenty of ways to add a little cash to your bank account!

6. **Connect with mystery shopping networks**. With mystery shopping, not only can you be paid for shopping, but you can also be reimbursed for your meal expenditures in restaurants when you conduct "shops" in restaurants and fast food places.
   - Your funds may be reimbursed if you're completing shops in hair salons, pet shops, and various other businesses. Thus, you get free services plus a few bucks extra when you mystery shop.
   - Mystery shopping requires you to have sharp observation, listening, and attention skills as you'll be asked to complete online questionnaires after you do a shop.
   - Mystery shopping companies are paid by various businesses to get usable, specific details about how their staff members are treating customers.
   - To find competent mystery shopping websites, use your search engine to explore.
   - Two reputable sites where you can apply to be a mystery shopper are Market Force and Shoppers' Critique International.

- Who knows, you just might get a free lunch tomorrow simply for offering your opinion about your restaurant experience!

7. **Sell items on eBay or Amazon.com**. If you're internet and tech-savvy, try selling some of your stuff you don't want or need anymore online. You can also make extra income from buying and re-selling items from various websites.

- You'll need a good digital camera and knowledge about how to upload your pictures to whatever website you're using to post your photos and text descriptions of what you want to sell.

- But be ready. You'll need packing materials, envelopes, or boxes to mail your items to the highest bidder.

- If you've run a small business before, you can most likely handle the online "business" of buying and re-selling items to earn extra income.

8. **Advertise your skills**. If you have special talents and skills, consider putting yourself out there in cyberspace.

- Although there's a number of ways to reach your client base on the internet, one of the cheapest and quickest ways to do it is on Craigslist.

- You can advertise on Craigslist today and get calls tomorrow, depending on the size of your local area. The closer you live to bigger cities, the quicker you can access your market base and make some extra income using Craigslist.

9. **Start a blog and include Google Adsense** or another advertising account. Adbrite and Publisher Network will

also pay you for clicks on your blogs. Some advertisers pay for page views instead of clicks.

- Starting and maintaining a blog can be a lot of work, depending on how you set it up, so reserve some time in your schedule several days each week for making new posts, answering readers' queries, and maintaining your blog.

- You can also sell products or services on your blog - either your own or another product for which you receive commissions from your sales. For example, Clickbank.com, Commission Junction, and many others offer many products that you could recommend to your readers. Search for websites that pay commissions and sign up for an affiliate account.

- Over time, your blog site visitors will build in number, which will boost your income.

10.   Sell your photographs. The amateur photography business is booming online.

- Sites like Imagekind and Photo Stock Plus will lead you through the steps to post your photographs online. An abundance of such photography sites exist, so examine several of them and their terms before deciding to post your snapshots on one or two of them.

- Keep in mind that some of these sites charge you simply to post your photos while others don't.

- Of course, a percentage of your "sold" price will go to the website you choose.

Using the Internet to boost your income can be very lucrative. Try out some of these ideas today to enjoy a more profitable tomorrow!

There are over 80+ ways you can make money from home & online. Some do require skills, whereas some require no skills at all, and they can earn you a nice chunk of change in a short amount of time or, depending on the niche, a ton of money over time. It depends on what you want to do and how much time you want to spend on the work at hand. These are just a few examples you can try out. There are many more out there. If you want to learn more about them, check out consultablindguy.com or the YouTube channel for more information. Now go on, get out there and start making your dreams a reality and make that cash flow work in your favor.

14 Ways To Make An Extra $1,000 Each Month In Your Spare Time

While most of us are thrilled to make another $1,000 each month, another $12,000 a year would make a huge difference for most folks. There are many different things you can do to supplement your income. Surprisingly enough, it's not that difficult. It's more a matter of commitment than anything else.

Getting Started:

Getting off on the right foot will help to ensure your success as you take on a new moneymaking venture. But before making your first dollar, remember to do the necessary preliminary work. That way, you're more likely to do well and make much more money in the future.

Take the time to go through these items before choosing your moneymaking method:

1. **Create a list of your special skills and knowledg**e. It's not necessary to know or be able to do anything special to make an extra $1,000 each month, but it doesn't hurthaving a unique skill-set can allow you to charge more for your time.

2. **What are your parameters**? **Do you have to earn money** outside of a regular job? Are your weekends free? What about your weekday evenings? How many hours are you willing to work?

3. **Do you have any friends or family that you can help?** Maybe you have a friend with a construction business that needs help on the weekends. Think about everyone you know. They might have something that would be perfect for you. Maybe you have a friend with a construction business that needs help on the weekends. Think about everyone you know. They might have something that would be perfect for you.

4. **Be willing to try something new. It's possible to** force your will on the marketplace, but it's a lot easier to simply provide what it needs. What do you hear people complaining about in your area? Find a need and fill it.

5. **Prepare to become a marketing machine.** Many of the methods we're going to suggest require finding clients. The work itself is pretty simple, but finding the clients is the more challenging part.
6. **Have fun**. It's one thing to make yourself miserable for a few months to reach a goal, but it's quite another to do it long-term. Find something that you actually like to do. Anyone can make another $1,000 each month. You might even be able to do a few different side jobs and eventually replace your full-time income. Even one successful venture might be enough in some cases.

The Money-Making Methods
Depending on where you live, all of the ideas in this guide could be viable options. However, some are more suited for certain areas than others. Hopefully, you'll find a method that appeals to you.

Create A Website And Sell Something **With WordPress, it's never been easier to set up your own** website. Gone are the days of needing to be a programmer to create a great looking site.
Selling something on a website is quite simple:
1. **When people come to your website, sell them** something. To make your endeavor more enjoyable, find a topic that really interests you and then capitalize on that interest.

- For example, there was recently a story of a woman that started her own blog about lighthouses and now makes a full-time living selling lighthouse related items and lighthouse travel tours.
- You can also sell a service. Think of something you can do better than the average person. There's no need to be an expert.
- You can also have Google Ads or something similar on your website and get paid when people click on them. The "pay-per-click" market is huge!
- Affiliate marketing can be lucrative. There are websites with thousands of digital products that you can sell like on Clickbank.com.
- On these affiliate sites, you earn a commission every time you make a sale. Commissions are commonly 50-70%. The product creator even provides a sales page where you send your customers.

2. .The real key is doing the marketing to get customers to your webpage. There are plenty of resources available to help you market your website.
- Write some articles related to the topic of your website and post them in the appropriate places. Posting to article directories would be a good start. Article marketing has always been a great way to drive web traffic.
- Write excellent content. Some of the most popular websites were never intentionally marketed in any way. If your content is good, people will come to read it.

- Social media such as Twitter, Facebook, Reddit, and similar websites are additional ways of creating a buzz.

Even if you're not technologically inclined, a website can be a great way to boost your income in your spare time.

Sell A Technical Service

As suggested in the previous method, many people are intimidated by internet technology. **There are many easy and simple services you could offer to people and businesses that they might not think they can do themselves.**

Selling technical services can include the following:

1. Create websites for businesses. A reasonable website can be created in just a couple of hours, and it wouldn't be difficult to find someone willing to pay at least a few hundred dollars for a website.
   - One website a week would easily be an additional $1,000 each month. It could even be much, much ore.
2. Create Facebook pages for small businesses. Smaller businesses often have no designated marketing employees. Many of those businesses are also too small to justify hiring a full-blown marketing firm.
   - Templates are available that would allow you to create a Facebook page for a business in a just a few minutes.
   - These Facebook pages can easily be sold for $100 or more. Two or three a week would meet the magical $1,000 mark.

3. Create YouTube videos for small businesses. A few simple shots with a digital camera can be made into a slideshow with free software and a little bit of time.
4. Create and operate Twitter accounts for businesses. Many small businesses would love to have a Twitter account, but they are unsure how to go about setting it up. The common methods for finding customers (in order of effectiveness) are: in-person visits, phone calls, email, and **snail-mail. You might be surprised how easy it is to find a client if you can muster the courage and stop by or pick up the phone.**

These services are all much easier than you probably realize. You can teach yourself everything you need to know very quickly.

"It is not the creation of wealth that is wrong, but the love of money for its own sake." - Margaret Thatcher

Do Taxes For Others

With the software that's now available, nearly anyone can do some else's taxes. You won't require a degree in accounting to put some numbers in a software program. **Many of the people working for the big tax firms each spring are just regular people working part-time.**

In the rare event that someone's taxes are too complicated once you start doing them, simply tell them the truth. Just as all lawyers aren't qualified to handle all cases, it's okay to admit you can't do the taxes of a multi-millionaire with extensive offshore investments.

This method won't work all year. It's going to be limited to a couple of months, but you can easily make more than $1,000 each month during that time. Think about other services you can offer to the same clients. If they're happy with your tax preparation services, maybe they'll give you the opportunity to do something else for them during other times of the year.

Remember to ask for referrals. The easiest way to find new clients is by receiving a recommendation from other clients you've worked with.

"All I ask is the chance to prove that money can't make me happy." - Spike Milligan

Rent Out Your Extra Room On Airbnb

Airbnb.com is a unique website that allows people to rent out space they own. It can be space in a treehouse, a walk-in closet with an air mattress, an entire vacation home, or a room in your home. If you have a livable space, someone would probably be interested in renting it from you. If the space isn't currently being used, it's really just a wasted resource.

Just a couple of tips:
1. Have a proper lease in place. Laws and customs can vary from state to state. Contact an attorney or your local real estate investors club for assistance.
2. Do a thorough background check before letting a stranger move into your home. There are services available to run background checks, credit checks, and every other type of check you can imagine.

Before letting anyone move in, you'll probably want to require a security deposit or rent upfront. Everyone seems to have a story about getting the 'money next week.'

3. Ensure you're comfortable with someone new living in your space. If you're uncomfortable, there's not a lot that can be done, depending on the lease terms.
- If you're interested in providing space in your home, think about how you want to handle the common areas. These would include the kitchen, bathroom, and living room. Also, figure out where they'll park their car.

Why waste space you're not using? Monetize it instead!

Write for Extra Money

Are you good with words? Do you like to write as a hobby? If so, capitalize on those writing skills. With all the content available online, there's a tremendous need for people to write that content.

Try these options:

1. **Freelance**. Approach website owners and offer to write some content for them. Pay rates can vary dramatically. Some writers can make a few hundred dollars per article.

2. **Join a content providing service**. Many websites are always looking for writers. Two of the more popular ones are Textbroker.com and iWriter.com.

- You can search through jobs and choose ones that appeal to you.

- You'll have to write quickly to really earn some money, but this is something you can do in the comfort of your own home.

3. **Write an eBook and sell it on your own website.** Many people have made millions of dollars by selling information. We'll cover more about writing and selling books on Amazon later.

4. **Offer to write ads for eBay sellers. Contact the sellers** of high-ticket items such as homes, cars, motorcycles, and boats. Offer to write a top-notch ad for them, in exchange for 1% of the selling price. You won't get paid unless it sells.

- For example, if you wrote an ad selling a $20,000 car, you'd be looking at getting paid $200.

Writing can be hard work, but it has very flexible work hours. You can easily work it into your busy schedule.

"There are people who have money and
people who are rich." - Coco Chanel

Tutor Or Give Lessons

Some tutors are making over $100 an hour! If you're good at **piano, golf, tennis, painting, or anything else that's marketable, consider giving lessons.** The best tutoring jobs tend to be in the nicer neighborhoods, since mom and dad are likely to have more disposable income. Get in touch with schools and even post an ad on Craigslist.com. Research the average fees for the service you're providing and offer a competitive price.

"He that is of the opinion money will do everything may well be suspected of doing everything for money." - Benjamin Franklin

Mow Lawns or Offer Other Home Maintenance Services

This could go along well with taxes. You could do the taxes in the late winter and early spring and then move into basic **landscaping. It's not difficult or uncommon to make $20 or more per hour mowing lawns.**
The following guidelines will make everything easier:
1. Stick close to home. You want to avoid having your profits eaten up by gas and other traveling costs.
2. It requires minimal equipment. All that's really needed is a lawnmower, trimmer, and transportation. The mower and trimmer can be purchased used for very little money. However, you might be able to use the ones you already own.

3. Create flyers and pass them out around your target neighborhoods. As you are passing out your flyers, be friendly. Also, offer a fair price.
4. You can also offer to do other "outside" services. Other than mowing lawns, there are other services you could offer. For example, you could do edging, planting flowers, picking up dog poop, washing cars, or cleaning out gutters.

- People who are elderly or live very busy lives are often looking for someone to help maintain the outside of their homes.

"After a certain point, money is meaningless.
It ceases to be the goal. The game is what counts."- Aristotle Onassis

Provide Pet-Sitting Services

Many individuals work all day, and their pets need to be let outside for obvious reasons. Some people go out of town and prefer to leave their pets at home instead of boarding them at a kennel.

If you like caring for pets, consider the following:
1. Offer additional services. Since you're already at the house, think about other things you can do that would be helpful. Some examples would be dog training, picking up dog poop, housecleaning, or mowing the lawn.
2. Be the vacation solution. If your customers leave own, offer to take care of their pets. Remember that you'll have to let the dog out at least three times each day. Consider

keeping the pets in your home or charge for each of the three visits. Even offer to get the mail.

3. Stick with clients that are close to home. It's not worth driving 20 miles each way to make $11 for letting the dog out.

Expand your animal services. Try not to limit yourself to just dogs. With a bit of reading, you could quickly learn how to care for cats, birds, hamsters, an iguana, and just about anything else. Taking care of other's pets is a low-stress way to spend your time. Call around and find the rates of other pet-sitters before you decide on your rates. Advertise everywhere you can think. It makes the most sense to advertise at dog parks, pet stores, and veterinarians.

Flip Items on Craigslist

This can be a very lucrative part-time business. In a nutshell, you find items on Craigslist.com that you're confident you can resell at a profit.

The following items will all but guarantee a profit:
1. **Look for poorly written ads**. Many sellers create poor ads that lack pictures. With a better ad, you can expect to resell the item at a higher price.
2. **Limit yourself to a few different types of items**. Maybe you have some knowledge of or interest in guitars, appliances, and jewelry. If you have knowledge in a certain area, you'll be able to spot a good deal on Craigslist when you see it.

3. **Make a lot of offers**. Many people price their items appropriately but are in a hurry to sell. That could be good for you because many of them will take nearly any offer to make some money quickly. You'll never know if you could've gotten a bargain unless you ask.

4. **Check on the free items**. It's competitive, but sometimes there are valuable items given away for free. Even a $20 item might be worth getting and reselling since it's all profit that goes straight into your pocket.

5. **Avoid getting involved with lower-priced items**. There's only so much profit to be made on a $10 item, but it's not hard to make $50 on a used refrigerator. Your time is valuable.

6. **You might need a truck**. Some items, like large appliances, will require a truck. But there are plenty of other items that are suitable buys if you don't have a truck.

"I'd like to live as a poor man with lots of money." - Pablo Picasso

Babysitting After School Hours

There are many children that go into after-school programs. Many other children are forced to spend the afternoon home alone until their parents return from work. If you like children, babysitting could be a profitable endeavor. You could offer to look after kids between the time they are finished at school up until their parents return from work. You can either pick them up from school or meet them as they get off the bus. All you'd really have to do is fix them a snack and supervise them while they do their homework.

Consider these ideas:
1. **Try to watch multiple children.** Watching two children pays better than one. Watching five pays better than two.
2. **Think about the third shift crowd**. Many single parents work third shift, and someone has to watch those children. What could be easier than putting a child to bed in your home and getting them ready for school in the morning? You could easily make $30 per night per child.

"A wise man should have money in his head, but not in his heart." - Jonathan Swift

Give Swimming Lessons

Swimming lessons is another gig that would dovetail nicely with the tax preparation idea. Many pools offer group lessons, but each child spends most of their time watching while the children take turns swimming for the instructor. **Many parents are**

happy to pay for private swim lessons. It would be easy to make $20-$50 per hour. Get certified as a swim instructor and get in the pool. If you're a parent, you can even bring your children to the pool. While you're at it, get certified as a lifeguard. This will give you even more job opportunities. In warmer climates, both of these can be done year-round.

"Money is better than poverty, if only for financial reasons."
- Woody Allen

Be A Freelancer Online

If you already have a regular job, there's a good chance you can get paid to do the same thing at home. Someone out there wants help doing whatever it is you do. Fiverr.com is a great place to find clients for your services. You can do anything from writing, to setting up websites, to transcribing, doing spreadsheets, or providing voiceovers. Avoid selling yourself short. There are many potential clients looking for the cheapest deal. If you have something of value to offer, ensure you're making the money you deserve. There are many other comparable sites that offer similar opportunities. Upwork.com is another example of a site where freelancers can get work.

"A bank is a place that will lend you money if you can prove that you don't need it." - Bob Hope

Become A Photographer

Photographers can make impressive money. If you have the skill, you can photograph weddings and other formal events. Family portraits are another way to make a decent buck.

Consider the following:

1. **Many websites utilize photographs**. Typically, you won't get rich selling one or two copies of individual photos. But if you think about it, if you sell 3,000 photos at $0.50, it can really add up. You can also sell each photo one time for $30 or more.
2. **Sitting fees**. One way photographers can get paid, independent of photo sales, is by charging a sitting fee for taking the photos. Many photographers go to people's homes for a photoshoot. You can charge an additional fee for the convenience of traveling to your clients.
3. **You can also create calendars and other items with your photographs.**
4. Take pictures of your travels and make a calendar. Becoming a photographer doesn't have to require extra fancy equipment. If you have a decent camera, that should suffice. Depending on the type of phone you have, you might even be able to use that for some jobs.

"Liking money like I like it is nothing less than mysticism. Money is a glory." - Salvador Dali

Write An eBook And Sell It On Amazon.

Some people write a new book every week! While you might not write a bestseller, if you pick the suitable topics, it's not unreasonable to make $1,000 or more from each book.

We already discussed writing, but this is a little different. The previous example was when you write an eBook for someone else and get paid just one time for that work. Although it is your work, you've been hired by someone to write it and therefore are turning over the rights. In this case, you're going to keep control and ownership of your writing. You will be selling it on Amazon.com. The best part is that you'll have the opportunity to get paid multiple times for the same work. Once an eBook is up for sale online, you can continually capitalize on every book for years to come.

This is more speculative since you're not guaranteed to make anything. However, the potential rewards are many times greater. Also, this is a more involved job than all the other suggestions.

Follow this process if you are interested in writing your own eBook:

1. **Fiction or non-fiction**. First, you need to decide if you're more comfortable writing fiction or nonfiction. Non-fiction will be easier since you can use other books as source material.

2. **Determine the best sellers in your niche**. Think about personal areas of interest and check to see which topics are doing well in sales.

- Now, look at Amazon and see how many books within each category are within the top 50,000 bestselling books. You'll want to see at least three books in the top 50,000. Any less, and it won't be worth your time. In that case, find another, more popular niche.
3. **Purchase the top three books in your chosen category and read them.**
4. **Make some notes as you read**. What you're ultimately doing is writing your own book from what you learned from those three. However, you'll also need to add unique ideas of your own.
5. **Start writing.** Keep in mind that a book doesn't necessarily have to belong. Some of the best-selling books have been very short. The best length, however, seems to be 125-175 pages. This may seem like a lot. But, keep in mind that one page in a word-processing program is almost two pages in a Kindle book.
- Each Kindle page should take approximately 15 minutes to write, so a 150-page book should take approximately 35-40 hours.
- Some Kindle book writers actually outsource the writing! Remember that sites like Upwork and Fiverr can be used to find writers.
6. **Read your book**. After your book is written, go back through and actually read it! Look for ways to enhance your work.

7. **Hire an edito**r. You should always consider hiring someone else to edit the eBook for you, even after you've read it over.
- Customers will get really turned off if there are errors in spelling, grammar, and punctuation.
- Bad reviews for your first book could negatively impact your future as an eBook writer.
- A second pair of eyes, especially those of a trained editor, is imperative to ensure that your eBook is error-free.
8. **Kindle books require specific formatting**. There are many templates that you can find online. Information about formatting your book can also be found on Amazon.com.
- Be careful about using images. First, always Insert the image, never Copy-Paste.
- Amazon charges you a download fee for each book you sell. That fee is based on the book file size, which is another reason to avoid too many images.
- Using a lot of images can increase your costs and decrease your profits. Images can also be compressed to smaller file sizes, limiting your expense.
- It would be brilliant to include hyperlinks in your eBook that point back to your website. You can then sell additional items to your customers.
- Hyperlinks will also let you capture email addresses for future marketing purposes. Prepare a free report and provide it in exchange for their email address.

- A good email list is worth at least $0.50 per address per month. A list of just 2,000 email addresses should be worth $1,000 a month.

Numbered lists can be a good idea, but bullet points aren't able to be displayed on older Kindle models. An asterisk or dash can be used instead.

9. **A good book cover is imperative**. A book with a poor cover doesn't sell well. Take the time to secure an attractive cover. The first option is to buy a cover.

- The most inexpensive option for purchasing a cover is to head over to Fiverr and search for Kindle covers. You're only paying $5, so keep your expectations in check. However, you might be pleasantly surprised by the quality.

- With fiverr.com, you may have to pay a few different people before finding a cover you like. However, at such an affordable price, it might be worth it to try out a few different designers.

- An option that costs a little more is visiting www.goonwrite.com. The covers from this site are ~ $35 each, but once a cover is bought, it's removed from circulation. There are other similar websites.

- There are also more expensive options. One of these is www.99designs.com. The cost for a cover is $300 or more. It's debatable whether or not it's worth spending that much for an eBook cover.

- Another source of covers is www.warriorforum.com. You're sure to find someone there that can create a great book cover at a variety of price points.

You can also make your own cover. There are several programs and templates available online that will help you to create a great cover.

- If you use a photograph to make your own cover, be certain that you have the legal rights to use it. Only use high-resolution photos, so your eBook looks professional.

10. **Now, it's time to upload your book to Amazon**! Uploading a book requires an account with Kindle Direct Publishing (KDP). You can set up an account at www.kdp.amazon.com.

- Amazon has excellent video tutorials that will walk you through all the steps. Enroll in KDP Select, which allows you to promote your book in some unique ways. It's free for the first 90 days.

- You're allowed 4,000 characters to describe your book. Use them wisely! A longer description looks more professional and gives your potential readers more information to make a good buying decision.

- The description doesn't have to be 4,000 characters, but be thorough enough to arouse the curiosity of the potential buyer.

- Regarding publishing rights, choose option-2, 'Not a public domain work.' You probably wouldn't want other people to be able to sell your eBook as their own, right? When you 'add categories,' choose the two that are most closely related to your topic.

- Keywords are critically important. You can add up to seven keywords, so always use all seven! The Google Keyword

Tool is a great tool for finding keywords related to your niche.

11. **It's advisable to set the price of your book between $2.99 and $9.99.** Amazon allows you to claim 70% of the cost as your commission within this price range. That commission drops to 30% if you price your book higher or lower.

- Now buy it! You'll get 70% of the money back anyway. Amazon is more likely to promote your book if they see buying activity occur quickly.

12. **Marketing your book is the next step**. KDP will allow you to offer your book for free. Three days is long enough to get your book out there. You're aiming for at least 2,500 downloads during that time.

- If people aren't downloading your free book, the cover probably needs to be changed. The next place to look is the book description. Is the description boring? People just want to learn more about your book if they're willing to spend money to purchase it.

- The best marketing for your eBook is good reviews. Tell all your friends and family to buy a copy and leave a good review!

Ask for reviews in the book itself. Put a simple blurb at the front and the end of the book requesting a review. Always thank your readers in advance for their help.

- You can also "bribe" your readers for reviews. Offer them something for free and strongly SUGGEST they leave a review. You can't offer the free item in exchange for a review, but you can give them something free upfront and then request a review.

- Facebook is another great tool for advertising your book. Post the book cover on your Facebook page and tell all your friends to pick up a copy. Also, remind your friends and family to leave a review. Ask your friends to like and share your post on Facebook. Even if they haven't purchased the book yet, they can still spread the word.

- Create a Facebook Page for your book. Search around and see what other authors have done. Be shameless in mimicking the pages that appeal to you. You can even give away free chapters of your book to "hook" some readers.

- You can also find Facebook groups related to your book topic. Join them. Most groups will allow you to post information about your book. Join the group as part of the page for promoting your eBook. Then your post will show up as your book page instead of your real name.

13.   **Have your own blog**. Every author should have a website dedicated to their writing. In order to be taken seriously, an author requires a website.

A central hub allows you to give away free chapters, post information about new books, and collect names for your email list. Have a separate page for each book.

- On your website, create buying links for each of your books that point back to Amazon. Update your website once a week to keep your readers engaged. That is where content comes in again.

- Create a social media hub on your website. Create links to your Facebook, Twitter, LinkedIn, YouTube, and email accounts. We haven't covered how to set up all of these, but there's more than enough information out there to guide you through the process.
- Videos can be a great way to market your book. Video reviews are great. That's what friends are for! You can also put up a video of yourself talking about your book.

If you're planning to continue writing books and want to write on a variety of topics, it's suggested that you create a pen name for each topic. It's hard to claim to be an expert on dog training, international investing, building model boats, and tutoring math. If you were to write all those books under the same name, no one is likely to take you seriously. You'll require separate email, Twitter, Facebook, YouTube, and LinkedIn accounts for each pen name. Writing and selling eBooks is a very viable way to make some real money. Remember to pick a topic that's already selling well. There's no reason to reinvent the wheel.

"Money is a strange business. People who haven't got it aim for it strongly. People who have are full of troubles." - Ayrton Senna

Conclusion

There are many ways to earn an extra $1,000 each month. The most crucial step is to commit to the method that best suits you. Consider your circumstances. If you live in a rural area, writing an eBook probably makes more sense than being a dog-sitter. If you live in a suburban area, but have a full-time job, being a dog-sitter may not be practical. Committing to a method means precisely that. You're planning to stick with that method and make it work. Most of these methods require expertise that you probably already possess. If it's not a perfect fit, try to mold the method to your strengths. Remember that marketing is the key. The work itself is pretty simple. The challenging part is finding clients, so you'll want to concentrate on doing some marketing every day. Marketing needs to be done regularly if you're looking for the most benefit.

Use every possible form of marketing. Focus on the methods that are likely to be the most successful, but there's no reason to be afraid to branch out into other methods over time. Always ask for referrals after you've made a customer happy. Give them a couple of extra business cards to hand out to friends, family, and colleagues. An extra $12,000 a year could make a huge difference in your life. How will you spend your newfound funds?

> "When I was young, I thought that money was the most important thing in life; now that I am old, I know that it is."
> Oscar Wilde

14 Ways To Make An Extra $1000 A Month In Your Spare Time Worksheet

Self---Reflection Worksheet Making an extra $1,000 each month is both reasonable and desirable.

Answer the following questions to gain a better perspective of moneymaking methods that would best suit you.

1. What would I do with an extra $1,000 each month?

_____

_____

_____

_____

_____

2. What unique skills or knowledge do I possess that are valuable to others?

_____

_____

_____

_____

_____

3. How much time do I have available to earn this extra money? When can I work?

_____

_____

_____

_____

_____

4. Do I know anyone that could use my expertise & might be willing to pay me for it?

_____

_____

_____

_____

_____

5. Do I have any hobbies that might be a good niche for money making activities?

_____

_____

_____

_____

6. ?What sort of service or product does my local area need

_____

_____

_____

_____

_____

7. What methods of marketing would be most applicable
to the niche I've chosen?

_____

_____

_____

_____

_____

15 Legitimate Ways to Work From Home

The "work from home" field is filled with scams and empty promises. However, there are ways to legitimately make money from home. The key is to leverage your strengths and ensure that any companies you're working with have a good reputation. Avoid doing too much work until you're paid for the first time. Then you should have an idea of whether the offer is legitimate or not.

Stay at home and pay your bills:

1. Be a consultant. Many small businesses don't have a need for a full-time whatever-you-are. But they might need someone with your skills and knowledge for a short period of time.

2. Transcriptionist. This type of work is available and can be worth your time if you can type quickly. There's software available that can transcribe with reasonable accuracy. Descript is 95% accurate, and it will cut your time down a ton. You might be able to make a decent hourly rate without leaving home.

3. Freelance work. Writing articles, creating videos, performing search engine optimization, or creating graphics are just a few examples of freelance work that's waiting for you.

4. Work for a call center. Some businesses want to take your call, but are too small to have bodies dedicated to answering the phones 24/7. You can work at home for a

call center and receive or make those important calls for the company.

5. Teach a language. English is in high demand, particularly in Asian countries. Italki is one website that will allow you to take advantage of your English ability and make $20+/hour.

6. Virtual assistant. The creativity of your employer will determine your tasks. You could be making travel plans, balancing the books, or researching chocolate cookie recipes. The tasks can vary from super simple to tedious and lengthy.

7. Rent a room in your home. There are several websites that will connect you with renters, both long-term and short. If you have space you're not using, consider monetizing it. Do be sure to contact an attorney for reviewing agreements.

8. Be a juror. Lawyers will pay you to review a case and give your opinion. Think of it as a practice trial before heading to court. Ejury is one such company that will pay you for your jurist skills.

9. Test and review websites. User Testing is the most popular company. You're paid $10 for a 20-minute task. That's $30 per hour if you stay busy.

10.   Take surveys. This field is full of scams, so be sure to check out the company before wasting your time. Never pay to join a survey organization. A few companies with good reputations include Harris Poll Online, Pine Cone Research, and Swag Bucks.

11.   Sell vegetables from your garden. At times, your garden provides more than you can consume. Visit the local farmer's market and sell your excess.

12.   Mechanical Turk. This is a service provided by Amazon.com. You can perform small tasks for money. Most of the jobs are very quick and easy. The pay is very low per task but you can complete multiple tasks per hour.

13.   Tutor at your home. $25/hour isn't out of line. There are also places to tutor online.

14.   Affiliate marketing. You can sell someone else's product online and get paid for each sale. For example, Amazon.com has an affiliate program. There are many more.

15.   Pet sitting. It's possible to earn $25/day or more for watching someone else's pet. Unlike daycare laws, most areas don't have a limit to how many dogs you can keep in your home! Rover.com is a popular option to connect with pet owners.

If you find yourself between jobs or need to make some extra money, working from home can be both convenient and lucrative. Many work at home offers aren't worth your valuable time, but others can provide a full-time income if you're willing to work online. Consider working from the comfort of your home. Always research before committing to any one source of generating income to ensure it's right for you and what the in's and out's are to ensure it's legit and worth your time.

8 Steps to Becoming a
Top Earner In Your Field

In most fields, whether medicine, law, business, consulting or accounting, there are a select few that make far more money than the rest. There are steps you can take to become a top earner in your field of employment. Is it luck? Do you need to be extremely charismatic? Do you require some special talent? No, no, and no.

Consistently being a little bit better than your peers and focusing on success is all that's required.

Separate yourself from the rest in these ways:

1. **Have a goal**. Achieving exceptional results requires a plan or luck. Luck is uncontrollable, so focus on creating a goal instead. Have a specific goal in mind that includes a particular dollar amount and deadline. Wanting "a lot of money" isn't a practical goal.

2. **Keep money in mind when making decisions**. When choosing a career, consider the earning potential. A personal trainer could decide to focus on bodybuilders or high school athletes. One that works with famous actors, executives, or professional athletes has far more opportunities to earn a significant income.

3. **Find a mentor**. A suitable mentor is someone that has accomplished what you wish to achieve. It would also be advantageous if they had a genuine interest in providing guidance and advice.

4. **Spend time with those with similar goals**. There are others with the same goals and aspirations as you. Seek them out and become friends. Find those that are already successful at the level you hope to attain. You'll learn things you're unlikely to learn from your current crowd.

5. **Seek to enhance your performance each day**. There are a few fields where the participants regularly attempt to improve their performance. Musicians, artists, and athletes regularly spend time getting better at their craft.

- How often have you seen a lawyer or a manager set aside time to boost their skills? Rarely, if ever.

- If no one else is striving to become more skillful, how much competition do you have?

6. **Increase your knowledge each day**. Gaining more knowledge will allow you to apply your skills more effectively.

- Thirty minutes each day is enough to get ahead. Spend this time reading books or researching your field online to seek a higher level of understanding

7. **Get used to being uncomfortable**. As you stretch yourself to think and do new things, you're going to feel that awkward twinge we've all felt. It's just a physical sensation, like a sore toe or a hand that's fallen asleep. There's no reason to let it control your thoughts and actions.

- Why would you quit because of a slightly queasy feeling in your stomach? Your subconscious knows which buttons to push to encourage you to quit. Avoid giving in.

8. **Persevere**. If there's one trait found in all top earners, it's perseverance. It's not difficult to be incredibly successful if you'll keep getting better and refuse to quit. In fact, it's just about impossible to fail. Some days are more promising than others, but great days are on the way.

Becoming a top earner is well within your reach. Have a goal and keep it in the front of your mind. Find a successful mentor. Continue to learn and increase your skills and knowledge. Persevere until your dream of becoming a top earner has been reached. My goal is to earn enough to get off disability, to share my knowledge with others who are differently-abled and those who are non-disabled to assist in your growth to be self-employed and be your own boss or able to have the extra income you desire. Whether it's creating content, affiliate marketing, email marketing, etc.

My mentors are Pat Flynn, who is an entrepreneur, best-selling author, and the owner of Smart Passive Income. My other mentor is Karma, who is also an entrepreneur, well known around the world by many as KarmaCashflow. I am also a founding member of the People of Video Society with Dan Currier of the Creator Fundamentals YouTube channel. Also, a member of the Nimminati with Nick & Dee Nimmin also well known YouTube creator's. I have many others I am associated with, but I would be here typing for hours to list them all. They are all mentors in one way or another and help me to further my knowledge to share with you. If you want to learn more about my mentors or more ways to make money, check out the website at consultablindguy.com or visit the social media pages or YouTube channel.

7 Steps To Affiliate Marketing Profits

Affiliate marketing is a lucrative and easy way to make money online. As an affiliate, you sell other people's products for a commission. So you don't have to create a product or offer customer support. Your only real job is to promote the product. What's even better is that you can set up your business in a way that everything practically runs on autopilot. Once you set it up, you can make money for several months, or possibly even years, without touching the website again.

Following this 7-step process will quickly get you making money in affiliate marketing:

1. **Affiliate marketing is a lucrative and easy way to make money online**. As an affiliate, you sell other people's products for a commission. So you don't have to create a product or offer customer support. Your only real job is to promote the product. Following this 7-step process will quickly get you making money in affiliate marketing: Choose your niche. This is certainly one of the most critical steps for success in affiliate marketing. If you choose a niche that's too large, there's likely to be too much competition for success to come easily. Choose a niche that's too small, and you'll never have enough customers to be really profitable.

Tips for choosing a niche:

- Sell solutions. What is a common challenge that many people have that you know how to solve? If you're familiar with the dilemma, it will be easier to market products that offer a solution.

- Cater to cherished hobbies. What topics are you knowledgeable about that many are fanatical about? Promote products related to popular hobbies and activities.

- Meet an emotional need. What are people afraid of? Most of us are afraid of being alone, missing out on the good things in life, or not being successful. Sell a product that resolves those fears.

- The three most successful niches tend to be love, money, and health. Narrow one of these broad topics down to a sub-topic. For example, in the love niche, subtopics can include getting back your "ex," finding "the one," dating success, and many more. You can narrow it even further by catering to one gender.

2. **Find your keywords**. Spend some time researching good keywords in your niche. The Google Adwords Keyword Tool is one of the most popular methods of discovering popular keywords that people use when looking for information or products in your niche.

You can also use keywordseverywhere.com as well to do your research; it's another great way to find the information on your keywords.

- What you're looking for is a keyword related to your niche that is getting a significant number of searches, but for which there is not too much competition. The Google keyword tool is pretty self-explanatory when it comes to these numbers. A good minimum is 1,500 searches per month.

  Your keywords will be the cornerstone of your marketing plans. All of your marketing efforts will revolve around these keywords.

3. **Choose a product**. There are several affiliate network sites, but Clickbank is certainly the largest. Also, take a look at Commission Junction. You want to consider how much you will earn per sale, but that's not the only important detail.

Take a look at the sales page. How does it look to you? Does the sales page peak your interest and make you want to buy the product? If you wouldn't buy it, you shouldn't expect anyone else to either. Ensure the sales page looks professional

Does the product have a guarantee or a warranty? How good is it? Would you be wary of buying this product with the guarantee or warranty that is provided?

- Perhaps most importantly: is this a product that people in your niche would be willing to spend money on?

4. **Get a domain name**. Your domain name also contributes to your sales success. This is the first place your keyword will come into play.

- Include your keyword in your domain name. For example, if your keyword was "lose 30 pounds in 30 days," your domain name could be "lose30poundsin30days.com." It's very likely that the domain name you want won't be available, but there are ways around this issue.

- For example, the domain name "lose30poundsin30daysnow.com" might work for you. Or perhaps, "lose30poundsin30dayseasily.com" would work well too. Just try to be sure that your keyword comes first in your domain name. Add anything extra at the end.
- Most studies have shown that .com endings are best. Most top affiliate marketers avoid other suffixes, with the exceptions of .net and .org.

There are many places to register domain names. GoDaddy.com is the most popular.

5. **Build a website**. The easiest way to a full-blown website is by using WordPress software. You can get it free at wordpress.org and look over the tutorials about how to upload the software to your hosting. Many hosting companies also have a "1-click" installation for WordPress.

- Post content on your site every day for the first couple of weeks, and then 2 or 3 times a week thereafter. This will keep your readers and the search engines coming back for more.
- Put a newsletter sign-up form on your website and communicate with your subscribers regularly. Your subscribers are your list, and your list is like gold. Cultivate a relationship with them, and they'll buy from you time and

time again. A popular autoresponder service is Aweber, and there are many more as well.

6. **Create lots of backlinks**. One way to make your website more relevant is to create a lot of backlinks. These are links that point back to your website. Search engines place a high value on these.

One good strategy to create backlinks and gain some readers is by writing articles and posting them in article directories. These articles will contain a short bio with a link to your website for promotion.

Other ways to create backlinks include posting on forums, posting on blogs, and registering your website with numerous website directories. Don't forget to create a Facebook page and Twitter account. Utilize websites like Squidoo, as well.

7. **Keep repeating the process**. One website and one product to promote are unlikely to create a large amount of income. It will be necessary to promote several products, each with its own corresponding website. You can stay within the same niche, or you can use a new niche each time.

- Once you have a process that works for you, it becomes easy. Simply repeat the process over and over again. Keep in mind that some of your websites might fail to make money. But a few of your websites will make a lot of money. So it only makes sense to create multiple sites with multiple products.

As you can see, making money with affiliate marketing is not that difficult. It can be time-consuming, but it's also possible to outsource a lot of the work. Many successful affiliate marketers hire someone to build their websites. They also hire people to write their articles. The most important part of the process is finding profitable keywords and products. Always ensure you are in a niche that appeals to have a sufficient number of customers. Remember that someone has to actually buy the product for you to make any money. Take note of what works for you and what does not. This process lends itself to constant improvement. Don't wait.

The sooner you start, the sooner you'll see some profits. There is no time to waste. Get out there and make your dreams a reality and start making the cash flow work in your favor. One thing to note when you do affiliate marketing. You need to disclose that the links you provide are affiliate links by federal law.

This is very simple to do by simply saying in your blog posts or content that " These links may be an affiliate link, and I may make a commission on your purchase at no added cost to you. " This will cover you from legal issues with the FTC (Federal Trade Commission) as well as the guidelines of most online platforms that you may be using to conduct your business.

Easy Ways to Make Extra Money

We could all use a little extra money. The obvious solution is to get a second job, but if you're already working 40+ hours a week on someone else's schedule, the idea of working more hours on a schedule might not sit too well with you. Also, most part-time jobs don't pay very well. So what can you do?

There are plenty of things you can do to earn extra money! Try some of these:

1. **Write articles**. Contact blogs about subjects in which you're an expert. Offer to write an article for them. Or try a site like textbroker.com or elance.com. The money can be good, and you have a lot of flexibility. You can work anytime of the day or night.
2. **Sell stuff**. Sell all the stuff you have that you don't want or need anymore. If you're really feeling rambunctious, ask your neighbors and friends if they have anything they want

to sell. You can ask for 10-20% of the selling price. Use eBay or Craigslist to get a good price.

3. **Re-write ads**. Contact sellers on eBay or Craigslist and offer to re-write poorly written ads for 2-5% of the selling price. Some folks make a lot of money at this. The trick is to stick to the higher priced items like cars, furniture, and similar things.

4. **Consult**. If you're an expert at anything, find a way to make some money on the side with it. Maybe you can do taxes in the spring. Or perhaps you have someother talent that a small business could use on a part-time basis.

5. **Tutor**.Tutoring can be a great way to make extra money. The hourly rate can be great, and it's pleasant, low-stress work. Put an ad on Craigslist or contact the local schools.

6. **Give a seminar**. This is similar to consulting, but instead of getting a good payday from a couple of sources, you can make a little money from a lot of people. You can probably get a lecture hall at a local university for a smal amount of money. Simply advertise and see how many people you can get to sign up.

7. **Start your own website.** If you can get traffic, you can make money. Start a blog or a simple website to sell a product or even someone else's product for a commission. Or, you can charge for advertising on your site. Research internet marketing and implement traffic-getting techniques. Add more websites once you establish some regular profit.

8. **Mow lawns**. It sounds like a job for a high school kid, but you can make $20+ in 30 minutes. $40+ an hour isn't bad! It certainly beats delivering pizzas.

9. **Deliver newspapers**. It's good money for the amount of time it takes. You can even get some exercise if you get a walking route.

10. Ask for a raise. If you think you deserve a raise, it doesn't hurt to ask. You're already putting in the time. Even a small raise is like free money.

11. **Walk dogs**. People love their pets and will pay $10-15 for someone to take their dog out at lunchtime for 15 minutes while they're at work. Some people work second shift and would love for someone to take Fido out for a walk at night.

This is just a very short list of ideas; I have 100+ you can probably come up with many more. Making a little extra money can really help to pay the bills, and you might even find something that you enjoy doing. Good luck! If you want the list of 100 ideas on ways to work from home or online head on over here: https://consult-a-blind-guy.ck.page/wfh100 an get the list for FREE.

Become a Self-Made Millionaire
by Following These 9 Practices

If you aren't lucky enough to inherit a million dollars, you'll have to create wealth on your own. Relatively few millionaires inherit their wealth, so you're in good company. Most millionaires didn't become wealthy by doing anything spectacular. They simply have a useful set of habits that they stick to religiously.

Start on the path to becoming a self-made millionaire:

1. **Deal with uncertainty.** Most millionaires don't have a "regular job" and are forced to deal with more uncertainty than average income earners. Be comfortable with uncertainty.

2. **Pay yourself before you pay your bills**. Save at least 10% of your paycheck before you sit down and pay your bills. If you pay yourself first, you'll adjust your spending to accommodate your bills. If you pay your bills first, you'll spend the remainder and save nothing. Save your money before you have a chance to spend it.

- The average millionaire saves over 20% of his income each month.

- When you get a raise at work, attempt to save 100% of that new income.

3. Live beneath your means. Most millionaires aren't big spenders. They buy used cars and avoid luxury brands. They live in more modest homes than they can afford.

- Becoming wealthy is most often the result of a moderate lifestyle, aggressive When you get a raise at work, attempt to save 100% of that new income. Saving, discipline, and time. These are all things that anyone can do. Consider the results when someone does the opposite of these things.

4. **Fire your boss**. Roughly 70% of millionaires are self-employed. Working for a big company can be comforting, but it's also expensive. You're selling your time at

wholesale prices. When you work for yourself, you have more opportunities to make a big salary. Start a small business on the side and make that your hobby.

5. **Spend time with other millionaires**. Spend time with wealthy people if you want to become wealthy. You'll be provided with more opportunities and learn how millionaires think. Their approach to money and the world is very different than those of the average person.

6. **Avoid debt that doesn't increase your income or net worth**. Millionaires avoid debt like the plague unless it provides financial opportunities. A millionaire might get a loan to purchase an apartment building or build a business, but she wouldn't borrow money for a vacation.

   - Avoid borrowing money unless it will strengthen your financial situation down the road.

7. **Have financial goals**. Most impressive things are accomplished by those with goals. Saving a million dollars is too big to happen by accident. Wealthy people that created their wealth have goals. What are yours?

8. **Get a mentor**. The vast majority of millionaires state that a mentor was a significant factor in accumulating their wealth. Everything is easier when you have a guide that has already accomplished your goal. Find a mentor and follow their advice. Networking is the key to finding an appropriate mentor. Put yourself out there.

9. **Avoid wasting time**. Every minute you waste could've been spent on earning more money or learning something relevant. It's important to have hobbies and interests

outside of building your wealth. But time spent on television and surfing the internet is neither beneficial nor satisfying. Use your time wisely.

You can adopt the most important behaviors of self-made millionaires. Is there anything in the list above that you can't do? With patience and the right habits, you can become a millionaire, too. With persistence, there's nothing you can't accomplish.

Remember to be patient and make your money work for you not against you. Besides working full-time for a company, you're only getting half the money you work for. Consider this, the first six months of the year, your income goes towards taxes. The other six months, your income is what you actually bring home. So essentially, you're working half the year for free, and the other half is yours to keep. Figure out your budget and then consider how you can cut things out or down to save more money. The more you can save, the closer you will get to your goal. Then figure out the estimate of your expenses, then re-figure your budget multiple times to come up with the best savings plan. Remember, if you're your own boss, " PAY YOURSELF FIRST " and everything else after that. Now go out there and make your dreams a reality and make that cash flow work in your favor. Want to learn more about how you can make money from home and online? Check out consultablindguy.com or the YouTube channel for more.

How Much Money is Enough?

If you ask a billionaire, he'll likely respond that no amount is enough. Others might reflexively say, "One million dollars." Those that are more thoughtful might have a different number. There comes a point that there might be a better way to spend your

time than chasing more money. You'll never know if you've reached that point if you don't define it. Studies have shown that happiness doesn't increase beyond an income of $70-75k per year. That's a comfortable living in most parts of the country, but it's not enough to drive a new Mercedes every three years and vacation in Europe with the family every summer. It would be tough to send your child to Harvard on a $70,000 salary. How much is enough? It depends on you and your circumstances.

Consider how much you need to live fully:
1. **How old are you?** How much longer do you expect to live? If you're 90, you probably require less money for the rest of your life than someone that just turned 30. There are actuarial tables that can tell you how much longer you're expected to live. Plan to live longer than expected!
2. **How much are your monthly expenses**? What would your expenses be if you were living the life of your dreams? Let your imagination run wild. What expenses would you have? A new bowling ball each year or a second house

inVail? A housekeeper? A thoroughbred? It's your life. Determine how much it would take to finance your ideal life.

3. **Who are you responsible for**? Do you have three children that will attend college in the next ten years? Do you have a spouse that doesn't work? Do you care for an aging parent? For how long do you expect to financially provide for others?

4. **What is your current debt situation**? Do you have 20 years left on a mortgage hanging over your head? Significant medical bills? Credit cards?

5. **When would you like to retire**, and how much do you need each month to live comfortably? How would you like to spend your retirement? Do you want to travel regularly? Play golf every day? How much would a typical month in retirement cost?

- Maybe you value your free time above all else and would be happy living a simple life with a Labrador retriever and a large vegetable garden, reading books all afternoon.

6. **What toys do you want to own**? A plane? A Porsche? A boat? A second home? Swimming pool? Motorcycle?

There's no set answer to the question, "How much money is enough?" It's completely dependent on your desires and circumstances. The number might be quite small or very high. It's your number. If you've never considered how much money you need, take the time to think about it. Money is great for a couple of things: primarily, solving problems and providing choices. It has limited value beyond those two purposes. It's a mistake to use money for establishing status. To be worried

about impressing your peers is best left to your teenager.
Needing money for the wrong things is limiting. It requires working longer and harder than necessary.
You could be doing other things with your limited time on Earth. Think long and hard about what is most important to you. Ensure that you develop an income, savings, and net worth to acquire the possessions and freedom that will allow you to live your life in the way you desire. Spend time addressing this critical issue. You might be able to quit working sooner than you think.

Get Creative With Making Money at Home

Have you lost your job or suffered reduced hours (and pay) because of the sluggish economy? As the person responsible for putting food on your table, you might not have the luxury of waiting for a lucrative full-time job to come your way.
Instead, start the process of finding other sources of income. Use your resolve to come up with creative ways to earn an income at home.

How to Identify Alternate Earning Opportunities
Use these ideas for identifying creative ways to make money at home:
1. **Survey your neighborhood**. Sometimes, answers to your challenges are closer than you know! There could very well be a need for your knowledge or skills right there in your

own neighborhood. How could you tap into these needs to earn from your abilities?

- Did you play sports while you were in school? Perhaps one of your local schools could do with an assistant coach to help expand one of their sports programs. This could provide you with some extra income.

- Since you already have a car that's sitting idle most of the time, why not start a carpooling service to take community kids to and from school or their after-school activities? It's very likely that parents will feel reassured knowing that their kids are in the hands of a trustworthy neighbor.

2. **Re-purpose one of your skill sets**. At your last job, you were likely called upon to do different tasks that were aligned with your skills. Take a minute and think about whether some of those skills could be applied to other areas.

- Were you the resident letter writer because of your way with words? If so, it's possible that you could take your skill to a content writing website, newspaper, or publishing house.

- Did you ever get involved with training new staff members because your boss felt you were an effective communicator? Offer your services to a skills training institution. You could even offer online training in various skills for a fee.

3. **Consider consultancy**. Some employers, while unable to hire new employees due to the instability of the economy, may still need valuable input from people like you in the

field. Hence, many companies are going the route of hiring consultants, instead.

- When companies hire consultants, they don't have to worry about employee expenses like health insurance, clothing allowance, and more. To do different tasks that were aligned with your skills. Take a minute and think They can get what they need without the costs and commitment of hiring an employee.
- That's where you come in! Offer your consultancy services and enable them to save money while you make money.
- You might be able to provide valuable input to the company right from your home computer.

Those who will remain afloat throughout this employment slump are people like you who are willing to think outside the box to make things happen.

Take advantage of earning alternatives like these and turn things around. Use these tips as a springboard to more ideas of your own. Who knows? You might just find your next great career!

Earn Extra Income by Freelancing on the Web

Who isn't looking for additional cash these days? Luckily, there are plenty of ways. Research the websites you're interested in. If a website passes your review you can make extra money by offering your services on the internet. Ranging from full-time to piecemeal freelance gigs, the array of online job choices is staggering.

If you're optimistic and confident, prepare to make plenty of extra money by doing some online freelance work.

Try these ideas to pick up some quick cash:
1. **Consider your skills.** Focus your efforts on your unique talents when looking for web work.
   - For example, if you're a fast typist, look for data entry jobs online. If you can spin a good yarn, try a writing job or two. If you're a skilled web surfer, find research jobs to fill the coffer.
   - Try Upwork.com and other popular freelance portals to find work.
2. **Use social networks for meetings**. With the advent of social media, you can converse with prospective employers. Ensure that others see your qualities through your social networking efforts.
3. **Be brave**. Diving in can be challenging and perhaps intimidating. To protect yourself, research the websites you're interested in. If a website passes your criteria and appears to be reputable, sometimes it's a great idea to simply jump in and accept your first online gig.
   - When you do, you'll be rewarded for your courage with some extra money.
4. **Learn to do transcriptions to earn steady, incoming wages.** Transcribing is an exploding online career. If you're a competent typist, you're more than half-way along the

path to earning extra dollars by typing out interviews, dictated books, and other info.

5. **Contact local businesses to offer them help** to post on their social media accounts. If you're an avid Twitterer and Facebooker, you could be paid to post regularly for business owners who don't have the time or skill to do it themselves.

6. **Look for websites that offer cash to endorse their products**. Become an affiliate of popular companies like Amazon and post their ads (coded with your affiliate number) on your Facebook page. Whenever someone clicks on your ad and buys the product, you earn a commission.

- If you have a lot of friends who enjoy a particular hobby, find a vendor of supplies you can all enjoy. Become an affiliate, post their ads, and earn commissions on their products.

7. **Utilize websites that reward you** for shopping on their sites. It's wise to be careful with this tip. You could spend more with your shopping than you make through the gift card reward. But if you're planning to purchase a gift anyway, you could earn a few extra bucks this way.

8. **Find a "micro-gig"** at the website called "Fiverr." What will you do for five dollars? Post it on the Fiverr website, and you might get a few takers. Explore the website to get an idea of the tasks people want done. Then, offer to do those tasks.

- Think about what you can do easily and quickly.

9. **Serve on a mock online jury**. At Ejury.com, you'll be paid to serve on a mock jury. Discover the experience of making a real difference with the other online jury members.

10.   **Do you have an endless thirst for knowledge** and trivia? Put your curiosity to work and make a few bucks at Cha Cha. Seek out correct responses to people's questions and get paid for each answer. If you're a tip-top researcher or web surfer, Cha Cha's for you.

If you have a computer and know how to type, you have a gold mine right in your own house. Achieve your financial goals by bringing in extra money from online sources. There are many other sites you can check out for freelance work. Check out Upwork, Rev, and craigslist, just to name a few. They have listings of just about every type of work under the sun that you could make some modest income from.

A Guide To Making Money With Fiverr

Microjobs are becoming more popular all the time. If you're looking to make some extra cash on a schedule that works for you, Fiverr (www.fiverr.com) is a great vehicle to accomplish exactly that. If you already have a service-type business, you can use Fiverr to find more clients. Fiverr is a website that allows users to sell and purchase services for $5. There are people that actually earn a full-time living from Fiverr alone. $5 might not sound like a lot, but there are many simple tasks you probably know how to do that only take a few minutes of your time. Perhaps there is something you could even do while watching television on your couch.

Follow this step-by-step plan for earning money with Fiverr:

1. **Look at the services being offered**. You're sure to get some great ideas. Scroll through the offerings and make note of those that you're capable of performing.
2. **Make a list of the services you'd like to provide**. Take some time and brainstorm your own ideas.

- Blog and article writing
- Voiceover work
- Editing
- Programming
- Reviewing Products
- Graphics
- SEO Work

Think about challenges people have and how you can solve them. A store owner might like to have a blog but doesn't have the slightest idea how to set up WordPress. Someone might want to remove red-eye from a photograph but doesn't know how to use the necessary software.

- Keep in mind the time it will take to complete the task. Do you want to work for $5/hour? It might be worth it if you're able to turn that client into a long-term client for higher-end services later on. That $5 graphics job might become a $1,000 job after they get a feel for your work.

3. **Create your gig.** Fiverr offers are referred to as "gigs." Fiverr has become quite competitive over the last few years. Optimizing your gig is important.

- Take the time to create a good title. Look at the other gigs and notice the titles that really catch your eye. Attempt to create an even better title.
- Be bold and include a video. You can describe your offering or even show an example of your work. Video improves your visibility tremendously.
- Use the tag field effectively. Consider all the terms people could use to locate your services.

4. **Promote your gig**. This is the real key to Fiverr success. Getting noticed is critical. Take advantage of the various social media platforms to promote your services. Use Facebook and Twitter at a minimum. You can also use blogs, articles, and forums to spread the word.

5. **Make use of the Fiverr forums**. Fiverr has a very active forum community. One of the best ways to find your first customer is to spend some time on there and comment on the various threads. Many Fiverr service providers are also customers. If people get to know and trust you, you'll be more likely to get some work.

6. **Be thorough**. Get all the information you need before getting started with your work. Delivering a custom greeting card with a green theme won't go over well if your client hates green. There is a messaging system built into Fiverr to foster effective communication.

- Fiverr prohibits communication outside of their website. This rarely stops the motivated, however. Moving clients away from Fiverr is an effective tactic for providing more expensive services.

7. **Be punctual and excellent.** Deliver your best work on time. It can be easy to procrastinate without a boss hovering over you. If you become popular, it's easy to have the jobs stack up quickly. Positive reviews contribute to long-term success.

There's a lot to like about Fiverr. With a good gig, it's possible to earn money at an impressive hourly rate. The greatest challenge is getting noticed among all the other service providers. There are plenty of quick tasks that can be performed, but there are a lot of other people offering the same services.

Optimizing your gig is critical. Spend the necessary time on your title and description. Be sure to include a video to improve your exposure. With a bit of work, it's possible to earn an impressive amount of money in your spare time.

A Case Study: Monetizing a Hobby Online

Many of us dream of finding a way to make money at our hobby online. Wouldn't making money on something you love be a thrill? Plus, if you set your business up properly, maintenance may take very little work. For example, Michelle turned her love of dolls into a part-time business with a full-time income. Michelle has always loved dolls. Even as she got older, this never changed. She collected them and even had several antique dollhouses. Her husband eventually got a little irritated at the cost of this hobby. Michelle decided she would show him. She brainstormed for a couple of days and decided she would finance her hobby by making money with it. Michelle thought this might actually be fun. Plus, she already knew a lot about her hobby, so she wouldn't have to learn much. She did have a lot to learn about putting a business online, however.

Here are the steps Michelle took, in order, to get her business going:

1. **She made a website**. Michelle knew nothing about web design, but a friend told her that she could use www.wordpress.org to make a professional-looking web page. There are tutorials on the site.

2. **Found some products to promote for a commission.** First, she went to www.amazon.com and signed up as an affiliate, which is free. This provided Michelle with specific links to various doll-based products she could advertise on her site. She also found products to promote from a variety of other places.

3. **She put those affiliate links on her website**. Michelle worked the affiliate links into her website text wherever it was logical. If she posted an article about a specific type of doll, she would include an affiliate link for where the reader could purchase that doll. If a reader bought the doll, Michelle received a percentage of the purchase price.

4. **Michelle wrote her own manual**. Because of her extensive knowledge, Michelle was able to write a how-to for doll collecting. She did all the work in a word processor and then converted the document to a .pdf file.

- Michelle then sold her manual on her site, too. She really liked this, because she got to keep 100% of the money!

5. **She marketed her site.** This is most important! After all, if no one knows the website exists, no one can buy anything.

- Michelle started her marketing campaign with a Facebook fan page, a twitter account, and some written articles. She posted the articles on over 50 free article directories, including www.ezinearticles.com and www.articlesbase.com.

- In the author's resource box for each article, she included a link back to her website.

6. **She signed up for Google Adsense**. Adsense provided advertising that Michelle could put on her website. Every time a site visitor clicked on an ad, Michelle received some money. Over time, with a lot of visitors, this money really began to add up. Eventually, she was making several hundred dollars a month just from Adsense income.

While this is not an all-inclusive list, these are the basic steps that Michelle and many others have used to start a business online. You can do this too! You will always need a website, a product or service to sell, and a way to get people to your website. Getting a consistent stream of visitors to your site can take time, but with persistence, you'll get there. Start thinking today about how you can make money online with your hobby. What products and services can you offer? What unique ways can you drive traffic to your website? The sooner you get started, the sooner you can spend your work-time doing something you love.

From Hobby to Home Business in Five Steps

Do you ever feel trapped in a job you don't find rewarding? The key to living a more fulfilling life is to go after your passions. Being someone's employee often requires you to put these passions aside so you can work towards their vision – not yours!

Becoming an entrepreneur is not for everyone. There are many obstacles between you and your dreams, including coming up with the willpower to get started on your project, finding the confidence to get through multiple mishaps, and devoting many hours of hard work to building your vision.Being an entrepreneur is hard work and can be disheartening at times – but owning your business can be a very fulfilling and freeing experience.

Follow these steps to follow your passions through your own business:

1. **Find your calling.** You could base your business on a talent you have, a hobby you love, or your desire to make a difference in people's lives.

- There is a popular belief that it takes 10,000 hours of work before one can be considered an expert in any field. This belief may not be true, but it shows that expertise requires time and hard work.

2. **Register your business and apply for necessary licenses**. Registering your home business is a very simple process.

- All you need to do is register your business name through the U. S. Small Business Administration and apply for a tax ID.

- You will also have to register your business through state agencies.Applying for licenses is necessary if your field is regulated – for instance, if you prepare food, work with dangerous chemicals, or provide services that require special qualifications such as legal advice or accounting.

3. **Create your business plan.** Creating a business plan is a systematic process that provides a blueprint for your business and will help you obtain funding for your project.

- Start by explaining what the purpose of your business is and how you'll achieve it.

- Explain what kind of products you want to sell or list the services you'll be providing.

- Define your target audience in as many details as possible.
- Create an outline for your marketing strategy and include your expected prices as well as how much profit you expect to generate.

4. **Explore your financing options.** Go over your budget and business plan carefully to assess how much money you require.

- Look for investors among your friends and relatives, or angel investors through local business associations. Borrowing money is usually your best option if you cannot find investors for your project.
- The U. S. Small Business Administration is a great place to get started with financing, but you could also contact your financial institution to learn more about the business loans they offer.

5. **Get to work!** Becoming a successful home business owner requires time, hard work, and real dedication.

- Besides spending some time on developing your products or services, promoting your business, and providing excellent customer service, it's also important to work on acquiring more skills that will help you become a better business owner.
- Divide the large goals from your business plan into smaller goals you can accomplish on ,a weekly or daily basis. This division will also help you assess your progress.
- Keep in mind that your goals might have to shift if your market changes.

The best way to launch your business and achieve financial stability is to put together a detailed plan with a series of small, manageable steps that will lead you to your goals. Use these five steps as a broad template for your project and add any additional steps that are relevant to your business. Want to know more? Still, have questions? You can check out my YouTube channel, and maybe that will answer some of those things, and you can comment with any questions you still have and I'll get back to you as soon as possible or maybe even do a video just for you to help clear up an issue you're having. Head on over to https://youtube.com/consultablindguy. I have been a crafter for years and sold plenty of items online and offline, so I know how the struggle goes when first starting.

Don't worry, you got this. Good luck!

How To Make Money With Your Passion

You might have heard of others enjoying a fun and fulfilling career related to their passion. They get to spend their time at work doing things they like! What about you? Do you feel as if you're chained to a job you loathe? Do you dream of making money with your passion? Take heart! Whether you're looking for a fulfilling career or wanting to bring in a second income stream, you can start making plans today for a successful venture making money from your passion. You can be pretty sure that there is something you love to do that someone would gladly pay you for right now!

There are three critical steps to making money with your passion:

1. **Determine all the ways you can monetize your passion.** When you start brainstorming, it's important to do so in a way that moves you toward success.

   - Most people immediately try to figure out why something won't work. However, if an idea is immediately attacked in this way, the idea tends to be dismissed too quickly.

Every idea – even the best idea – will have challenges associated with it, so record all your ideas without prejudging them.

   - Capture as many ideas as you can and then take a few days, maybe even a week, before you approach those ideas critically. Give your brain some time to really ponder on them for a while. A few nights of sleep can create some spectacular results.

- Give each idea at least a few minutes of consideration before making a decision. Many excellent ideas are quickly ignored before they are thoroughly investigated.
- Be open-minded. Because we associate our passion with 'fun,' we don't really consider the financial value that activity might have to others.

2. **Know that you're already an exper**t. One common challenge you may have is the belief that you don't know enough. But you don't have to be the world's leading expert to be valuable and get paid.

- Ask yourself the following question: "Do I know enough about this subject to be able to teach the average person enough to at least get them started?
- If you can answer 'yes,' then you know enough to charge people money for your expertise. It's similar to being a math tutor. You might not have a Ph.D. in mathematics, but you could still probably tutor a 5th grader and get paid for it.
- There are plenty of people out there that are the equivalent of a 5th grader when it comes to your area of expertise. **Being an expert is relative. You are already an expert compared to many**.
- So, if you could sit down and teach the average person something of value, you already know enough to make money at it. That doesn't mean you shouldn't continue to educate yourself and improve your knowledge and skills.

But it does mean that you can get started making money as soon as possible.

3. **Believe you can do the impossible**. Many things are commonplace today that were considered to be impossible not that long ago.

   The four-minute mile is a common example. It was considered to be impossible for a long time. Then it was accomplished, and over 15 additional people did the same thing over the next three years. Even high school kids have broken the 4-minute mile barrier.

   - Of course, making money from your passion is not impossible, but most believe that it is. So you have to think you can do what you feel is impossible.

   - The easiest way to do this is to surround yourself with people that have already done it. If you can see others that are doing what you want to do, it's like brainwashing in reverse. **If you see their reality every day, you'll believe that you can do it, too.**

If you can understand how these three steps can work for you, it's only a matter of time before you can make your living with your passion!

Who Could You Be Helping Right Now?

Keep in mind that there are things that you love to do that you can do better than the average person. There are also people out there looking for your expertise. If you can simply find each other, you're all set.

1. **Do some research on others who make money with their passion**. You'll find that few of them are in danger of being the next Bill Gates, yet, they do very well! That should be reassuring to you. **There are plenty of opportunities for 'regular' people with a passion in a field to excel.**

2. **Your biggest obstacle is not a lack of skill, experience, or credentials**. It is simply the result of too little creativity or courage. With enough creativity and courage, anything is possible. **Focus your energy on those two items**. It improves all aspects of your life.

Tips For Success

Even though you'll be enjoying pursuing your passion in your new business, it's still a business, and you'll want to see it bring in profits.

Endeavor to develop these attributes for success in putting your passion to work for you:

1. **Successful people have a relatively accurate perspective about what is possible.** Consider this: if your perspective on everything in the world were actually accurate, you'd most likely be wealthier, happier, and more capable of bringing your dreams to life. We all have perceptions that are inaccurate. **Strive to imagine what you can really do.**

2. **Understand what steps need to be taken.** Many of us waste our time on activities that don't have much impact.

Determine which activities are priorities for profits and spend more of your time on those activities.

3. **Complete the tasks that you know must be done**. Not all business tasks are pleasurable, even if you're passionate about the business. However, successful folks do these necessary tasks quickly and enthusiastically.

Make That First Dollar

Psychologically, it's very powerful to actually make some money at your passion – any money at all! Even if it is just $1, it demonstrates that you're capable of getting paid for your passion. **Don't underestimate the power of getting paid for the first time!** Be persistent until that first payday happens.

Conclusion

Making a great living at your passion is something that anyone can do – even you. First, you must believe that it's possible. Go find some people that are already doing what you want to do. They're out there, and finding them with the Internet is easy. By spending time with them, even electronically, you'll begin to believe that you can do the same. Brainstorm all the possibilities with an open mind. Take a week before you start really looking at the ideas critically. What seems like a bad idea on day one can look pretty good on day eight. Take action and make that first dollar. A simple sale can make all the difference in the world. One dollar, and you're off to the races. **Give yourself the chance to make money doing what you love**. You can do it!

Top 8 Tips for Making Money From Your Artistic Creations

Is it possible to earn a living as an artist? Actually, it's entirely possible. After all, many others have done it. While the starving artist cliché might be more common than financially comfortable artists, it certainly can be accomplished. For an up-and-coming artist, there are many challenges to be met, but all of them are solvable. Those that become successful apply effective solutions.

Using these tips will help you make a living from your artistic endeavors:

1. **Realize that talent alone is insufficient.** We all know incredibly talented people that have nothing to show for it. There is a business aspect to any type of art that must be managed if you want to be successful.

2. **Choose your art and money beliefs with care.** What do you believe about money and art? Are those beliefs going to support you in earning money? If you have the following beliefs, it would be wise to work on changing them:

   - All artists are starving artists.
   - The only artists that make money are sellouts.
   - Money corrupts art.

3. **Find other artists that are successfully making money.** Successful artists are generally quite agreeable about giving advice and support.

   - Why start from scratch when you can get the inside scoop from a true expert? Use other artists as valuable resources!

4. **Create art that people want.** If you look at the art that sells, it's not necessarily the most original, super-beautiful piece of work that's ever been created. It's simply art that people enjoy. Look at popular movies and books. They're not always great, just enjoyable.

5. **Get your work out there.** The starving artist has 100 things uncompleted or completed but not visible to the general public. You have to publish your art in some fashion if people are going to be able to buy it. Give them something to see. Remember that "art" comes in many forms.

   - If you're a writer, consider writing a book for Kindle.
   - If you're a painter, take your work to the local art fairs.
   - If you make movies, get something on YouTube.
   - If your art is making wedding cakes, take some pictures and put them on your website.

6. **Seek to be visible and then seek to be paid.** If necessary, this might even mean giving your work away for free until you become better known.

   - Show off your work to anyone that you think might have an interest.
   - Once your art is visible and has reached a sufficient level, start charging for the privilege of enjoying your creation.

7. **Most mediocre artists are poor artists**, so be excellent. Most artistic fields are competitive. The good news is that most artists aren't truly committed. There is a lot of mediocre competition.

- Persistence is enough to enjoy more success than 90% of the people in your chosen field.

8. **Be a consumer of art**. When you find something you really like, purchase it. If you would like others to support your artistic endeavors, you should do the same for them. Supporting others will help you believe that you deserve to be supported as well.

So get out there and become well known in your field. That means getting some excellent work completed and feeding it to the masses. Find a great mentor and spend as much time with them as possible. If you're persistent, you're likely to succeed. Enjoy a healthy income while doing what you love to do!

Make Money From Your Hobby
How to generate an income from doing what you love

Introduction

Have you ever wondered what it would be like if you could earn money from doing your hobby? If you really think about it from a financial aspect, it makes good sense. You likely already have all the tools it takes to enjoy your hobby, and you probably want to sharpen your skills and get better and better at your hobby. And more likely than not, you're willing to invest additional money into whatever tools are necessary, and the time it takes to practice your cherished activity. Right? Getting paid is just the icing on the cake. Not to mention anything you spend on tools will be tax-deductible. Making money from your hobby is a pretty smart thing to do. After all, when you love to do something, you'll want to do it all the time. If you want to earn money from your hobby, there are some strategies to use to achieve this goal. Selecting the hobby that provides the best chance to earn money, starting small, saving receipts for tax purposes, and developing your skills to perform the hobby are integral strategies to take to make money from your hobby. Let your creativity run wild and consider the following strategies to make money from your hobby.

Choose The Hobby That's Right For You To Develop An Income Stream

To earn money from a hobby, you've got to find the hobby that fits you. Consider your answers to the following questions to help you pinpoint which of your hobbies you want to cultivate in order to make money.

1. **What do you like to do in your spare time?** Think about all the hobbies you enjoy. Feel free to list them out. They might be as wide-ranging as jewelry-making to woodworking and building websites. The important thing here is that you recognize what it is you love that you can make money doing.

2. **Are you willing to take a class**? Consider the activities you truly thirst to learn more about. If you strive to discover more about a hobby, it just might be the one to help you make money.

- Some people have begun practicing hobbies on their own with little to no formal instruction. If you love doing your hobby and want to make money at it, hopefully, you'll think it's a good idea to further your skills with some expert instruction.

- However, your decision to gain more information about your activity will be affected by the level of skill and know-how you already possess and your internal drive to further explore the activity.

3. **Are you able to create something that you can sell?** Many hobbies involve making an item that is then usable. For example, if knitting is the leisurely activity you enjoy, you'll be creating wearable and other assorted items like scarves, sweaters, and purses to sell.

4. **If not, will you be selling your skills instead?** If you love to paint scenery on walls, you'll be creating beautiful land and seascapes in people's homes. You'll be selling your time, paint supplies, and efforts yet leave people with a lovely finished product. Other hobbies where you'd be selling your skills are planting gardens for people and organizing closets.

5. **Is your favorite hobby online or offline?** With the advent and widespread popularity of the internet, even more types of hobbies are available for people to develop online.

- One such example is building websites. Even though some people are trained to do this type of work, others have learned to build websites by actually completing the process on a do-it-yourself web-building site. Some have even taken on building websites for their friends and family.

- So, when you're considering which of your hobbies to convert into an income stream, ensure you explore your online activities as well.

6. **Keep your mind wide open.** Remember that many activities you love to do can be considered a hobby to use to make money.

- Ponder this: a person who loves to organize her shelves, closets, and garage helps all her friends and family organize their homes. Why not consider organizing homes a hobby that she can do to make money?

- As you review your hobbies, think about those activities that bring you feelings of joy and completeness. When you identify one or two, examine those hobbies from the position, "Will someone pay me to do this job or make this item for them?"

Selecting the activity that will pay off most likely will be pretty easy to do. If you consider the above points, you'll narrow your choices to the one that you believe will bring in the most bucks.

"I do what I did as a hobby as a kid, you know, and make a living at it. And I just feel like I'm one of the luckiest guys in the world 'cuz I get paid to make toys and play with them." –Rick Baker

Hobbies To Consider

A wide range of hobbies can be utilized to develop another income stream. If you're lucky enough to enjoy several hobbies, you'll be deliberating which hobby would be wisest to select as your money-maker.

Outdoor Hobby Examples

1. **Boating**. Become a tour guide by taking visitors to your community out on the water. Start by charging less than the bigger boats and more established companies.
2. **Fishing.** If you love to fish and you own a boat, establish a business of taking people out on your boat to fish. Provide them with fishing poles and bait and charge them by the hour.
3. **Decorative Painting**. People that have a knack for doing special paint applications and design on patio floors, driveways and stucco walls will definitely make extra money with these talents.

Craft Hobby Examples

1. **Woodworking.** Those individuals who've been making their own furniture since completing Shop class in high school are in a position to truly embrace their love of producing furniture. Design your own pieces and sell them. Create customized pieces that your customers request.
2. **Knitting and Crocheting.** Yarn-related hobbies have been popular for eons. Even beginning knitters knit lovely scarves, baby blankets and purses that sell. Develop your own particular "brand" by producing purses with curly knitted cords affixed at the clasp or two-toned baby blankets. Use your personal design sense to make extra cash with yarn-related hobbies.

3. **Jewelry-Making.** Men and women alike have enjoyed the fine craft of making adornments for people of all ages. Whether you like working with beads or doing detailed metal work, selling the jewelry you make, such as rings, earrings, bracelets, chokers, and necklaces has been known to bring in some very big bucks.

Online Hobby Examples

1. **Creating websites.** Hobbyists who have this know-how or have learned by doing will really enjoy themselves and earn money by helping others to produce the websites of their dreams.
2. **Art design**. Believe it or not, experimenting with computer art software can eventually help you develop a nice income stream in the area of graphic arts. If you love toying with such programs and can create some dynamic art, you might be able to sell it online.
3. **Photography.** With today's user-friendly digital cameras, practically anybody can take good photos. But if you take great photos and have an eye for the unusual shot, you can definitely make money online with this talent.

Check out the various websites that allow you to post and sell your photos. Some will require you to pay a few cents to post photos while others are free to post and will take a percentage of your profits when a snapshot sells. Whether you choose an outdoor hobby, a craft hobby or an online hobby to establish your small hobby business, you'll enjoy the adventure of endeavoring to make money by practicing your hobby.

"It was just a hobby. I didn't expect it to turn into a business."–
Phil Katz

Start Small

As you begin to prepare yourself to earn money with your hobby, the following points will be helpful.

1. **Recognize you're starting a small business**. Converting a hobby into a money-maker is the same as beginning a small business.

2. **Limit spending**. Whenever you start a small business, it's important to keep the lid on upfront expenditures. Since the whole idea is to bring in cash, you'll want to refrain from getting too elaborate with spending in the initial stages of your hobby business.

3. **Examine your tools and knowledge base**. Think about whether you can start your hobby business with the tools and knowledge you already have. Of course, this would be the best and lowest cost method to earn money from your hobby.

4. **Focus on doing what you do well.** Spend some time performing and/or making the items that you do really well. Make an effort to stay focused on what you know and what you do best when you're first turning your hobby into an income stream. Your confidence will soar as you see the demand for what you do is growing.

5. **Give it a year**. After you see how your hobby business fares in the first year or so, examine whether it would be financially feasible to expand your repertoire.

- If consumer demand for your service, skill or products grows over the year and people have asked for a wider range of services, skills or products, you'll be more confident about investing your dollars to broaden your horizons and make more money.

Start small with your hobby business by recognizing it's an actual small business, limiting spending and taking a look at the tools and knowledge you already have. Then, concentrate on what you know and do well and allow your hobby business one year before making any major investments into it.

"It feels important to go to school; not necessarily to further my education, but more like a hobby." –Mandy Moore

Save Your Receipts And Keep Records

One of the great things about turning a hobby into income is that any costs you incur to perform the hobby are tax-deductible. It's pretty exciting when you think about claiming all your hobby-related expenses on your taxes every year. Also, keep accurate records of all your costs and income. Doing so will make things much easier, come tax time.

Here's a shortlist of some of the items you can claim:
- New equipment costs. Any equipment or tools required to make or perform your hobby is deductible.

- Supplies costs. Whether it's yarn, wood, textiles, or whatever, if you need it for your hobby business, it can be claimed.
- Travel costs. If you travel to display and sell your goods and services, present at seminars, or teach classes, those costs are considered business-related expenses.
- Printing costs. Any marketing materials you require, such as business cards and other related flyers, are deductible.
- Office supplies and postage costs. In the event you use these items to contact prospective or past customers, claim the expenses on your tax return.
- Monthly internet connection costs. If your business is online-based, paper-clip these bills together to claim on next year's return.

Get a spiral notebook or some files to keep all your business records together. Write down what you sell and the money you earn. Make helpful notes as you go along so you won't forget something important. If you start out keeping what few records you'll have, it will get easier. Because making money from your hobby constitutes a small business, save every receipt related to it. Document your mileage and other costs associated with your hobby. And keep records of every item that sells and the amount you earned. You'll be pleasantly surprised at the money you'll save at tax time if you save your receipts and keep accurate records.

Develop Your Skills

Because you want to excel at your hobby to make more money, you'll hopefully be willing to focus on developing your skills further. Taking responsibility to increase your expertise is an important element in the process. Explore the wealth of information that's out there about your chosen hobby. Read, watch videos, join a group, and discuss the hobby with other aficionados of the skill. Make it your number one goal to develop all the skills required to do your hobby flawlessly.

1. **Read about your hobby.** For nearly every hobby, you'll find reading material to educate and introduce you to new elements and facets of the activity.

2. **Watch videos online.** Since anything and everything can be found on the internet, look for videos of people practicing and discussing your hobby of choice. Soak up as much information as you can about what you love to do.

3. **Join an interest group**. If you're not already a member of a group that shares interest and time in your hobby, join one now. You'll be exposed to the work of others. You'll begin to establish relationships with others who do the same work. You might even gain additional knowledge from other group members about how they've made money.

4. **Talk to others who do the hobby**. In the event, a group isn't available for you to join, find a mentor who has practiced the hobby for years. Perhaps you'll meet someone who you think has better skill and knowledge than anyone else.

Developing your hobby skills is an important aspect to earning as much money as you can from the hobby. Reading, watching videos, joining groups, and communicating with others who do the hobby will help you gain knowledge and know-how about the hobby and develop your skills even more.

"I took up a sort of a hobby of just hanging around the local library. I'd pick out an author, and I would read all their books."
–Tom T. Hall

Tap into Your Creativity

Turning your hobby into an income stream requires you to "go deep" when it comes to creating your product or practicing your hobby skill. One of the unique aspects of making an item to sell to others is showing your own individual creativity. For example, if you make furniture, create your own signature scroll to include in all your furniture pieces. Allow your creativity to flow. To show a personal sense of originality when performing a service, consider doing something special to highlight your work. For example, provide customers with a snapshot of your results at their home and sign the photo. Leave a "thank you for your business" card after you've finished. Show off your abilities and efforts to make your product or skill interesting and even fun for your customers. Make a concerted effort to tap into your creativity to accentuate your hobby talents and impress your customers.

"I have an expensive hobby; buying homes, redoing them, tearing them down, and building them up the way they want to be built. I want to be an architect."
–Sandra Bullock

Perfect Your Skills

If you want to successfully make money doing your hobby, hone your skills. Practice, become known as the expert in your area, present at seminars, and instruct others on how to do the hobby. All of these efforts will help you fine-tune your skills and excel at what you do.

1. **Practice**. As they say, "Practice makes perfect," so it's recommended you spend many hours performing your hobby if you plan to build your income stream.
   - If your chosen interest is wood-working, make as many shelves, chests and tables as you can. The more you do, the better you'll become. You'll learn to cover up errors, correct mistakes, and make your pieces even more attractive.

2. **Become the resident expert.** Although reading was mentioned earlier, if you want to truly perfect your skills, get your hands on all reading material related to your hobby.
   - Make the decision to strive to know everything there is to know about your special activity. Establish a goal to become a "walking encyclopedia" for your chosen craft.

3. **Present at hobby seminars**. In your hometown and the surrounding areas, you might find opportunities to present to people eager to learn more about your hobby. Even if

you don't get paid to present at first, it's still a wise decision financially.

- If the invite is local, it won't cost you anything to get to the place to present. Once you're there, you're going to meet many people interested in your hobby. This means you can cultivate new customers. (See "Market Your Skills" section).

4. **Teach others.** If given a chance, instruct others about how to do your craft. In so doing, you'll develop your reputation as an expert in the field.

Hone your hobby skills by engaging in the above activities. Your hard work will pay off in dollars.

"We've been doing this for ten years and it's been a hobby for a lot longer than it's been a job." –John Campbell

Set Your Prices

Hopefully, this strategy won't be too difficult. Take a look at how others price similar goods or services. Consider how much time you'll expend to do the labor to produce the product or complete the service. Be judicious in your record-keeping. List out the services or goods you'll plan to make and sell, placing your charges for each item.

Keep in mind that when first starting your business, you might get more business if you keep your prices low. Of course, you can always adjust them later, doing so in small increments until you reach the price level you desire.

Market Your Skills

Selling your hobby wares or skills happens whenever potential customers "see" you and your work. In order to gain exposure, it's necessary to develop a plan to market your skills. Take a look at these marketing ideas to see how they'll fit into your new small business.

1. **Develop simple marketing materials**. Think business cards and maybe one flyer. If possible, make them yourself on your own computer to save money. If you're unable to produce marketing materials yourself, go to your local office supply store (like Office Depot, Staples, and Office Max), and inquire about costs to have 500 business cards printed.

   - At the very least, get business cards. You'll find them helpful to leave at various businesses or to give out to prospective customers. Your customers need to know how to reach you, and business cards conveniently and cheaply provide that information.

2. **Use the internet**. If you're willing to travel to perform your hobby skills for others, or your finished products can be easily shipped, it's recommended you have a web presence. You stand to put your face, product, and skills in front of millions of potential customers when you use the internet. Consider making a website to market your skills and wares.

3. **Establish a presence in your community**. If you want to earn money through practicing your hobby, make yourself known in your local community. Appear at street festivals.

Set up a table at the local health fair. Whenever your community gets together, be there. Your best place to find loyal customers is in your local community.

4. **Join the Chamber of Commerce**. Although you might not be sure you want to take this step, you'll be surprised at how many other small business owners you meet.

5. **Chamber members are incredibly supportive** of one another and often even call each other to do business. Plus, they refer customers to one another.

   - Depending on the type of hobby business you start, joining the Chamber of Commerce will help you make money from your craft.

6. **Display at trade shows**. If you want to make some cash from performing your hobby, take every opportunity to get your face and product out there where it can be seen. Trade shows make this possible. When you take part in local trade shows, you might be able to share displays with other local small businesses. Doing so means you will also share display costs.

7. **Network**. For any small business to be lucrative and successful, it's necessary to network. Getting to know as many other people in the same business or related ones widens your own financial opportunities.

   - Use your contact with one business owner to pave the way to establish other connections. Show your social side to market your hobby business to increase your income.

8. **Make media contacts.** Send out letters to local radio and television shows that you're interested in being interviewed to discuss your hobby and/or products. Keep in mind that such media usually want topics to be discussed and will not be interested in simply helping you sell your goods and services.

   - However, approach media representatives with the idea of educating the public about your hobby and sharing your expertise. Media representatives will usually give your business a "plug" at the beginning or end of the program you present.

9. **Get to know other small businesses.** You've probably deduced by now the importance of knowing what other small businesses are sprouting and flourishing in your community. Ask to display your wares or at least your business cards and flyers at their businesses. Be willing to display their cards as well whenever you're setting up to market and sell your own stuff.

10. **Stay in touch**. No matter where you're displaying goods or advertising services, have a sign-up sheet for prospective customers to list their names, addresses, and e-mail addresses.

    - To simplify further, just ask for names and e-mails if you plan to avoid making contact using the U.S. Mail. If you have a diversity of products and services, make a column on the sign-up sheet for customers to note their specific interests in your products.

- Then, follow up by mailings or e-mails to periodically "remind" them of your hobby services or products.

Take part in local business conventions and seminars of all types. Any time you can display what you're selling, you might make a contact. And remember, that any costs you incur to put up a display table can be claimed on your income tax as an expense.

"Making money is a hobby that will complement any other hobbies you have, beautifully." –Scott Alexander

Know Your Community

Be savvy about your community and what it offers. Get familiar with any businesses that already exist that relate to your hobby in any way. Also, become acquainted with as many individuals as you can where you live and "work" with your hobby. Approach business owners and ask if you can leave some of your business cards in their shops to be displayed and distributed. Depending on the type of business, you might even be able to place some of your products there to be sold on consignment. Again using knitting as your hobby, let's say you find out about a new business that sells yarns. Wouldn't it be wise to make contact with that business? Think about how your hobby pursuits might relate to other businesses already established in the community. You can help each other if you take the time and make the effort to know your local bailiwick.

Getting acquainted with your community's inhabitants will allow you to create products or perform hobby skills that will sell locally to keep your dollars flowing in. So, get to know the people as well as the businesses where you live. Stay educated about your community.

"Life's a hobby." –Joshua Lederberg

Provide Excellent Customer Service

To grow your hobby business, it's necessary to give your customers exactly what they want. Review these quick tips on some important elements of customer service.

1. **Be approachable.** Prospective customers are drawn to business owners who're smiling, friendly, and easy to talk to. Make eye contact, be open and demonstrate the ease with yourself and your product or service.
2. **Listen.** People shopping at your display table or walking by will provide you with the information you need to make your business successful. What questions do they ask you? What do they want from your hobby product or service? What are their comments about your work product as they walk away from you?
3. **Apply the knowledge you gained from customers.** Figure out ways to give your customers what they want. If a hobby item you're making is selling well, make more of them. If customers say, "I wish this one came in blue," take their phone numbers and call them back after going right home and making some blue ones.

4. **Return calls and e-mails promptly**. Nothing will kill a new business quicker than ignoring or delaying contact with a potential customer. Call or e-mail people back a.s.a.p. Show you care about your hobby and your business.

5. **Guarantee your hobby goods and services.** Keep in mind that you want happy customers for a number of reasons—they'll keep coming back for more, and they'll tell everyone they know about your wonderful products, services, and work ethic. You'll receive your customers' honest feedback if you're respectful of their wants and needs.

"Golf isn't just my business, it's my hobby." –Lee Trevino

Summary

Planning to make money from your hobby is a realistic goal. If you have a great time practicing your hobby and friends and family have taken positive notice of your skills and products, maybe it's time to establish a small hobby business. If you select the right hobby for you, start small, develop your skills, and tap into your creativity, you'll be well on your way to developing an additional income stream from your hobby. If you perfect and market your skills, know your community, and provide the best customer service, you'll be successful in making money from your hobby.

Discover all the joys and financial benefits of making money from your cherished hobby.

"Today is life-the only life you are sure of. Make the most of today. Get interested in something. Shake yourself awake. Develop a hobby. Let the winds of enthusiasm sweep through you. Live today with gusto." –Dale Carnegie

**Make Money From Your Hobby
How to generate an income from doing what you love
Worksheet**

The ability to make extra cash when you want to provides an excellent financial safety net. Using your favorite activity to create an income stream means you'll spend more time practicing an activity you love and make money doing it. Use this worksheet to help you determine how you could earn money with your hobby.

1. **Hobbies. List the pursuits you know how to do well and enjoy doing.**

_____

_____

_____

_____

_____

_____

_____

_____

Circle the hobby above that you enjoy the most. If you've gotten compliments on doing the activity or on your finished products, that's the hobby to plan to convert to a money-maker.

Whether you'll be selling your labor or an actual finished product, write down here what you plan to do or create.

_____

_____

_____

_____

2. Skill development. Circle which methods you'll use to further develop your skills:

Read   Join an interest group

 take classes

Talk to others in the field

Watch videos

3. Perfecting your skills. How will you perfect your skills?

   More practice Read even more

   Present at seminars Teach

4. Show your creativity. Write ideas here on how to "brand" your merchandise or services.

   _____

   _____

   _____

   _____

   _____

5. Set your prices. Record here how much you'll charge for each service or product you plan to offer initially. Could you offer a free trial?

   _____

   _____

   _____

   _____

   _____

6. Marketing your skills or products. Explore the various ways to market your product. List which marketing methods you plan to use.

_____

_____

_____

_____

7. Explore your community. How much do you know about your community's small business environment? Does your community have a small business association? Write down the information you discover, along with contact information of business owners you may want to meet that participate in your hobby or a related field.

_____

_____

_____

_____

_____

8. **Customer service. Providing great customer service from the very beginning is crucial when starting your hobby business. What will you do to ensure you give good customer service? What bonuses, freebies, or oyaltybuilders can you offer?**

_____

_____

_____

_____

_____

_____

_____

_____

Turning Your Hobby Into
An Income Stream

If you're like most people, you probably dream of having a job that's enjoyable and fulfilling. Maybe the solution is to turn something you love into a way to pay the bills. You may be thinking, "There's no way I can make money from my hobby." But you might be surprised! Just think how great it would be if you could make money from the one thing that you actually choose to do when you have free time. What could possibly be better than that? You might not be able to fully replace your regular job right away. However, you could earn a few hundred dollars a month or more for something you would be doing anyway. And that can make a big difference.

The two basic routes to making money from your hobby are:
   1. **Teach**. Someone out there would like to learn what you know. Don't make the mistake of believing that you have to be one of the world's top ten leading experts on something in order to make money at it. Nothing can be further from the truth!If you know more about something than anyone on your street, you can certainly make money teaching others.
   * Some ways to teach include:
      ○ Giving seminars (online or in person)
      ○ Selling articles related to your hobby
      ○ Writing and selling a book or e-book

- One-on-one coaching
- Setting up a website that provides educational information and sells related products and services.

2. **Sell a related product or service**. Hobbies require supplies. Other people may as well be purchasing those supplies from you. If your hobby is collecting something, you can buy and sell whatever it is you collect. Or think of businesses related to your hobby. For example:

- If you love animals, you could sell your services as a dog sitter.
- If you love boats, you could sell boat plans or rent boats to vacationers.
- Do you love design and interior decorating? Do you like to watch design shows on TV? You might not be on television anytime soon, but you probably know more about decorating a house than the average family does. Certainly you could charge a few hundred dollars for a consultation.
- What if fishing is your passion? How about owning a bait and tackle shop? You could be a fishing guide. You could sell fishing lures online.
- Do you love to travel? Take lots of pictures and write about your adventures. Travel magazines and websites are always looking for good content. You could also start your own travel website.

The real key is to take time to think about all the ways you could possibly make money related to you hobby. Then you can choose to do so in the most enjoyable way possible. The hardest part of getting started for most people is marketing; you must market yourself and your business to get clients or customers. So be bold.Tell your neighbors and family members about your plans. Post an ad on Craigslist.com. Make a website. People have to know you're out there so they can hire you or purchase from you.

Imagine the excitement you'll feel the first time you cash that check for doing something you used to do for free!Once you make a little money from your hobby, the wheels will really start turning, and you'll be surprised at all the other ideas that come to mind. Start today by making a list of all the ways you could possibly make money at your hobby. Have fun, and good luck!

Balloon Animals

Have you ever wanted a second income opportunity that's fun and pays well for your time? Making balloon animals at parties or local businesses that cater to young children might just be the idea you're seeking. Making balloon animals can be both fun and lucrative. It's also a great business you can do alone or with a partner. The cost to get started is minimal. You'll need less than $30 worth of supplies to get up and running with your first gig!

Learn Your Craft
Learn how to twist a balloon like a pro:
1. **Get balloons and a pump.** The simplest option is to head over to Amazon.com and search under "balloon animal supplies."

- 100 suitable balloons cost around $9.
- Purchase a quality pump and a backup! A good pump may cost you $9 or $10.

2. **Watch instructional videos on YouTube**. You can purchase a book, but it's easier to learn how to create balloon animals from a video. It's also free. Here are a few examples to get you started
   - https://www.youtube.com/user/balloonanimals
   - https://www.youtube.com/user/TrulyTwistedBalloon
   - How to make a dog balloon animal: http://www.youtube.com/watch?v=oEbBgIK7M3g
   - How to make a balloon animal swan: https://www.youtube.com/watch?v=bnhDHV9F56Y
   - Even the most complex animals are easy to create with a little practice.

3. **Practice!** When you're performing for an audience, you won't be able to look at an instructional video. Be able to produce at least 15-20 animals from memory. You can reuse balloons in your practice.

Make flashcards for each type of animal you wish to learn. Randomly go through the cards and practice making each one. When you're able to create each animal five times from memory, you're ready for action.

- Stay sharp. Make at least a couple of balloon animals each day.

4. Continuously add to your repertoire. Try to add a couple of new animals each week. You'll be surprised how much you can learn in a few months.
   - Avoid getting stuck in practice mode. If you want to boost your income, you need to get out there. You don't have to be the world's leading expert at twisting a balloon before you start making money!

INTEGRATE RELATED SKILLS FOR MORE OPPORTUNITIES

At many venues, it will benefit you to have a partner with a related skill with which to further entertain the kids. Or, learn another fun skill yourself! Multiple talents give you more options and add to what you can offer.

Consider these skills:

1. **Kids love magic.** You don't need an elaborate set with the ability to saw a person in half. Children love magic that they can view up close.
   - Card tricks
   - Make a coin or other object disappear.
   - Any sleight of hand trick is popular.
   - YouTube can be a great source for instructional material. Books are also popular. There are also websites dedicated to magic tricks.
2. **Paint faces**. There are a plethora of face painting kits available online. Be safe! Be sure to use paint designated for face painting.

- Again, it will be necessary to practice. Find a few willing volunteers and get all the practice you need.
- You might think you need to have artistic skill, but face painting is quite simple. Just follow the guide and you'll be fine.
3. **Temporary tattoos.** Depending on the type of tattooing you choose to do, you might need a little artistic ability. There are a variety of kits available for making temporary tattoos. Get the practice you need to ensure your little customers are happy.

What else can you think of that children would enjoy? What do your own children love to do? Twisting balloons might not be enough to keep children entertained. Develop a second skill and keep those kids mesmerized. Consider finding a friend to be your partner. Now that you have two skills that will delight both children and their parents, it's necessary to find clients.

Find Clients And Get Paid
Build your business with these marketing strategies:
1. **Approach restaurant owners.** Think about the restaurants in your area that cater to families. There's an excellent chance they'd love to hire you. Parents love it when their kids are happy and occupied. You might even turn a restaurant with poor food into a popular destination.
- Be prepared to show your work. Bring your pump and balloons.

Have photos available of your face painting or tattoo skills.
- If magic is your thing, be prepared to do a few tricks.

- Create a flyer with all the necessary information.

Visit restaurants when the owner or manager is least likely to be busy. Avoid arriving during regular meal hours.

- Consider using regular mail, email, and the phone, too.

2. **Consider other possible clients**. Aside from restaurants, you might also target children's museums, zoos, toy stores, bookstores, and birthday parties.

3. **Market your business** with a variety of methods. Be creative and make full use of social media:

- Facebook
- Twitter
- LinkedIn
- YouTube
- Instagram
- Reddit

4. Let your friends and family know about your new business. Pass out business cards to everyone you know. Provide a few extra so that they can pass them along to others.

5. **Approach party supply businesses**. Ask if you can hang a flyer in their store and give them referral commissions. You'll never know if you don't ask.

The toughest part of any small business is marketing. Fortunately, there's never been a better time to market your business inexpensively. Use all the resources available to you, and you'll be able to find all the clients you want.

A balloon animal business can be run on a part-time basis and provide a great boost to your income. Making children laugh and smile is certainly a more enjoyable way to make a buck than your typical part-time job.

Hand Crafting Jewelry

Even if you know little to nothing about jewelry or the process of making it, you might be a good candidate for this fun and unique business if you:
- Have previous experience with arts and crafts
- Have a good level of manual dexterity
- Would like to learn a business that can be conducted entirely online with good income potential

While there are pieces of jewelry that require a tremendous amount of skill and experience to produce, there are also projects accessible to almost anyone with the manual dexterity to hold a bead and a piece of string. Don't allow your lack of experience stand in the way!

Getting Supplies

Making jewelry is a popular hobby, so there are plenty of options for getting the supplies you need. A quick search online will reveal an endless number of jewelry suppliers. These suppliers are among the most popular options:
- http://www.joann.com/jewelry-making/
- https://www.riogrande.com/
- http://www.firemountaingems.com/
- http://www.jewelrysupply.com/

I personally as a native craftsman use some trading post sites for my supplies These suppliers provide beads, gems, cord, wire, leather, clasps kits, looms,design tools, and hand tools.

- http://crazycrow.com
- http://wanderingbull.com
- http://nocbay.com

How to Make Jewelry

The best approach to learning how to make jewelry is to either find someone to teach you or to take advantage of the many videos available online. Many of the suppliers of jewelry-making supplies and tools also provide videos so you can learn how to use their products.

YouTube has thousands of videos for jewelry-making enthusiasts. Look for the most popular videos and learn the proper techniques.

Look at Your Competition

Check out your competition. You'll not only get great ideas, but you'll also gain a better understanding of the landscape.

- What types of jewelry are others offering?
- What seems to be most popular?
- How can you improve on the jewelry provided by others?
- Can you build a better website to sell your jewelry?
- What platforms are utilized to sell? Etsy? eBay? Others?
- Do your local craft fairs and flea markets sell jewelry?

Getting Organized

Fortunately, you don't need much. Beyond a place to work, access to a camera and computer, and organizational skills, there's little else required. A lack of resources isn't an obstacle for anyone interested in making money with jewelry.

Ensure that you have the essentials:

1. Find a place you can work undisturbed. A desk or table that can be dedicated to your jewelry-making adventure is ideal. After your spouse or child sends 300 beads rolling onto the hardwood floor, you'll understand the need for a dedicated space out of the way of household traffic.

2. Work on your photography skills. It's also important to be able to capture the beauty of your jewelry with a camera. If people can't see your jewelry, they won't purchase it. Taking high-quality photos is critical. No one will pay for jewelry presented in a blurry photo with bad lighting.

3. Ensure that you can upload photos to the internet. A cell phone can be used, but a computer is far more convenient. You'll also need an internet connection. Slow internet access can present a challenge if you're uploading many high-resolution photos.

4. Storage containers for your supplies. Avoid the belief that you can store all the cord, wires, and beads in their original packaging. The packaging was designed for display and shipping, not for use over days, weeks, or months. Tupperwaretype containers can suffice.

- Of course, there many jewelry-specific options. Find a solution that works for your budget and needs. The more budget-conscious might rely on several Ziplock style storage bags.

You don't need much to get started! Jewelry-making is a business that can truly be started on a shoestring budget. There's no reason to get carried away. Get what you need in order to get started.

Marketing Your Business

Marketing is the key to success. Assuming you have an attractive product, your success depends on your ability to get others to see and purchase it. Marketing may even be a bigger part of your success than the quality of your product.

There are multiple ways to market and sell your creations:
1. **Social media**. Social media can be a powerful way to move your product. The best options include Facebook and Pinterest. Both allow photos, which is critical to your success.
2. **Selling platforms**. eBay, Etsy, and Amazon spring quickly to mind. However, it's not enough to post your products and wait for the money to roll in. Your social media, website, and marketing campaigns can all point to these platforms.
   - Each platform requires its own marketing plan. A search online will result in endless advice for marketing your products on eBay, Etsy, and Amazon.
3. **Your own website**. You can sell your jewelry without the fees charged by the selling platforms. This can also be your

greatest source of leads. There's a lot of information on search engine optimization available to make your website visible to those who are looking for handmade jewelry.

- Include a shopping cart and other shopping tools on your website to make buying easy.
- The quality of your website will also be attributed to your jewelry, so ensure the website is a pleasing experience to your visitors.

4. **Craft shows and flea markets**. These vary from city to city. Go check them out and see if they're viable options for you. Be creative and think of other ways to let people see and purchase your jewelry. Marketing will take quite a bit of time until you have a loyal client base. Be diligent and patient in the meantime.

Conclusion

Nearly anyone can create and sell jewelry. While you may not have the design skills of a professional, there are people out there that would love to purchase your creations. Jewelry-making is an easy business to get off the ground. The costs are minimal, and minimal skill is required for the simpler projects. If you'd like to make money from the comfort of your own home and put your creative skills to work, making jewelry can be a great way to boost your income.

Hand Crafted Greeting Cards

A handcrafted greeting card business can help you bring in additional income. It's a fun business that doesn't require a large startup cost. Greeting cards are popular items that allow you to use your creativity. You can design and sell your own greeting cards for a profit. You have the option of selling the cards at brick and mortar locations or online stores. Greeting cards have an unlimited style and design potential, so you can use your imagination. They make fun gifts and can be customized to fit a variety of needs. This guide will help you get started making money from your own handcrafted cards.

Required Supplies
Consider these supplies as you build your business:
1. **Scissors**. You'll need strong and sharp scissors to make greeting cards.

2. **Colorful paper**. You can find colorful paper in a variety of sizes and styles. You may want to purchase different types as you develop your business.
3. **Card stock.** This heavy paper is excellent for greeting cards. You can find card stock in many different thicknesses and strengths. Just go with the ones you like best.
4. **Envelopes**. Customers prefer to have greeting cards with matching envelopes. Add designs or special embellishments to the envelopes to coordinate with the cards.
5. **Glue**. You may need more than one type of glue for your business. You can find glue sticks, glue pens, rubber cement, glue rollers, glue dots, and hot glue. You may also need craft glue or paper glue.
6. **Glitter**. If you decide to use glitter on your cards, you can save money by purchasing it in bulk. Glitter is available in many shapes and colors.
7. **Cutting mat**. A cutting mat will protect your tables as you work on creating the cards.
8. **Craft knives or paper cutte**r. These will give you perfectly straight edges.
9. **Decorative paper trimmers**. Decorative trimmers make the edges of your cards wavy or other shapes. They provide variety in your designs.
10. **Adhesives and tapes**. Glue isn't the only option for attaching embellishments or other items to your cards. Adhesives and tapes can also help.

11.　**Ink and ink pads** for calligraphy or stamps.
12.　**Card punchers.** They punch out different shapes and patterns such as hearts, stars, or circles.
13.　**Beads.** Beads add a unique touch to your greeting cards. You can find them in many colors, patterns, and sizes. Some even resemble jewels.
14.　**Ribbons and threads**. Use these for additional decorative touches.
15.　**Rubber stamps**. Rubber stamps come in hundreds of shapes, sizes, and pictures.
16.　**Stickers**. You can also use stickers to decorate your cards.
17.　**Pens, markers, crayons, and colored pencils**. You may want more than one type of writing utensil.

You don't need to get all of these supplies at once. As your business expands, you can purchase additional supplies.

Getting Started

Greeting cards are a competitive industry, so you'll want to find a niche or unique way to stand out. You can turn this into a profitable business, but it takes research, time, and dedication.

Get a good start with these steps:

1. **Research successful greeting card businesses**. The first step is to discover how others who are successful have developed their ideas. See what's working and do that.
2. **Develop your niche**. Reflect on your artistic talents and think of ways you can incorporate them into your cards. Do you excel in calligraphy or make beautiful pastel drawings?

Find a niche that uses your unique skills to make your greeting cards special and unusual.

3. **Consider the tax implications**. Before you start your business, it's wise to look into tax requirements and taxsaving strategies. Depending on your state, you may have to pay both federal and state taxes on your earnings. Plus, how will you handle sales taxes?

- An accountant or tax attorney can provide excellent advice on how to set up your business to take advantage of workat-home tax deductions and keep up with the taxes.

4. **Make a business plan**. It may be tempting to jump right into making cards and selling them. However, a business plan will help you set and achieve your goals.

5. **Buy the supplies**. After buying the supplies, you can begin to experiment with designs. You may want to test a few of your ideas with friends and family.

Check business license rules. Your location may require a business license for home operations. Your accountant can also help you with this. Set up a home office or dedicate an area for your business. Successful businesses thrive in their own spaces. You can use a home office or simply use part of another room in your home for the business. It takes several steps to set up your handcrafted greeting card business. Once you're ready to make cards, it'll be easier to have these steps behind you.

Finding Customers

Greeting cards can be purchased at many retailers. Even gas stations carry a small amount of cards. Plan ahead to find places where you may be able to get customers. Prepare a customer strategy before you create a large supply of greeting cards.

You can make this business work by targeting customers and making cards that fit their needs.

Try these tips for finding customers:

1. **Create your own greeting card website.** By creating your wn site, you'll be able to control all of the design and rketing aspects.
   - Come up with a catchy domain name.
   - Show a variety of cards on the site.
   - Make it easy for customers to buy directly from the website.

2. **Join established online businesses**. You can join websites such as Etsy or eBay to sell your handmade greeting cards. You'll have less control, but these popular sites bring traffic and customers. You can still set your own prices on these websites.

3. **Ask local gift shops to carry your cards.** Work out a deal with local shops.

4. **Sell your greeting cards at fairs.** Local fairs attract art lovers, and they may be interested in buying your handcrafted cards.

5. **Sell your items at card trade shows**. Greeting card trade shows bring together many crafters.

6. **Sell your cards at craft shows**. They're a popular way to reach customers and show off your products.
7. **Contact local art galleries**. They may be interested in displaying handcrafted cards.
8. **Offer greeting cards to businesses.** You may be able to sell your cards to local or national businesses. Businesses often end cards to employees, clients, and customers. Offer your handmade creations and build your customer base. Consider both small and large businesses in your area.
9. **Sell your cards in stores.** You can ask stores to display your cards and sell them. Reach out to a variety of shops such as grocery stores, clothing stores, craft stores, and others.

You can find customers who are interested in greeting cards in many locations. It's important to diversify and have multiple locations that carry your cards.

Marketing Your Business

Marketing is an essential part of a successful handmade greeting card business. Target your audience and use several techniques for greater exposure and success.

Consider these marketing tips:

1. **Find a niche** or make unique items that get attention. Greeting cards that stand out will help you achieve business success.

2. **Offer extra services.** Bring in more customers by offering extra services:
   - You can address and mail the cards for your customers.
   - You can offer to customize each card with their names, unique poems, or other messages. You can also include photos or keepsakes with each card.

3. **Advertise in local newspapers and magazines.** Place ads with pictures of your cards.

4. **Advertise online**. You can purchase ads from multiple sources online. Consider buying ads on social media sites such as Facebook. You can link to your social media profiles, offer coupons, and link to your website.

5. **Join local craft organizations and support groups**. They can help you network, find customers, and grow your business. You can also share your cards with them and learn more about handcrafted items.

6. **Find sales representatives** who work with crafters. You can hire a sales rep to promote your products and sell them.

7. **Consider the National Stationery Show.** This annual event draws many card makers. You can exhibit your greeting cards or simply attend the show to network. You can even enter to win awards at the show.

8. **Contact local reporters.** Discuss what makes your handcrafted greeting card business unique and get publicity.

9. **Reach out to local charities.** They may need greeting cards for a variety of reasons. Partnering with local charities will gain exposure for your business. You can help others while more people learn about your cards.

10. **Contact schools.** They may be interested in selling your cards for fundraisers.

11. **Find other local youth groups.** They may want to sell your cards to raise money   for their groups or charities.

12. **Join craft forums online.** Interact with other crafters and owners. Share ideas, ask questions, and get craft ideas. Learn about new products and marketing opportunities in your area and on a national scale.

13. **Enter design competitions**. You can find competitions online or in magazines. Craft and art magazines have competitions for handmade items. You can also enter competitions sponsored by art galleries, guilds, and craft shows.

14. **Contact doctors' offices**. Dental and medical offices send out reminder or appointment cards throughout the year. They may be interested in other types of cards that they can send to their patients

15. **Reach out to new, small businesses**. You can partner with them and offer your cards. New businesses may be interested in promoting their brands through unique, handmade cards.

- You can offer promotional packages that include mailing cards to potential customers in their neighborhood. You can also provide birthday cards or anniversary cards that they send to registered customers.

16. **Partner with artists or photographers**. Do you know other creative people who are starting their own businesses? You can work with them and incorporate their art or photos into your cards.
    - Together, you can market and sell the finished greeting cards. You can feature their work and offer customers customized art or photos.

17. **Partner with jewelry makers**. Did you know that greeting cards that have extras are more popular? You can partner with jewelry makers and add their handmade items directly to your cards.

Marketing your handcrafted greeting card business is a longterm process. For the best results, reach out to new customers and markets regularly. It also helps to stay aware of the trends and use technology to your advantage.

Conclusion

A handcrafted greeting card business can be a fun way to use your creativity and make money at the same time. You can start the business with only a small amount of supplies, but it's important to develop a good marketing plan. Greeting cards are available from many retailers and companies, so you're in a competitive industry. However, you can stand out in the industry with unique, handmade cards. A handcrafted greeting card business can become a sizable source of income for your family as well as a rewarding way to use your talents.

Soap-Making Business

Soap is a versatile product that everyone uses and needs. A soapmaking business can be a fun way to increase your income. You can start the entire business at home and find many venues in which you can sell your products. You can customize your soap with herbs, oils, and original fragrances, so you will stand out. If you enjoy handcrafts, this business may be just what you're looking for! You can do it as a hobby that also brings in some extra money, or you can take it full-time and grow your business to a point where it brings in a full-time income. Use this guide to help you get started!

Required Supplies

A soap business requires several essential supplies. You may also want to buy extra oils, herbs, fragrances, colorants and other items to make your soap unique.

Consider these supplies for your soap business:

1. **Molds**. Molds come in many different shapes! You can purchase a variety of molds or even make your own.
2. **Spoons and mixing utensils**. You will need clean utensils to stir your soap mixtures and add different liquids.
3. **Fragrances**. Use them as they come to add standard fragrances to your soaps or mix and match them to come up with unique and original fragrances of your own.
4. **Goggles.** Soap mixtures can be hot, so you want to protect your eyes from any spills.
5. **Gloves.** Purchase gloves that fit well and keep your hands safe from the different mixtures as you work.
6. **Colorants**. They add color to your soap and make it stand out.
7. **Oils.** You may need several types of oils to make your soap, but it will depend on the recipe you use.
8. **Lye**. If the recipe calls for lye, then you want to stock up on it.
9. **Blender or mixer**. You may want to invest in a blender or mixer to make your soap. They can speed up the process.
10. **Scale**. Soap recipes often require specific weights of ingredients, so you may need a scale.

11.   **Labels and stickers**. Quality labels will show off your brand with a perfect finish.

12.   **Bags, boxes, or other wraps**. How will you package your soap? You may want to invest in plastic bags, boxes, or a variety of other wraps.

13.   **Melt-and-pour soap base**s. You can purchase kits with these bases to speed up the process.

14.   **Measuring cups**. Silicone or plastic cups will work fine to measure ingredients.

15.   **Thermometer.** Soap recipes may require a specific temperature.

16.   **Butters.** They can add extra moisture to your soap. After you've selected a recipe that you'd like to try for your soap, you can pick up the required supplies and make plans. You can buy preassembled soap-making kits or purchase individual items and build your own cache of ingredients and supplies.

Getting Started

Soap can be an easy way to increase your income and provide customers with high--quality, handmade items. However, it's important to create a business plan for your best profits. You'll also need space in your home or other area to make the soap. Lastly, you'll want to consider the markeBng and branding aspects of your business.

Follow these steps to get started:
1. **Make a business plan**. As you work on your business idea, you'll want to have a plan for how to create and sell the soap.
2. **Check local, state, and federal laws**. You may be required to get a permit or other paperwork before you can start selling the soap. In addition, you may have homeowner association restrictions in your area that limit home businesses.
3. **Consider business insurance**. Your state or city may require you to have business insurance before you can sell your soap.
4. **Educate yourself**. Before you can start making or selling soap, you have to learn how the process works.
   - You will need to find soap recipes that fit your business. The internet has tons of recipes you can try.
   - Test the recipes that interest you. Try out your ideas for customizing your soaps with your own unique ideas.
5. **Purchase supplies**. A typical soap-making kit that includes all of the supplies can cost $500 to $800. You can usually purchase supplies for $1,000 or less and set up the business at home to save more money.
   - For example, some kits cost $800, but you can make 400 bars of soap with them.
6. **Determine costs and potential profit**s. How much will the soap business cost long-term?

- For example, if you buy an $800 kit and make 400 bars of soap, then you can price each bar at $4. This will give you a total $1600, so you make a profit of $800.

A soap-making business requires an investment of time and money. You can calculate your potential return after you buy supplies and figure out the costs.

Finding Customers

cented soap is a popular product, but how will you compete with major brands and boutiques? It's important to consider your customer base and where you'll sell your soap.

Consider these tips for finding customers:
1. **Create your own website**. A website can help you reach customers around the world and build your business.
   - Advertise your website and products to find customers.
2. **Join an established website**. If you don't want to make your own website, then you can join a website for sellers. You have multiple options including Etsy, eBay, and others. You can also find sites that specialize in handmade products.
3. **Get a stand or booth at a farmer's market.** These markets often welcome handmade soap products.
   - Farmer's markets attract customers who value unique, handmade products. can set up a booth and sell your soap. You can also use the opportunity to sign up

customers for a list and have soap shipped to them on a regular basis.

4. **Join local fairs**. The fairs may allow you to sell your soap and reach new customers.
5. **Make deals with small, local boutiques**. Many boutiques welcome new merchandise that is handmade.
6. **Consider getting a cart at a shopping center or mall**. You can sell soap from a rolling cart or stand at the mall.
7. **Join flea markets.** They may be willing to let you sell your soap.
8. **Make deals with hotels and bed and breakfast venues**. Do you have local hotels or bed and breakfast inns that may enjoy stocking their rooms with handmade soap?
9. **Check out gift shops**. Local gift shops may be interested in carrying handmade soap for their customers.

It's important to consider multiple customer bases and reach out to different locations. You can build a thriving soap-making business by finding new customers on a regular basis.

Marketing Your Business

Soap can be purchased at any retail or online location, so you'll have to stand out from the crowd. Your marketing and advertising plans will play a big role in the success of your soapmaking business.

Try these marketing tips:

1. **Create unique branding**. Your individual brand needs to be special and help you stand out from other soap manufacturers.

2. **Consider making unique soa**p. If you want your brand to stand out, then the soap has to be unique too. You can customize it in several ways and find different shapes, colors, and fragrances that work.

   - You don't have to make boring square soap bars. You can make soap into any shape depending on the mold you use.
   - You can buy molds that create soap that looks like cars, dolls, trees, flowers and many other shapes. You can also practice and make your own molds or order custom ones from retailers.
   - Make your own, unique fragrances by mixing several standard essential oils or other fragrances.
   - You can even offer fragrance-free soap for people with sensitive skin.
   - You can add various kinds of butters to your soap to turn it into moisturizing soap.
   - Your soap can be customized with ingredients such as honey, aloe vera, goat milk, almond butter, olive oil and others.
   - You can make your soap colorful and unique. You may want to consider fun colors such as pink, blue, green, purple or neon shades. You can purchase different colorants and mix them together.

3. **Make unique labels for your brand**. If you want customers to remember your soap, then you need labels that clearly carry your brand name.
   - Your labels should state that the soap is handmade and point out the other features.
   - Is your soap moisturizing, chemical-free, natural, or organic? Communicate these features on your label.
4. **Advertise online**. You can purchase social media ads and other types of ads to promote your business.
5. **Advertise in local magazines or newspapers**. They may be less popular, but you can still reach customers this way.
6. **Attend small business events**. These events give you the chance to talk about your business and share business cards.
   - You may also learn more about running a small business and networking with others.
   - You can build connections with local stores and boutiques that may be interested in carrying your soap.
7. **Join soap-making forums online**. One of the easiest ways to learn more about the business and pick up marketing tips is to reach out to other soap makers.
   - Online forums dedicated to making soap can help you learn more about the process.
   - They can introduce you to others who have years of soapmaking experience. You can ask for advice, tips, or simply listen to their wisdom.
   - You can learn more about advertising and marketing related to soap.

8. **Consider retail distribution on a bigger scale**. Can you get your soap into top retail stores around the country?
   - For many soap makers, it's a dream to sell their products in stores such as Whole Foods. However, it's not easy to get retail distribution, and it requires money and effort.
   - You also need a great deal of inventory before you can join big retail stores.
9. **Consider niche markets**. You may already be making unique soap, but it may not be enough. Niche markets can help you find more customers.
   What type of niche market for soap can you join?

For example, one niche market for soap would be vegans. You can also make special soap for pets or exclusive, allergen-free soap.
10.   **Consider joining the Handcrafted Soap and Cosmetic Guild**. This guild is an exclusive organization for people who make handcrafted items.
   - The guild can help you market your soaps and learn more about advertising.
   - It can also help you save money on insurance and other soap-making products. You can join other soap makers and learn from them.
   - The other benefits of joining a guild include shipping discounts, listings in directories, and promotional help. You may also benefit from the online stores available from the guild or the discount merchant services.

11. **Get interviews and make press releases**. You can discuss your business with local reporters or bloggers who cover soap.

- You can discuss running a small business or offer advice to others in interviews.
- You can also put out your own press releases and announce new soap fragrances or shapes that you create.

Conclusion

A soap-making business can be an interesting way to increase your income. You can do the business at home, but you can sell the soap to people around the world, thanks to the internet. Soap-making requires skill, time, effort, and a small amount of money to get started. However, you can build a fun, successful business that brings in a consistent income every month.

Gift Baskets

Have you ever considered making and selling gift baskets? Probably not, but maybe you should! Gift baskets are easy to make and have an excellent profit margin. There's not much to creating a gift basket other than purchasing the basket, the gift items, and putting them all together in an attractive arrangement. Creating and selling gift baskets is great way to make money, even if you don't have a creative bone in your body!

There are many opportunities to sell gift baskets:
- Birthdays
- Holidays
- Get Well Soons
- Anniversary
- Jus because
- Corporate clients, who give gift baskets to their own clients and employees

Gift baskets are popular all year round. Everyone has several opportunities each year to purchase a gift basket. Why not let them purchase these baskets from you?

3 Steps To Success
Step 1: Preliminary Research and Decisions
Gift baskets can contain nearly anything:
- Fruit
- Candy

- Cheeses
- Jams and jellies
- Gourmet cooking supplies
- Lotions and beauty supplies
- Wine or Microbrew beers
- Hobby supplies

You might even come up with your own ideas. Search online and get a few ideas. Also determine how much you'd like to charge. Look at local offerings and find a competitive price point. Since you're a oneperson operation, your overhead is minimal. You can undercut your competitors and still turn a nice profit.

Step 2: Find Suppliers

You're going to need baskets and items to place in your baskets. You might be able to find many of the items locally, depending on where you live. You might have to outsource others. By limiting yourself to just a few types of baskets, you won't need to keep as much inventory on hand.

A few basket suppliers include:

- Almac Imports
- The Lucky Clover Trading Company
- Willow Group, LTD

There are also numerous suppliers for gift basket items. Google has all the information you need. It really depends on the type of items you intend to put in your baskets. Some suppliers specialize in gourmet food items, for example. Once you've determined the contents of your baskets, you can find the right suppliers.

Step 3: Find Customers

You have two main groups of customers: Those over the age of 18 and businesses. Most 15-year olds aren't going to purchase a gift basket. One large corporate client can keep you busy! Between giving gifts to their employees and customers, you might have all the work you can handle.

Find and keep corporate clients:

1. **Create a brochure**. Brochures are less expensive than you think. You can even make brochures on your own with your personal computer.
   - Approach every business that you believe might be interested. Introduce yourself and drop off your brochure.
2. **Drop off a free sample**. You might want to consider dropping off an example of your work at the front desk. Once you do something for someone else, they're much more likely to do something for you.
3. **Ask for help**. Do you have a friend that works for the big pharmaceutical company in town? She might know the right person to approach at her company. She might even do the heavy lifting for you and speak on your behalf.
   - Think of everyone you know and where they work. You know someone that can help you to get your first corporate client.

4. **Approach likely partners**. You might find a flower shop that doesn't offer gift baskets. They might be willing to advertise your services for a commission.
5. **Be reliable**. It's important that you are 100% reliable. You might not get a second chance.

Corporate clients can be more challenging to land, but you won't need to spend a lot of time fishing for other clients either. Be patient and diligent. One large client can be all that you require.

Finding non-corporate clients:
1. **Word of mouth**. You already have a friend or family member willing to give your service a try. They'll also happily spread the word about your business. If everyone you know would tell 10 other people, you'd be all set.
2. **Advertise**. Advertising online is inexpensive. You can get a domain name for only $10, and webhosting for less than $10/ month. Create a simple website with attractive photos. Look at other successful websites for good ideas.
   - Utilize online classifieds and social media websites. Advertise daily until you have the clients you require.
3. **Persevere**. Advertising will require a lot of your effort until the business is off the ground. If it were easy, everyone would be doing it. Expect that finding clients will take time.
4. **Treat your clients like gold.** It's much easier to sell to a happy former customer than it is to find a new one. Be grateful for the clients you have and treat them extremely

well. Follow up with them occasionally and see if they'll have any gift basket needs in the near future.

Starting any new business can be a challenge, but selling gift baskets is a simple idea that anyone can do. Everyone knows someone with a birthday, and everyone celebrates several holidays each year. Take advantage of these common events and provide a great gift idea at a reasonable price. Determine the types of gift baskets you want to offer and get busy finding your suppliers and customers. Provide a good product and service and you can boost your income significantly.

MAKE MONEY WITH PODCASTING

There are many types of content marketing. Blogging is very popular. Writing articles and eBooks are other ways to market yourself and your products. Social media is also very popular. Podcasting is another option. A podcast is a digital audio file that you can stream from the internet or download and listen to. Podcasts can be free or sold for a fee. You can set up a podcasting site or "channel" and make daily podcasts like a radio show.

Reasons to consider podcasing:
1. **20% of adults report listening to podcasts** at least occasionally. That's a lot of people you can reach with your voice!

2. **Podcasting is much less crowded than blogging**. The blogging landscape is very crowded. Get out of that space and consider starting a podcast, instead.
3. **People can do other things while they listen**. Think of all the activities that can be performed while listening to a podcast:
   - Work out
   - Wash the dishes
   - Take a walk
   - Mow the grass
   - Drive
   - Sit in a bus or train
   - Vacuum the carpet
   - Sit by the pool
4. **There's more intimacy**. The written word is no substitute for the spoken word. With a podcast, you can connect on a whole new level.
5. **You can reach a new crowd**. Many people won't read a blog, but will listen to a podcast.

Podcasting has many advantages over the other forms of online marketing. You can provide value in a new and more meaningful way. Podcasting is even easier than blogging, because you don't need a website to get started.

Getting Started Wit Podcasting
You can get started quickly with only a couple of tools:

1. **A quality microphone**. Fortunately, a good microphone in this day and age is only around $50. The Snowball by Blue

Microphones is the most popular. Do a little research and find a quality microphone. Remember that you're only recording your voice. You don't need a microphone that can handle the crushing volume of a drum set.

- In a pinch, a combination headset-microphone can work well enough to get started. Move up to a better microphone when your finances allow.
- The headset combo is also a good option if you're interviewing others. Remember that you have to be able to hear the other person without the sound spilling over into your microphone.

2. **A computer to store the recordings**. Actually, there are many alternatives to a computer, but you'll need a computer to upload your podcast anyway.

That's all you need to get started. There's no excuse! A simple microphone and your computer are all you need to make a high quality podcast. Start looking for a microphone today. You can get started on your first podcast immediately.

Creating your first podcast:

1. **Choose a format**. There are a few ways to conduct your podcast:
   - Go solo
   - Have one or more guests
   - Most podcasters stick to a single format and occasionally change it up. Your listeners will probably grow to expect and like a particular format, but don't be afraid to vary it on occasion.

2. **Prepare.** Unless you're very talented, you'll want notes, if not a full script. If you're interviewing someone, have questions ready.
   - Consider the purpose of the podcast. What are you trying to share, teach, or explain? Perhaps your podcast is strictly for entertainment purposes.
3. **Record in a quiet space.** People don't enjoy listening to anything with a lot of background noise. It's distracting and shows a lack of professionalism.
4. **Edit appropriately.** There are many audio programs available for cutting and pasting sections of your podcast. Many of them are free. Ensure that any guests who participated in your podcast have the opportunity to review your edits before making the podcast public.

What could be easier? It can be a little more intimidating to put your voice online than writing a blog post. But that also makes it more effective. You're putting a part of yourself out there for the world to experience. Once you've recorded your podcast, it's time to make it available to others.

Getting Your Podcast Out To The Masses
You can send out your podcast in several ways:
1. **Create an RSS feed**. You can upload your podcast to a single site and it will automatically be delivered to your subscribers.
2. **Use iTunes**. iTunes will also deliver your podcast to subscribers. People will also be able to search for it. You can choose whether or not to charge a fee.

- After uploading to iTunes, you can expect it will take approximately 5-7 days until your podcast is available. There is a review process.

3. **Upload your podcast to other sites**. Soundcloud is a popular platform and provides multiple sharing options.

4. **Use social media**. Tell everyone about your latest podcast. Get every listener you can find. They're all potential customers.

Use your imagination. Market your podcast any way you can. Every loyal listener is potentially another dollar in your pocket. Marketing is the key. Now that you have a podcast and listeners, the next step is monetization. It's time to boost your income.

Making Money With Your Podcast

1. **Sell your own products**. Do you have a course or other product for sale? You can use your podcast to promote your products. The show can be about your product, or you can casually mention it during the show. In your podcast, entice people to visit your website where they can buy your products.

2. **Sell affiliate products**. Don't have any of your own products? Sell someone else's. This is a great way to lure guests to your show. Let them tell your audience all about their life-changing doo-dad. You can take a piece of the action with an affiliate commission.

3. **Sell your podcast**. You can also charge for your podcast. Some podcasters put out a few free episodes and then sell

the rest. Some make a short version available free of charge, but charge a fee for the full episode.

4. **Charge for advertising**. Make money by charging other companies for advertising on your show. This works especially well when you've built an audience. Find companies who sell products to your target audience. Run a prerecorded commercial or promote the company in the context of your show.

There are other ways to make money with your podcast. Find sponsors. Get donations. Use the podcast to build your brand and market your services. Whenever you have an audience, the possibility for making money exists. The possibilities are only limited by your imagination! Consider podcasting as a means to boost your income. There are many ways to monetize your podcasts. All you need is a microphone, computer, and a little free time. Provide value, and the money will follow. This is just the tip of the iceberg, if you want to get into the nitty gritty of making money with a podcast you may be interested in watching some videos by Pat Flynn. He is an entrepreneur who went from being an architect to being one of the top podcasters around the world. And he has a couple courses on how to get started podcasting and how to increase your listenership and income from podcasting. If you're interested you can check out his YouTube channels Pat Flynn & Smart Passive Income as well as his website at https://smartpassiveincome.com You can also check out the info I have on my website https://consultablindguy.com/powerup

Passive Profits:
Do It Once and Profit Forever

Introduction

It's practically universal to want to increase your income. Regardless of how much money someone has, they would still like to make more. If you're like most, you swap your time for money. Even highly paid, successful doctors and lawyers are limited because they have to trade their time in exchange for payment. Doctors can only see so many patients in a week. Their potential income is limited by time. Passive income is money coming in that requires you to invest very little time. You may spend some time initially, while you're getting it all set up. However, once it's up and running, you'll continue to receive income for a long time to come.

A few examples of passive income include:

1. Rental Income
2. Dividends, pensions, or interest from investments
3. Earnings from a business that doesn't require your involvement (affiliates and silent partnerships)
4. Royalties or cash from an artistic creation (a book or song you wrote, or even a painting)

Imagine the power of building a few passive income streams that will provide you with reliable profits for the next ten years, or even longer. Passive income is one of the greatest ways to build wealth. You can create an unlimited amount of extra money in this way.

"Many people take no care of their money till they come nearly to the end of it, and others do just the same with their time."
- Johann Wolfgang von Goethe

Rental Income

Most of us have purchased a home or condo at some point, but most of us haven't purchased a property for the sole purpose of earning money. There's a difference. When you're shopping for a property to live in yourself, you're interested in certain features. However, these features may be irrelevant to you when you're shopping for a rental property.

Check out these different types of rental properties:

1. Single-family homes and condominiums. These common properties are well-known by everyone.
2. Multi-family properties. This includes everything from a duplex to a giant apartment building. These have some advantages over single-family homes because you can rent to multiple tenants simultaneously.
3. Commercial property. Any building that's zoned for commercial use would be included. You could be talking about a small barbershop, a giant shopping mall, or an office complex.
4. Industrial. This would include factories and similar properties.

Getting Started

If you're a first-time landlord, it might be easier for you to start with a residential property because of the familiarity. Commercial properties tend to boom and bust more dramatically, and they require a different level of expertise. Industrial properties tend to be quite expensive.

Choosing the best type of residential property to purchase can be determined by your location and interests:

1. Single-family homes and condominiums. These are best suited to areas with low purchase prices compared to rents. Determine if the money generated from the rental income is enough to pay the mortgage, as well as all the other expenses. Remember you want some profit left over, too!

- The common expenses include: Insurance, maintenance (roof, painting, upgrades, and so on), property taxes, and management fees (if you hire someone else to manage your properties).
- Look for homes with 3 bedrooms. Everyone that's looking for a 2-bedroom home can live in a 3- bedroom, but the opposite isn't necessarily true.
- The most lucrative rental homes are typically in slightly lower middle class areas. This part of town will normally have solid rents, but the price of the property is quite low. Do the math on a variety of properties and you'll find the best deals. Keep in mind that these areas may have poor appreciation though.
- The real disadvantage of single-family homes and condominiums is vacancy. When the property is vacant, it brings in zero dollars. This is one of the areas where multi-family properties have the advantage.

2. Multifamily properties. There are several advantages to multi-family properties:

- There's a decreased cost per unit. A building with four units will typically cost much less than four single-family homes. But, you can collect rent from four different tenants.
- Maintenance costs are potentially lower. For example, replacing the roof on a four unit building will cost less than replacing the roofs on four different houses.
- Vacancy is less of an issue. Having one vacancy doesn't eliminate all your income.

- There are disadvantages, too. In a single family home (and a duplex), the tenants are normally expected to mow the grass and shovel the driveway. In a multi-unit building, you'll be expected to take care of the maintenance responsibilities. Larger buildings will also require some onsite management.

Profit Analysis

Research all potential investments to ensure you're pending your money wisely. Many people treat investing like gambling. However, if you do your homework, it will be far from a coincidence if things turn out well.

Take these factors into account:

1. The median home price in your area. Simply, this is a home priced in the "middle." Half of the homes in the area are more expensive and half are less expensive. In most cases, the best rental homes will be 30-75% of the median home price. This information is readily available.
2. Check the average amount of rent for different priced properties. Look at the different price points nd make some comparisons.
3. Figure out the cost per unit for different multifamily properties. Look at different price-points and calculate which type of property will be the most profitable to rent.

Getting a Good Price

Nearly any property can become a good rental opportunity, if purchased at a decent price! If you're looking to purchase a rental property, the keys are to know the price you want, ask for it, and be patient. Be prepared to shop around and make many different offers. Someone out there is waiting for you to come along and buy that property. Even if you offer less than the asking price, someone will eventually say yes. A lower price means a greater cash flow and more equity. Advertise and seek out properties. The best deals usually aren't advertised. Call the "for rent" ads in the paper and ask the owner if they're interested in selling. Place an ad stating that you're looking to buy a rental property. You can usually find a property at 65% of the fair market price, if you look hard enough.

Finding Tenants

One of the keys to success is finding good tenants. Most of the horror stories you hear about rental properties are the result of unfavorable tenants.

The ideal tenant will have the following attributes:
1. **Verifiable and sufficient income**. Your tenants need to have a money source so they can pay the rent on time each month.
2. **Good references**. Good tenants leave a trail of happy landlords. Check with the last few places they've lived. Be most concerned with payment history and the condition of the property after they moved out.

3. **Meet and get a good feel for them**. Do you get the impression they'll be reliable and trustworthy? Follow your intuition when you meet potential tenants.

Long-Term Considerations

1. **Continue renting the propert**y. After the mortgage is paid off, you can keep renting out the property. But now all the money will be yours.
2. **You can refinance**. Some landlords like to refinance their properties and pull the equity out. You can then invest that money and you'll still have the rental income.
3. **Sell it**. Depending on the housing market, the time may come when selling is the best option. You can then purchase more properties when the market falls again.

Other Items

You'll likely require the following supports:

1. **An attorney**. Attorneys can be invaluable when purchasing real estate, and even more so in dealing with tenant issues.
2. **A tax expert**. Since rental properties can create some unique tax issues, it's a good idea to consult a professional that deals with taxes. For example, you probably aren't able to deduct your mortgage interest. However, you can deduct the depreciation of the uilding, but not the land.
3. **Real estate investors club**. You're almost certain to have at least one real estate investors club in your area. The club members can provide a wealth of information, including great references for a lawyer and tax accountant.

Real estate can be a great way to generate a relatively passive income. When you own property free and clear, there's a lot of money to be made.

Dividends, Pensions, or Other Interest From Investments
With a large enough investment, it's possible to pay your living expenses from the interest. While it can take a significant amount of time to accumulate enough assets to see a significant amount of money, it's entirely possible long term.

Ponder these tips about investments:
1. **Start saving and investing early**. Even $100 a month can result in a huge nest egg, if you start saving and investing early enough. Go online and work with some interest calculators to see various scenarios that could work for you.
2. **Leave your savings alone**. To accumulate wealth, avoid withdrawing it for any reason.
3. **Focus on growth early on**. Your early years are the time to focus on stocks. Later on, you can focus on other investments as your retirement nears.
4. **Take full advantage of any retirement accounts**. Look into any pension plans your employer offers. If you're self-employed, you'll have different retirement options available.
5. **Think about taking your profits from other sources of passive income and investing them**. The key to maximizing your wealth is reinvesting your profits into other projects that will provide even more earnings. One thing to

remember is that if all of your money is invested in other forms of passive income, you may lack the liquidity you'll require if an unexpected expense comes along. Therefore, it's a good idea to set up an emergency fund equivalent to several months of living expenses.

"Financial peace isn't the acquisition of stuff. It's learning to live on less than you make, so you can give money back and have money to invest. You can't win until you do this." - Dave Ramsey

Earnings From a Business That Doesn't Require Your Involvement

Most of us dream of owning a business that would pay us at least $100,000 per year. But if you're running the business, other opportunities are limited. You'll once again be strapped for time. But, what if you had that $100,000 business and could hire someone for $50,000 per year to run it? You'd still be making $50,000 and have all your time free.

Consider the other opportunities you could still pursue in this scenario:

1. **Start another business**. Consider how much you could earn if you owned several businesses, but didn't have to spend a lot of time running them. You could just keep adding businesses to your portfolio.
2. **Spend your time expanding your business**. Most business owners are too busy running the business to expand it. If you spent 40 hours a week expanding your

business, how big could it grow? How much would you earn then? Maybe you could franchise and have hundreds of franchise owners giving you money each month.

3. **Create another source of passive income**. Maybe you'd like to own a business, several rental properties, and 25 websites.

If you're interested in passive income, it's important to pick profitable businesses that are suitable to you and your circumstances.

Remember to keep these things in mind:
1. **A suitable business is one that requires little time and expertise**. Pick something that can be handed off to another person, while you're creating an additional stream of income.
2. **It's scalable.** Some businesses are easier to grow than others. Think of a business that you can duplicate and grow easily.
3. **Pick something profitable**. Choose a business that will generate enough income to allow you to hire someone else to run it while still providing you with a decent income.
   "Business opportunities are like buses, there's always another one coming."– Richard Branson

Create Something Once That Could Pay You Forever
Think about book authors. They can write a book, put it on Amazon.com, and then sell it for the rest of their lives. Songwriters get paid for writing a song, as well as profiting each

time the song is performed or played on the radio. So, would it be a good idea for you to write a book? Let's consider it!

Implement these easy steps and write your own book:

1. **Pick a topic.** There are two basic choices: fiction and non-fiction. Ideally, you'll do a little research and pick a popular topic. You might know everything there is to know about the mating habits of bumblebees, but is anyone interested enough to purchase a book about it?

2. **Formulate an outline.** One of the easiest ways to write a book is to create an outline and then fill in the blanks.

3. **Start writing.** A typical page is around 350 words, making a 100 page book about 35,000 words. It's easy to write a couple thousand words each day, and in two to three weeks, your book could be finished and ready to sell!

4. **Edit.** After you're done writing, it's helpful to edit your own work first. Then it's a good idea to hire an editor to look it over. You want your book to be error-free.

5. **Upload the book** to Amazon.com. All the information about the uploading process is on the website. Pay special attention to the pricing information.

6. **Tell everyone you know about your book.** Ask your friends and family to buy your book. Post it on your Facebook wall. It's entirely reasonable to make a few hundred dollars a month from a few weeks of part-time work. If your book becomes popular, you can make thousands of dollars.

7. **Keep writing.** Many writers create books in multiple categories. For instance, an author might write romance

novels, dog training guides, and books about international travel. Many authors will use different pen names for each category. Potential buyers may be doubtful of your expertise if you claim to be an expert in multiple categories, so a pen name for each industry works well to avoid this issue.

Related Ideas

If you like the idea of writing, but would rather tackle something shorter than a book, you could write articles and post them on revenue-sharing sites. Basically, people read your articles and are exposed to advertisements as they do. You get a percentage of that advertisement revenue made by the website that is hosting your article. It can take a decent amount of time to write enough articles to generate a real income, but many people make a full-time living using this method. Again, it's important to find popular topics! The more times your article is read, the more money you will generate. These articles can continue making you money for years! What about photography or art? There are similar revenue sharing sites for photographs and other types of artwork. Any time someone buys your photograph, you'll get a commission. You could also have your own website to sell your work. In this case, you wouldn't have to split the money with the revenue sharing site, but you'd have to generate your own traffic.

"The important thing is not being afraid to take a chance. Remember, the greatest failure is to not try. Once you find something you love to do, be the best at doing it."
– Debbi Fields

Sell Affiliate Products With Your Own Website

If you'd like your own website, but you're hesitant to deal with customers and shipping, consider selling affiliate products, where you make commissions from recommending other people's products.

You can find plenty of things to recommend on websites like ClickBank.com and Amazon.com:

1. **ClickBank**. ClickBank has electronic products, such as e-books, videos, and audio programs you can sell. After signing up with ClickBank, you'll be given an affiliate ID. Each product has a landing page (sales page), and a link is generated. If anyone buys a product after clicking on your link, you'll earn money.

   - You'll usually earn 50-70% of the purchase price.
   - It can be challenging to pick products because there are so many to choose from. The most popular categories are love, weight loss, and money because they are universal. However, these categories can be competitive.
   - Pick a product based on your ability to generate web traffic. It might be wise to start with something less competitive until your SEO chops are up to the task.

2. **Amazon.com**. Amazon has a similar program, but the link you provide to your customers will take your buyers to Amazon's website. Again, you make a commission when someone makes a purchase after following your link.

- The percentage that Amazon pays out in commissions is very small. Therefore, it makes sense to go after larger ticket items, such as flat screen TVs, so you can make more money.
- You could create a website that reviews flat screen TVs, and then simply provide your affiliate link to the Amazon page.
- Create reviews from the ones already on Amazon. Read multiple reviews and then incorporate the information into a single review.
3. **Other sites.** Search on the internet for "affiliate products." You'll be surprised to find out how many different products have affiliate programs that will pay you a commission for each product you "sell."

Making money as an affiliate has numerous advantages:

1. **There's only a minimal cost to become operational.** There's nothing to buy upfront and no inventory to store. Your only expenses are web hosting and a domain name. A domain name costs $15-$20 or less per year. Web hosting is around $6 per month for upto 25 domains.

2. **Someone else is dealing with the customers**. Since another company is providing the product, they also handle the complaints. In our previous examples, ClickBank and Amazon will deal with any customer issues.

3. **There are an unlimited number of products to sell**. You can sell t-shirts, vitamins, lawnmowers, travel packages, and anything else you can think of.

4. **The company providing the products deals with collecting payments and delivery**. Everything is taken care of for you. In most cases, you'll be paid your commission once per month.

Affiliate marketing has a very low barrier to entry and can be a great way to start generating passive income. Your websites will require a minimal amount of work once you get them created and ranked on the popular search engines. You could even do this without a website. If you have an email list, you can send out a mass email and direct your customers to the product. Anytime you have a website, do what you can to capture the visitors' email information. A good email list is extremely valuable.

You can also sell your own digital products. You could even sell them on a site like ClickBank and let them do the work for you.

"Money is always there but the pockets change; it is not in the same pockets after a change, and that is all there is to say about money." - Gertrude Stein

Putting It All Together

While it's possible to earn a lot of money from just one source of passive income, it's generally better to have several.

Discover the reasons why multiple income sources will serve you well:

1. **You'll learn to practice diversification**. Just as you spread risk with your investments, it's best to do the same

with your passive income streams. It's best to have several unrelated sources of passive income, just to be safe.

- What if all of your passive income is from real estate and the rental market tanks?
- What if Google changes its search algorithm and all of your web pages stop ranking for the relevant search terms?
- What if the revenue-sharing site you're using shuts down?

2. **You'll increase your odds of success**. Many of your attempts to generate passive income are likely to come up short. However, others will pay off much better than you ever imagined. The more opportunities you give yourself, the more likely you are to hit it big.

3. **You'll get to know more people**. Others can provide great opportunities. The more sources of passive income you build, the more people you'll get to know, which means more revenue from networking. Swap e-mail lists and partner with others. Avoid trying to do this all alone.

4. **You'll likely find something that you're good at**, love to do, or both! Give yourself the chance to find something you excel at or are passionate about. When it stops feeling like work, you'll be happier and more successful.

Other Ways to Combine These Examples

Perhaps you'll decide to start out by purchasing and renting out a duplex. It might take a couple of months to find a suitable property, in a good location, at an affordable price. But eventually, you'll find a great tenant and start making some money. Then, you could save and invest part of that positive cash flow. The rest of the income could be used to purchase several domain names and web hosting. Spend a month or two to build your websites and drive traffic to those sites through search engine optimization. You could either become an affiliate or sell your own products. Since you probably had to write some articles for your SEO, you might continue writing and posting them on several revenue sharing websites. While you're on vacation, you might take a few great photos of the Rocky Mountains. Perhaps you can create a calendar with those pictures and sell it on your own website. By now, you might have enough money to start a small business, and so on.

"Everyone needs a certain amount of money. Beyond that, we pursue money because we know how to obtain it.
-Gregg Easterbrook

Conclusion

Passive income is a great wealth builder because it removes time constraints. Even wealthy professionals are limited by time. Passive income is one way to circumvent time limitations. There are many ways to create a passive income and we've only covered a few. You can probably come up with several more on your own with a little creative thinking. If you're lacking passive income sources, start adding them today. The sooner you get started, the sooner you can build your bank account. If you can build a passive income source that pays just $5 per day, you'll earn over $1,800 in the first year. That's a great return for part-time work. Imagine if you found more sources like that. Initially, you may feel like you're making little headway, but after several months you'll be astounded at the wealth you're creating. Consider what interests you. Wouldn't it be ideal to use your passion to generate income? Imagine making money while spending time working on things that resonate with you. What could be better? Start generating passive income today. Do it once and profit forever.

"Make every thought, every fact, that comes into your mind pay you a profit. Make it work and produce for you. Think of things not as they are but as they might be. Don't merely dream - but create" - Robert Collier

Making Money in Your Spare Time

Making money can be very difficult for some people. Even if you have a good job, you may not have enough to pay all of your bills and still have money left over. There's a way around that, though. You can make some extra money in your spare time. You don't need to dedicate all your leisure time to making money, either. Just a few hours a week would be enough. You could use your evenings after dinner or a day on the weekend. It's not about getting rich or replacing your day job - it's just about having a little extra.

Even fifty or a hundred dollars a week might make the difference between paying a bill or not.

Where Do Your Talents Lay?

Everyone is good at something. Even if you aren't sure what kinds of talents you have, think about what you like to do. Do people compliment you on your singing voice? Your cooking? Your handy work? The compassion that you have for children or the elderly? You have the potential to make money from your passions, interests, and skills! It's not as hard as a lot of people make it out to be. What kinds of hobbies do you have? Do you write? Take pictures? Paint or draw? Can you teach or tutor others? Are you handy? Make a list of what you're good at and what you enjoy doing - sometimes, these aren't the same things.

Choose an activity from your list and then try these strategies to use this talent to produce income:

- Advertise your services in the newspaper so you can find people who need help.
- Post your information on Craigslist, and online classified ad sites where people hire others.
- Start a website or blog where you can offer your talents and services.
- Network with others who do the same things, so you can get ideas and advice.
- Attend community events and hand out business cards.
- Create a portfolio of your work and start showing it to others.

You never know when you might be able to make a connection that leads to something great. If you're not prepared, that chance could slip away. Rather than wait for that moment, be ready in advance. Start preparing now, knowing that making money in your spare time could take a little while. It may not happen overnight, but it will happen when you remain committed to it.

Yes, Attitude Does Matter

Remember that how you act can make a huge difference in whether someone hires you to do something. Even if you're the best in the business, a bad attitude won't get you very far. Stay positive, even when you get turned down for work. Keep your head up and continue to improve. When people see that you're committed to making money in your spare time and you're actively looking for work, you'll find people who will buy from you or hire you to do something. Get letters of reference from people who hire you and use them in your portfolio to show future customers.

Word of mouth is also vital, so do your best job every time. If you make a mistake, admit it, and then work to make it right. People appreciate honesty, and you'll get more work from those who see that you're a quality person with the right mindset. These attributes can actually help you go farther than the actual level of talent you have. So let your talents inspire you, rev up your can-do attitude, and you may be surprised how easy it really is to bring in some extra money in your spare time!

How To Make Your First $1,000 Online

Making money online has a certain allure. It immediately conjures up images of working from a coffee shop for a couple of hours and then driving away in a convertible sports car that costs more than the average home. While this vision is certainly possible, most people struggle to even make their first $100 online. And sometimes that $100 requires a lot of work, but a goal of $1,000 is still small enough to be believable, and the time will be well spent. One of the best ways to get started making money online is to build and lease websites that target local web traffic.

Building and leasing a website has several advantages:
1. **It's quite easy**. While it's challenging and expensive to get a website to show up on the first page of search results for the search term "ipad for sale," it's not difficult to rank a website for the term, "kansas city dentist."
2. **You build passive income**. Ultimately, you can make money in your sleep. Once you get everything set, it should only take a minimum amount of work to keep the money coming in.
3. **It's scalable**. Since there's a minimum amount of maintenance required, you can keep stacking cash flows on top of each other. Just keep building, ranking, and leasing websites.
4. **You have options**. For example, a website for a "kansas city dentist" might bring in $500 per month. But "new york

city lawyer" might be worth $5,000 a month. A smaller city hair salon might bring in $150 per month. You can start small and be rather certain of success.

The primary disadvantage is time. In most cases, it will take several weeks to a couple of months to rank a website. However, there will be less than 8 hours of work in many cases. Google likes to see things evolve over time. You can't just put the 8 hours in on day #1 and be done.

These steps will put you on the path to earning your first $1,000 online:

1. **Find a city**. A good size city for your first website will have a population between 100,000 and 400,000. Here is a list of cities by population.
   - A smaller city than that is likely to have too little web traffic for the work to be worth your time.
   - If the city is any larger, it might have too much competition for your first website.
2. **Find a good niche**. You're looking for a niche where a single customer has a significant value to a business. For example, a single dental patient is worth approximately $750 per year to a dentist, on the average. But a customer might only be worth $25 per year to a greeting card store. Some good niches to consider:
   - Dentists
   - Plastic surgeons
   - Plumbers
   - Architects
   - Optometrists and Lasix eye surgery centers

- Home Builders
- Chiropractors
- Lawyers
- Massage therapists
- Landscaping firms
- There are many others

3. **Research**. Use the free Google Keyword Tool to perform your research. There are instructions on the website. Look for a niche with low to medium competition for your city. It should also be worth $500-$1,000 per month. You can determine the value by looking at the search traffic for the keywords in question and multiplying by the suggested bid price.

   - When you see search results in Google, the first couple of results are usually paid for. The client is paying Google a certain amount of money every time someone clicks on that search result. The "suggested bid" price is comparable to that cost per click price.

   - If your website gets 200 visitors per month that search for "xyz city dentist" and the suggested bid price is $5, that traffic is worth $1,000 to someone. Remember to include all the relevant search terms during your research. You don't have to find a single term worth $1,000.

   - Keep going until you find a niche and a city that work.

4. **Create a website.** You might not know much about creating websites, but with the free Wordpress software at wordpress.org, a good-looking and effective website is

easy to build. You can find many good tutorials online. In a nutshell, you will need to:

- Purchase a domain name and web hosting. The domain name should be related to your niche. Most experts advise sticking with .com, .net, and .org. Web hosting is easy to find for a few dollars per month.

- Some good domain registrars are godaddy.com and namecheap.com. For best results, it's a good idea to obtain your webhosting from a different service than where you get your domain name.

- Build your website over time. Put up a post or page of content per week. You can hire someone to write articles for you for a few dollars. For example, if your niche is real estate agents, you should have content related to home loans, school districts, moving, the local real estate market, and so on.

- Use pictures and YouTube videos. You can find royaltyfree pictures online and you can simply imbed existing YouTube videos on your website.

- Include the search terms you found while doing your research. Sprinkle these keywords throughout your website.

- Educate yourself. There is a lot of information online about search engine optimization. Plus, there are many ways to market your website. The Internet is full of information about both of these topics which will bring more traffic to your site.

5. **Once the website is ranked on the first page of a search**, find a client. Finding someone to lease your website really is the easiest part. Approach your possible clients and show them what you have. Show them the traffic you're getting and the cost per click. Offer to sell them the traffic at 40 cents on the dollar.
6. **Add their personal content to the website**. Change your ictures for theirs. Add their business hours, address, and other relevant information. Make the changes slowly over a couple of weeks. Continue to update the website in some small way each month, just to keep it current.
7. **Collect your money**. Set up a system that works for you. PayPal is very easy, but expensive.
8. **Repeat**. Once you get the hang of it, you'll only be spending about an hour a week for approximately 8 weeks to build a website. That means you can build a lot of them imultaneously. Your websites should be simple.

It's quite easy to build a significant income using this basic method, but it may take some time to develop a system that works for you. It's important to learn about search engine optimization. The good news is that there typically isn't a lot of competition at the local level, so you don't have to be an expert. The only thing stopping you is yourself. Spend a little time each day and go through the above process. There is not a single step that's difficult. Your own doubt is the only issue. Get one success, and then you can give yourself permission to quit doubting. There are people that make over $100,000 per month building and leasing local websites. Get your share of the pie!

Start with a $1,000 goal and build from there – all in your spare time.

Make Money Online Within A Week

Making money online is an attractive idea. Who hasn't dreamt of having a website that makes hundreds of dollars a day? While having such a website is certainly possible, it would be difficult to set it up and start making money right away. Many times, you need something faster, like a way to bring in some income right now. To make money quickly online, you only have to know where to look and what types of services to offer. You can start putting money in your bank account today if you really try.

Consider these ideas to quickly start making money online:
1. **Sell photos**. Sites like iStockPhoto will let you upload your original photos, and you earn royalties every time someone buys the right to use your photos. You can save a lot of time by studying what's currently selling well and getting your own related pictures on the website as soon as possible.
   - You're not likely to make a ton with this endeavor, but you have the opportunity to earn money while you sleep, which is never a bad thing.
2. **Write articles for websites**. Websites are always struggling to find good content. Consider what you know a lot about and write about that. Speed can be important;

most websites pay small amounts for their content articles, but the money can be pretty good if you can write 5 or 10 articles each day.

- If you can sell your work to larger, mainstream websites, the money can be great, but the work isn't as easy to get.

3. **Mechanical Turk at Amazon.com**. You can't make a lot of money here, but you can start earning within minutes. Most of the tasks only take 30 seconds to finish and only pay a few cents, but if you have a free minute here and there, you can use those minutes to bring in some extra funds. You might be able to pay for a couple tanks of gas each month.

- Check it out at https://www.mturk.com/mturk/welcome This can be a good way to use downtime while you're watching TV or eating lunch at your desk.

4. **Be a virtual assistant.** This is something you can do part time or full-time. Typical tasks might include making phone calls, doing web research, website maintenance, general email maintenance, audio / video editing, and anything else your 'boss' can think of.

- Websites like elance.com and similar sites provide a marketplace where you can both list your services and look over the thousands of freelance projects offered by website owners.
- You could also contact potential clients directly and let m know what you can do for them.

5. **Sell stuff on eBay**. eBay is a great place to sell things. Typically, you'll get more money for your item there than you will anywhere else. You can clean out your attic and garage, but that won't last forever. Look for deals at garage sales, auctions, craigslist, and more to buy cheaply and sell for a profit.

You'll never make more money per unit of time than you will by negotiating, so don't be afraid to offer less than the asking price. Even paying $3 less is significant when you consider it only took 5 seconds. That's over $2,100 an hour! Beat that.

6. **Sell affiliate products with videos**. Most affiliate marketers try to make money with websites and articles. Both can take a long time to get indexed by the search engines and start drawing targeted visitors. But videos on YouTube can get indexed quickly.

- Find an affiliate product at a site like http://www.commissionjunction.com/ or http://www.clickbank.com/ then make a short video promoting that product and include your affiliate link. Anytime someone buys something, you get paid a commission.

- This is another task where you can do the work once and get paid for an extended period of time.

- Plus, your work adds up. If you make 5 short videos each week, for example, in a month you could have videos up promoting 20 products and in a year you would have over 250. Let YouTube and other video sharing sites work for you 24/7.

7. **Become a Wordpress expert**. Wordpress is by far the most popular blogging and content management software and is quite easy to use. With a little research and work, you could quickly become an expert compared to the average user.

   - Sell your services; these could include simple things like Wordpress and theme installations and transferring installations to a new website. Offer to troubleshoot problems for an hourly rate.
   - Go offline to find clients. Many of your local businesses don't know the first thing about creating and managing on online presence. See if any of your local businesses need a website or online marketing assistance. A simple Wordpress website can easily be sold for $500. Find 2 businesses a week and you're making a decent living.
   - Offer to do their website maintenance and marketing. Consider that those big yellow page ads can cost several thousands of dollars each month, and that's the type of marketing costs these business owners are used to. It's ossible to find clients that pay you $1,000 a month to handle their online marketing and website maintenance tasks.
   - By selling a couple of websites each week and gaining a few $1,000/ month clients, you're looking at some real money.

8. **Submit websites to social media**. Many website owners are willing to pay others to submit their websites and blog

posts to the various social sites. See www.socialmarker.com for some ideas and a simple way to submit the content to numerous sites.

9. **Check out www.fiverr.com.** This website allows you to post services ('gigs') for which you can charge $5. If you can find omething that people want and doesn't take long to complete, there is the opportunity to make some extra money quickly.

   - Many of the people posting gigs are really looking to find clients that will hire them directly for more substantial work later. Maybe $5 doesn't make sense for the simple service you're providing, but that client might hire you for several hundred dollars at a later date.

10. **Create Facebook profiles for businesses**. Businesses are beginning to see the potential marketing benefits that having a Facebook page can provide, yet many business owners don't have the time or desire to do this work themselves.

There was recently a report about a person that would call businesses after hours and leave a message that basically said, "Hey, I made a Facebook page for you, if you'd like to see it call me back at 555-1234." That phone number went to a free Google voice account that would take a message. However, he never made a profile until the business called and left a message. Then he would quickly make a simple profile, call them back, and offer to sell the profile to them. If you're looking to find some extra funds quickly, try a few of these options.

Some of them don't pay a lot, but sometimes flexibility is the most important thing. Spending a little time working while you're watching TV each evening can make a positive difference in your income. There are also options to start making a lot of money quickly, like providing web services to local companies. This is the kind of thing that could easily and quickly be turned into a fulltime income. Making an income online requires work, but if you put your work in the right place you can earn money very quickly and possibly very significantly. Get set up with PayPal so you can accept payments online to make it as easy as possible for people to pay you. Remember that it's much more financially secure to have multiple streams of income, especially in a bad economy. If you ever lose your primary source of income, it's nice to have other sources that you can depend upon. Become an online entrepreneur today and increase your bottom line.

Part-Time Gift-Wrapping Service

This is the perfect time of year to start a gift-wrapping service. Many people simply don't have the time, patience, or expertise to wrap presents. With the holiday season upon us, it's a great time to make some extra money, and the money from wrapping presents for others can be considerable. Even if you're terrible at wrapping presents, you can still make the business work. You might need a little training or a helper, but a current lack of skill never stopped anyone that was determined.

Learn How To Wrap

Wrapping is a unique skill that requires some expertise. Take the time to perfect your skills.

There are several good ways to learn how to wrap like a pro:

1. **Classes.** This is perhaps the best way to learn. You'll get immediate feedback and expert assistance. Search around for classes in your area.
2. **Purchase DVDs**. There are a few DVDs available that will provide instruction.
3. **Free Online Videos**. YouTube and a variety of other websites are full of instructional videos that will help you to perfect your gift-wrapping skills.
4. **Ask a friend.** Everyone seems to have that one friend that can wrap presents like a professional. Ask for a lesson and consider asking them to help with your income-boosting activity.

It's important to learn to wrap well. Pay special attention to those oddly shaped gifts that can be challenging to wrap in an attractive manner.

Start Marketing

Now is the time to start lining up clients. Many people might think they don't need gift-wrapping services but will change their mind closer to the holidays when time is at a premium. Anyone you know is a good prospect.

Consider these marketing ideas:

1. **Utilize social media**. Lots of people use these platforms, and you can find customers without spending a dime. Create accounts for your gift-wrapping service and post regular updates.
2. **Craigslist.** Nearly everyone searches on Craigslist when looking for something unique. Someone is sure to search for your services, and your ad will be waiting.
3. **Contact local stores**. While stores that already offer giftwrapping services won't be interested, most stores don't have these services. Drop off a pile of business cards. You might even want to offer a commission on each customer the store sends your way.
4. **Contact local businesses**. Many businesses provide gifts to all employees. It might be the perfect client. All the gifts are likely to be the same and require the same wrapping paper. You could get a lot of business from one client.

Word of mouth and a little marketing can be enough to keep you busy this holiday season. Start letting people know of your new service. Put together a simple marketing plan and work your plan.

Supplies

You can't wrap presents with duct tape and trash bags and expect to get paid. You'll need the right supplies to do the job correctly and professionally. Many of the necessary items can be found locally. You might have to order others online.

Stock up on supplies:

1. **Wrapping paper**. You'll need a wide variety of styles to accommodate all of your customers. A present for a 6-year old requires different paper than a gift from a boss to an employee.

    - Stock up on cartoon-themed paper or other paper suitable for children. Some children like reindeer and others like snowmen. A variety of children's paper will make your parent customers happy.

    - You'll also require wrapping paper more suitable for adults. Try to get a variety of plain and patterned paper. Your customers will enjoy having options.

    - It's possible that you might be asked to wrap presents for weddings, birthdays, work gatherings, or New Year's Eve parties. It might be worthwhile to have a few options for these types of events, too.

    - Look online for wholesalers. Nice wrapping paper can be quite expensive for a small quantity. You'll earn more if your supplies cost less.

2. **Tape, scissors, ribbons, bows, and name cards**. Stick to the basics. Instead of carrying every color of ribbon and bow, stick to neutral colors or colors that complement many of your styles of wrapping paper. You'll save a lot of time and money. A variety of "to-from" tags will ensure that you have something suitable for everyone.

3. **A place to work**. The living room floor might work if you don't have pets or kids. A large table in a spare room is

ideal. A dining room table can work well, too. Be creative and you're sure to find the right space.

- If you're really serious, you can rent out space in a retail rea. For a first effort, it might be better to keep things at home.
- Some gift-wrappers will travel to the customer's home and rap there when requested. Charging an additional fee would be appropriate.
- Perhaps a friend has a spare room you can use. You might even get a helper out of the deal.
- The basement and garage are also viable options.

Fortunately, with a gift-wrapping service, you'll need little more than a place to work, a few inexpensive supplies, and a telephone. There are few businesses that require less to get started.

Conclusion

A gift-wrapping service fits in perfectly with the holidays and can generate a great cash flow for the amount of time invested. Everyone has presents to wrap over the holidays and many people lack the time, skill, or interest to do it themselves. Even if you're all thumbs, you can still learn to wrap well enough to charge others for your services. Start practicing now! Develop your client base. Let everyone know about your business before the holidays. Many people will be too busy to take notice later.

The Keys To Successful Moonlighting

A second source of income is always welcome.
Or maybe you have dreams of escaping your regular job and want to start your own business. Well, it would be great to have that business going reasonably well before you quit the first job.

For your best results, keep these ideas in mind as you create that second income:

1. **Brainstorm.** Consider all the possibilities for your second income. How many hours can you give to it each week? Does it need to be on the weekends only? How much money can you expect to make? How long will it take to start making money?
   - Come up with a big list and then evaluate all your options.
2. **Value your time**. Be smart; it really doesn't make sense to take a part-time job making minimum wage. Anyone can do better than that with a little bit of work and planning.
   - Even something simple like walking a dog pays around $15 for a half-hour walk. There's no reason to flip burgers for $7.50 an hour. You'd get some exercise and have the opportunity to enjoy the outdoors, too.
3. **Consider your strengths.** Whatever you choose to generate your second income should either be something that you're good at or truly love. If you love doing it, you'll

learn to be good. Also, if you love it, it won't really seem like work.

Ideally, you'll both love it and be great at it. For example:
- If you're an accountant, doing something related to accounting makes sense.
- If you love to clean, a house cleaning service might be a great idea.
- If you love dogs, you could offer dog walking, training, or grooming services.

4. **Be thrifty**. Be careful about spending a lot of money to get started. One of the keys to being successful at your own business is to improve along the way. What if your first attempts don't work out so well? It's important that your early mistakes be inexpensive mistakes.

5. **Be timely**. Try to find a way to generate some income quickly. Remember, it's likely to be challenging at first.
- You don't want to finally find out that your initial plan won't work after toiling for 3 months. Design a plan that will give feedback quickly. You can then fine-tune your approach and eventually put more long-term plans in place.

6. **Schedule time daily.** A tremendous amount can be accomplished with just a couple of hours each day.
- Turn off the TV. Work on your side business during your lunch break. Make phone calls during your commute. Every little bit helps to get your freelancing business going when you're first starting out.

7. **Focus on activities that directly generate income**. Avoid getting caught in the trap of staying super busy on the things that don't contribute to your income. Many times, the most important actions are the least enjoyable.

- Keep in mind that in many cases, financially successful people simply spend a lot of time doing things that the average person doesn't want to do. Things like cold calling and giving presentations are good examples of this concept.

8. **Protect your first income**. Be careful with who you share your plans. If you have a professional position, many employers frown upon having another income. They feel that if you have extra time, you should be spending it on your first job. If you have a good-paying job, it might take awhile to replace that income.

- Be careful about using your company cell phone, computer, copier, and other items that belong to your employer for your new business. Technically it's theft, and while you're unlikely to go to jail, it's entirely possible you could lose your job.

9. **Be persistent.** Successful people have typically failed far more times than the average person.

- Keep working and improving. If something doesn't work the way you expect, try something else. If you simply change your approach until it works, how can you fail?

10. **Consider all the possible sources of income**. What else could you include in your business to make even more money? What are some related services you could offer?

Avoid getting caught in the trap of staying super busy on the things that don't contribute to your income. Many times, the most important actions are the least enjoyable.

Let's Look at an Example

Suppose your current job has you working nights. You decide that you can spend a few hours during the day on your second income. After making a long list of ideas, you like the idea of starting a dog-walking business. You love dogs, and it's something that has nearly unlimited potential. After all, there are a lot of dogs in any city. You're also available when most people are at work. It seems perfect. All you need is a phone and a leash, so it's easy and inexpensive.

How will you find clients?

- You might get started by going to the local dog park and talking to the dog owners
- Hand out business cards or give them a simple flyer you made on your computer
- Post the offer on Craigslist.org
- Hang a flyer in the Laundromat
- Contact the local veterinarians and ask for referrals
- Make a Facebook page
- Consider all the people you know that have dogs and all the people your friends and family know that have dogs

It's easy to see that there are a lot of free and very inexpensive ways to find clients. You can consider spending more money after you start making money. You might start out walking only 5 dogs Monday through Friday. If you charged $15 for each dog, that would be $375 a week or $1,500 a month. How hard do you really think it would be to find 5 busy people that need their dog walked around lunchtime every day? How could you grow this business larger? You can't walk 100 dogs a day and your time is limited. People don't need their dogs walked 30 minutes after they leave home or 30 minutes before they get home. There's only a small window in the middle of the day that makes sense unless people are on vacation. You could expand your business by hiring others. Imagine a team of dog walkers working for you. A lot of people would be happy to earn $10 an hour walking dogs. If they each walked 5 dogs, they could bring in $75 an hour to your business, so that extra $65 goes in your pocket. Do the math; it adds up quickly!

What additional services could you offer that would allow you to generate even more income?
- Water the dog owner's plants
- Bring in the owner's mail
- Feed and give water to the dog
- Pick up the droppings in the backyard
- Brush the dog
- Give the dog a bath
- Train the dog
- Transport the dog to the vet

You could have a list of these services with a fee schedule and give it to each of your clients. Not only will it make more money for you when your clients tack on these extra services to their bill, but they'll be grateful for your fine customer service! You'll be going over and above what other dog walkers might offer them.

As you can see, starting a sideline business that you can grow into something meaningful can be relatively easy and fun! There's also the possibility to earn a lot more money than you're making now. Create a plan now for a business you'll really enjoy and get started as soon as possible. You'll be amazed where you end up!

Handyman Services

Have you ever had a list of simple home improvement projects or repairs that you just didn't feel like doing? Or maybe you lacked the time required to get them done. General maintenance and repairs are a common challenge that you can turn into a powerful income boost. All homeowners and businesses need simple repairs and maintenance performed from time to time. You don't need any special skills to perform most of these tasks. There are many tasks you can do that others would rather not.

Consider providing these services:
- Changing lightbulbs, especially those that are difficult to reach. The lightbulbs in stairwells and vaulted ceilings can be challenging without a ladder or the right extension tool.
- Changing furnace filters. A furnace filter can cost less than a dollar and takes just a minute to change.

- Painting is a task that few like to do. Have you seen how much painters charge for their time?
- Installing new doors, door handles, and cabinet hardware are also easy tasks.
- Hooking up computers and other electronics. Some people find technology confusing and struggle to figure out which cable goes where.
- Fence repair.
- Cleaning gutters, replacing electrical outlet covers, hanging pictures, unclogging sinks and toilets, installing light fixtures, and more.

Most of these jobs are simple and don't require a lot of time. A full-time contractor can be very expensive. You can provide an easy solution at a price that works for you and your customers. It's easy to see how just a few hours of your time each week could add to your income in a meaningful way. You don't need much to get started: just a few simple tools and a couple of customers.

Set Up Your Business For Success

1. **Determine your customer base**. You can provide your services to homeowners, landlords, and even commercial customers.
   - Smaller office buildings can be potentially good clients. They often have the money to spend and aren't large enough to have full-time maintenance staff. You could fill that gap perfectly.

2. **Determine the services you can and can't provide.**
Which services do you feel comfortable performing? Which
do you not? You might not be comfortable with electrical
repairs, for example.
   - Consider all the possible handyman services and
     make a list of services that matches your interest and
     skill-set.
3. **Take inventory**. Do you have the tools and equipment
necessary to do the work? A simple toolset and a ladder
can go a long way. Figure out what you have and what you
can add to your toolbox economically. A few suggestions:
   - Hammer
   - Ladder
   - Adjustable wrenches and socket set
   - Selection of screwdrivers
   - A test-light and multi-meter for electrical projects
   - Wire strippers and spare wire
   - Variety of nails and screws
   - Drill
   - Portable power saw and saw horse
   - Shovel
   - Painting supplies
4. **Make a list of potential customers**. A business isn't a
business without customers. Make a list of every one in
your area that's a potential client. Pay particular attention to
those people that you already know.
5. **Form a company**. Depending on your area, you may need
to form a company to limit your personal liability. You may

also be required to be bonded and insured. Do the necessary research to determine if you need to create a formal company.

6. **Decide on your rate.** Determine what a professional contractor would charge and set your rate as a percentage of that rate. Be sure to set a minimum rate, too. You don't want to drive across town for a 15-minute job unless you're getting a minimum return.

You have everything you need to get started. All you need are a few customers. Finding customers is often the most challenging part of any business. Expect that some hard work will be required. Remember that if your rates are fair, you'll find customers happy to do business with you.

First Customers

1. **Contact everyone you know**. Pick up the phone or send a mass email. Inform everyone that you're starting a new business and that you're looking for clients. Ask them to spread the word.

   - Consider offering a referral fee for any leads that result in new customers. A small financial incentive can work wonders.

2. **Utilize free marketing opportunities**. In the modern age, there's never been a more convenient time to market your business on shoestring budget.

   - Craig's List and other online classifieds. Many of these services are free. Take advantage of them.

- Social media. You've heard of the popular websites: Facebook, Twitter, You Tube, Pinterest, LinkedIn, and Snapchat. Make your presence known.
- Create a website. You can create a free website on www.wordpress.com. It's so easy that anyone can do it.

3. **Pick up the phone**. Let your fingers do the walking and begin contacting appropriate businesses. Be prepared to make a lot of phone calls. Just remember that you only need one good customer!

4. **Make fliers for residential customers**. Walk the local neighborhood and pass out fliers. If you have the funds, consider hiring a couple of high school kids to do the work. Delegate when possible.

Now that you have a few customers, be protective of your reputation. Word spreads quickly! Always strive to provide excellent work at a reasonable price. Remember to always ask for referrals. After you've found a few customers, you may not have to advertise your business any longer Providing handyman services is within the abilities of any do-ityourselfer. You can make a great income and save your customers a lot of money over hiring a professional contractor. Put your skills to work and boost your income

Local Tour Guide

If you've ever traveled, you may have used a tour guide to make things a little easier. A tour guide is also likely to know those offthe-beaten-path attractions that only a local would know. At any time, there are people visiting your city that are in need of a tour guide. Could you make money by escorting visitors around your city? It has become common to use peer-to-peer accommodations through websites like Airbnb.com. Providing tour services through similar platforms is a logical next step. This business model is quite new. You can be one of the few people in your area, so the competition is minimal. Traditionally, commercial tour companies have provided this type of service. However, it's very possible to provide these services yourself. Typical pay rates are $15-25 per hour. Just a few hours each week is an effective way to boost your income.

There are 2 basic business models you can follow:
1. **Go it alone.** This requires marketing for clients and developing the necessary infrastructure to run your business. Marketing, communication, and billing are the primary functions that require addressing.
2. **Use one or more of the peer-to-peer travel services.** Recently, several peer-to-peer travel guide platforms have emerged that make the process of finding and servicing clients much easier.

The use of peer-to-peer tour guide platforms will allow your business to be up and running quickly. Fortunately, there are several options. Consider using all of them.

Peer-To Peer Travel Platforms

There are several internet platforms that can make running your business much easier and more effective. You're able to accomplish many tasks with a few simple clicks. These platforms are a great way to advertise your business, communicate with clients, and even perform billing functions.

These platforms can get you started:

1. **SnappyGo**. This platform is a little different from the others. Rather than offering your personal services, you can create travel and activity itineraries for others.
   - The advantage of this platform is your ability to serve several locations. Maybe you live in Miami, but attended college in San Francisco, and lived for several years in Houston. You can provide information on all three cities.
   - Strive to offer ideas that go beyond the guidebooks found in the travel section of the bookstore.
   - SnappyGo will take 30% of your income for use of their platform.
2. **HipHost**. HipHost will take 20% of your pay, but customers on HipHost are reminded to tip, which will help your bottom line significantly. This is a great place to offer your tours.
3. **Shiroube**. This is one of the largest services. There are more than 5,000 guides in 3,000 cities.

- You're able to offer guide services or provide tips, information, or itineraries.
- At this time, Shiroube is still free and doesn't take a commission. But Shiroube also doesn't provide a payment platform for your customers to pay you.

4. **Vayable**. Vayable is perhaps the most user-friendly and offers a secure payment portal. Plus, Vayable only takes a 15% commission. Vayable also charges a 3% service fee, but your clients will pay this.

Some of these platforms are popular in particular areas. Take a look and determine which of them make sense for you. They're all free to join and advertise, so it makes sense to utilize them all. Using a portal can launch your business almost immediately.

Creating Your Tours

1. **What does your area have to offer?** Do you live in wine country? Near ski resorts? Is your city known for its microbreweries? Surfing? You could offer horse rides or hay rides on your farm. Make a list of the interesting activities in your location.
2. **What do you like to do?** Many people have hobbies that can be enjoyed almost anywhere. Would you enjoy taking clients on a motorcycle tour? Bicycle tour? Walking tour of the downtown area? Shopping? Pub crawl?
3. **What do your friends like to do?** Your friends and family might have a few good ideas, too. Perhaps your sister is an expert on the local wine tasting scene.

4. **Consider focusing on a specific demographic.** Senior citizens often have different interests than children or young adults. Who can you serve?

5. **What can you do at different times of the year in your location**? Depending on the season, your city might have different activities to offer. Christmas light displays in various neighborhoods, cross-country skiing, or snowmobile tours could be good winter activities. Taking visitors to the secret swimming hole could be your focus in the summer.

There are bound to be local activities that would appeal to your city's visitors. Take advantage of your city's offerings and consider your own interests. Become an expert on the most interesting aspects of your area. Whether your city is known for being the home of a US president or the producer of the largest watermelons in the world, be sure your knowledge is up to speed. The more tours you're able to offer, the more interest you'll receive from travelers.

Other Ideas To Find Clients

Finding clients is the lifeblood of any service-based business. Advertising on the peer-to-peer platforms might be enough to keep your business going. But there are other options if you're willing to do a little work.

1. **Approach local hotels**. Most visitors to your city will stay at hotels. Visit the hotels in your area and offer to partner with them.

- The hotel can inform guests of your tour guide services, and you can split the profits with the hotel. The guests are happy, and the hotel and you are both making extra money. That's a true win-win situation.

2. **Approach local Airbnb providers**. Peer-to-peer lodging is very popular now. Offer a commission for any business they're able to send your way.

3. **Start a "things to do in xyz" website.** Of course, you're going to list your tour guide services as one of the options. Be sure to include the major attractions in your area, as it will help to rank your site in the search engines.

Conclusion

Becoming a local tour guide is a great way to put a few extra dollars in your pocket. If you live in a popular area, it's possible to generate a healthy, full-time income. What can you offer visitors to your city that they would never find on their own? What do you like to do? Answer those questions and you'll be on the fast track to extra income.

Niche Authority Blog

The basic model of blogging has become so popular that it's challenging to make an income. There are hundreds of millions of blogs! On the popular blogging platform Tumblr, there are over 245 million blogs. That's just on Tumblr alone! So how could you stand out from the crowd? Consider creating a niche authority blog – an informative blog that is targeted toward a specific audience. The combination can be highly lucrative. With consistent work, it's possible to create a nice income stream and have fun in the process. You'll also enjoy the prestige of being an expert in your chosen field. Starting a blog is simple and inexpensive. All you need is a few dollars, some free time, and a consistent work ethic.

Getting Started
Choose Your Topic

What would you like your blog to be about? It's possible to create a successful blog on nearly any topic. Expert status becomes even more important when the topic is highly competitive.

Choose your niche and blog topic:

1. **Make of list of topics that you're passionate about.** Blogs need to be updated on a regular basis. It's recommended that you add new content at least weekly. That's a lot of writing over the long haul.
   - It only makes sense to choose a topic that you'll enjoy studying yourself. As you learn more and more about your passion, and share your knowledge with others, you'll become quite an authority.
2. **Think about what you'd like to share with the world.** What are the topics you enjoy sharing with your friends? Think of a blog as a conversation between yourself and the world.

3. **Avoid topics that make you emotionally upset**. As your blog grows, many people will disagree with you. You'll need a thick skin. Avoid topics that tend to upset you.

4. **What do you enjoy reading about in your free time?** As they say, if you find work you enjoy, you'll never work another day in your life. That might be a little optimistic, as any blog will be tedious at times. But combining your hobby with an income stream is more enjoyable than most jobs.

5. **Choose keywords**. A niche website is highly targeted. Think of specific search terms that others would use to find your content and include these words in your posts. Choose keywords that many people are using in the search engines. There are several good keyword tools available online that help you find these popular search terms.

   • For example, instead of targeting the general term "quarterback," or even "NFL quarterback," you might choose to target, "How to read defenses like an NFL quarterback." You're looking for highly defined traffic.

   • It will also be easier to rank your website high on the search engine results pages with more specific keywords.

Now that you've decided on a topic you'd enjoy sharing, it's time to put your blog on the internet.

Obtain A Domain Name & Web Hosting

Head on over to a domain provider and find a domain name that is relevant to your topic. Two popular choices are GoDaddy.com and NameCheap.com. In general, it's best to stick with the three most common top-level domains: .com, .org, or .net. It's possible, but more challenging, to be successful with the less common options.

A domain name costs approximately $15/year. Finding web hosting is the next step.

These hosting companies are popular:
- HostGator
- Bluehost (This is the service I use for my Domains & Hosting)
- GoDaddy
- Dreamhost
- Arvixe

There is little difference from one company to the next. "Shared" hosting will be fine to start your blog with. You won't need your own server until you have a huge amount of traffic to your site. Choose a plan you like. Although some of these companies sell both domain names and hosting, it's better to avoid buying your domain name from the same company that hosts your website. You can usually find hosting plans for less than $10/month.

Install WordPress & Pick A Theme
WordPress is the fastest and easiest way to hit the ground running. It will serve as your blog platform. It's free, and you'll find plenty of excellent instruction on the WordPress.org website and YouTube. One of the most important aspects of your blog is finding a suitable theme. There are thousands from which to choose. WordPress itself has a large selection of free

themes. There are also themes produced by other companies that range dramatically in price. Look at other blogs, find one that really catches your eye, and search for a similar theme. Some themes can be more suitable for certain types of blogs. Some are especially good for a portfolio or photos, for example. Find a theme that works with your content.

Create Content

It's finally time to write! Decide on a schedule and stick to it. Your loyal readers will come to expect new content on a schedule. It's possible to work ahead, load your new content, and have WordPress post it to your website at particular time and date.

Create content that appeals to your readers and the search engines:

1. **Present the information that you feel is important and interesting**. Look at what your competitors are doing. Which website is the best? How can you do even better?
2. **Use appropriate keywords** here and there throughout your posts. For example, if you were writing about how to train a dog to sit, the search engines would expect to see one or more of the following words: dog, sit, treat, command, leash, listen, hand signal, train, and so on.
3. **Use multiple forms of media.** Include a mixture of text, photographs, and videos.
   - Create some videos on your topic, post them at YouTube, and embed the YouTube videos in your blog posts. Google owns YouTube and this tactic gives you

225

more exposure plus helps in your search engine ranking.

4. **Develop your own voice**. Let your articles and blog posts show your personality. Connect some of your content to events in your own life. This approach makes your site unique and attracts loyal readers who can relate to you.

The quality of your content will ultimately determine its popularity. Take the time to create the best content you can. Your readers will love you for it.

Establish Yourself As An Authority In Your Field

You might falsely believe that you're not an expert on anything. You might also believe that it takes years to reach expert status, but that simply isn't true. You're already an expert if you know more than most of the general population about a topic. Fifteen minutes of daily study is more than enough to expand your knowledge even more.

These actions will establish you as an expert:

1. **Guest blog.** Find the most influential blogs in your niche and ask to write an article for them. You might even get paid! Most importantly, all the readers of that blog will be exposed to you and your information. You'll also receive a valuable link back to your website.

If a known expert in your field publishes your work, you're considered an expert by default.

2. **Write well**. Writing is a skill that takes time to develop. If your grammatical skills are on par with that of an 8-year

old, find someone to edit your work. You could also hire someone to create your content for you. There are many websites dedicated to providing content to others.

3. **Link to authority websites.** In your content, link to other websites that are considered respected sources of information. If your niche website is dedicated to selling vitamins, a link to medical studies on Harvard.edu or Jama.com will show the world that you're current and relevant.

4. **Submit your work to more authoritative publications**. If you could get an article published in the New York Times or The Atlantic, you'd gain a tremendous amount of respectability in your area of expertise.

5. **Call talk-radio stations and ask to do a show about your topic**. Many stations are on constant lookout for content of their own, and would be happy to invite you. In addition, look for popular podcasts about your topic on the internet and offer to be on an episode.

Look at the other experts in your niche. How are they presenting themselves as experts? Once you're known as an expert, the rest is much easier.

Consider these advantages of being an expert:

1. **You'll make more money.** When you're considered an expert, you have credibility. It's much easier to make a sale hen people respect and value your opinion.

2. **The need for marketing decreases**. Experts require less marketing. Everyone already knows who you are. Imagine

people searching for your name rather than searching for "the best alligator shoes."

3. **Others want to partner with you.** When you're an expert, other bloggers, companies, and experts will be interested in working with you. You'll have far more opportunities, and those opportunities will come to you.

4. **You can create your own brand**. Rather than selling products for others, you can sell your own products. This is much more lucrative and fulfilling.

Spend the necessary time to develop expert status. Stay current, reach out to others, and post compelling content. Associate with other experts and authority websites.

Monetizing Your Blog

Blogging can be fun, even without an income. But boosting your income makes blogging even better. There are many ways to monetize your site. Keep in mind that no one wants to read a blog overpopulated with advertisements. Monetize your site, but avoid getting too carried away.

It's time to start making money:

1. **Build a list.** Send out a regular newsletter to your readers. Include interesting information and sell products in your newsletters. Sign up for an account at a good autoresponder service like Aweber or put an autoresponder plugin on your blog. Include a signup form on your front page.

2. **Affiliate marketing is a simple option**. You can sell products created by others and take a cut of the revenue. Look at clickbank.com and JVZoo.com for ideas. There are any other options.
3. **Google AdSense** is another way to monetize your blog without a lot of work. You simply insert a small bit of code provided by Google into your website. Google will fill that space with ads that are related to your content. When one of your readers clicks on an ad, you get paid.
4. **Amazon.com is a slightly different type of affiliate marketing.** You can sign up at Amazon.com to be an affiliate. You'll receive a small percentage of any sale made through your affiliate links.
5. **Sell your own product or service**. You could sell an e-book, physical product, or service. This can be very lucrative. You can even sell ad space or outbound links on your website to others.
6. **Charge a membership fee**. This can be a tough sell, depending on your topic. But imagine 10,000 subscribers each paying a few dollars a month to access your content.

Monetizing your blog is critical if you want to create an income stream. Be creative and take advantage of the best opportunities for your content and readership.

Marketing Your Blog

Let the world know about your blog! Take the time to market your blog consistently.

Allow new readers to find you more easily:

1. **Comment on other blogs.** Find other blogs about your topic and make relevant and helpful comments about the content. Include a link back to your blog.

2. **Link to other blogs on similar topics**. Conscientious blog owners keep track of their inbound links. You could make a valuable friend and receive a courtesy link back to your website.

3. **Guest post**. Most blogs are happy to have someone else ccasionally provide content. You might even get paid. At the very least, you can have new eyeballs read your material. Of course, you get to link back to your blog. This can be a great way to find new readers.

4. **Use social media**. Google is increasingly emphasizing social edia activity. Create a Facebook and Twitter account, at least. Use them regularly and encourage others to spread the word.

5. **Partner with other website owners in your niche** or a related one for a promotion. Each of you can promote the other's product in their newsletter. This will bring both of you new readers plus affiliate commissions. Pick a product that know your audience would like.

6. **Actions that establish you as an authority also bring you new readers**. For example, speaking on radio shows and podcasts spreads the word about your blog.

Remember that a certain percentage of readers will stick. Therefore, the more new first-time readers you can find the more long-term readers you'll get. Marketing must be done consistently to be effective. Set aside a few minutes each day to perform this important function.

Conclusion

A niche authority blog can be a great way to boost your income. A profitable blog can be created quickly, easily, and inexpensively. Choose a topic that resonates with your interests and be smart with marketing and creating compelling content. This could be the start of a new career. I bet you would be surprised that everything in this book is from my blog. That's right my blog has been turned into a book. Think about that, it has gone from a blog post to a compilation of blog posts into a book. Remember that part about self publishing and kindle E-Books. See what I'm getting at now. You too can post enough and then repurpose your posts on your niche into a E-Book or printed book. Just a reminder if you want to get into self publishing check out my friend Dale L. Roberts on YouTube and social media at Self-Publishing with Dale. He has plenty he can show you about publishing a book and even blog posts so you can make a book of your own. I even cover a bit of this topic on my YouTube channel at Consult A Blind Guy as well as my blog at https://consultablindguy.com/blog

OUTSOURCING-GET MORE DONE IN LESS TIME AND MAKE MORE MONEY

Outsourcing has become a popular way to have a service performed at a low cost. While many people boost their income by performing outsourced tasks for others, it might be smarter to be on the other side of the equation. There's much more income potential. If you're performing work yourself, you're ultimately limited by your time. However, if others are doing the work, you're only limited by your ability to manage all the moving parts.

Using Outsourcing To Your Advantage

Reflect on these ideas for making extra income by outsourcing:

1. **Arbitrage**. Arbitrage is an ancient concept. If apples on one side of the mountain are selling for $3/dozen but for only $1/ dozen on the other side, it's quite easy to purchase them on the less expensive side and simply carry them to the other side to sell for a higher price.

   - Consider the many services that outsourcers provide: article writing, graphics, voiceover work, YouTube video creation, website creation, and more.
   - There are many online outsourcing platforms where you can find someone to do whatever work you desire: Upwork, Fiverr, and Rev are just a few of the options.
   - It's possible to find high quality work for very little money with a little effort. For example, it's not uncommon to find someone willing to build a website

for $100. You can also find people willing to pay $1,000+ for a website. Simply assign the work and keep the difference.

- Imagine getting a bunch of clients that require a website and then passing the work on to a freelancer. The only real work you have is finding clients. You can hire additional freelancers as the need arises.

2. **Free up your time for more important tasks**. If you're a one-man or one-woman operation, you know how challenging it can be to do everything yourself.

- Besides making the product or performing the service, you have to market your business, find customers, handle sales, manage billing and collections, keep the books, and do everything else that a solo operation entails.

- It's rare to find someone that is good at all of the tasks that are critical to running a successful business. One weak link can limit everything else.

- If you dislike sales, there are people that can handle that aspect of your business for you. Think about all the tasks you do that would be relatively simple to teach to someone else.

- Find one or more freelancers that can handle those tasks for you. Tip: sales can be a great place to start, because it's possible to find someone willing to work on commission. They can pay for themselves.

- With more available time on your hands, you can be more productive and increase your income.

Outsourcing can be a great way to boost your income, but finding a skilled freelancer for your needs will require some effort or a little luck. Since luck is difficult to predict, it only makes sense to rely on effort and an intelligent process.

Finding A Freelancer

1. **Define your needs**. It's nearly impossible to satisfy your needs if you don't know what they are. Consider the tasks that are simple, you don't enjoy doing, or you're not particularly good at performing. Ideally, you'll find a task that meets all 3 criteria!

   - Choose one task to outsource. Pick the one that makes the most sense. Remember that you can also outsource the actual product or service itself. Maybe you're one of those lucky business owners with too much business to handle.
   - You can always outsource additional tasks later, but just start with one.
   - What characteristics does your outsourcer need to possess? What type of experience would be ideal? How skilled does he need to be? How many hours per week will you need help? What personality characteristics would you like to see?

2. **Create your listing and post it**. A simple search will yield a wide variety of outsourcing platforms. A few things to keep in mind:

- Be wary of posting or providing your main email address, Skype ID, or phone number. You're almost certain to be inundated with unwanted attention.
- Remember that you also have the option to look through the listings to find someone who looks like they have the skills you need at a fair price. The most effective strategy is to do both.

3. **Evaluate and interview.** The evaluation process will depend on the type of work you need performed. A résumé may or may not be necessary. Samples of prior work are important in most cases. Choose a few of the best candidates and interview them.
   - Skype is a great way to conduct interviews. There's so much that can be gathered from actually seeing someone and their body language.
   - Pay attention to whether or not the candidate is on time. If they're late for the interview, can you expect them to meet deadlines consistently?
   - Have a few questions prepared to test their knowledge. Every field has its own lingo. This is one way to discover those pretending to have expertise they don't truly possess.
   - Interview all your best candidates before making a decision. The first candidate might be great, but the third might be much better. You'll never know that if you don't interview everyone.

4. **Give the best candidate a small trial job**. If they can't do an adequate job, the sooner you discover that fact, the

better. Be sure to provide all the information and guidance they need to do their best. This will also help you to clarify in your own mind what you need from them.

- If you find someone with a positive attitude and excellent skills, it's your responsibility to mold them into what you need.

5. **Provide feedback**. It's unlikely that anything will be perfect right out of the gate. Constructive feedback is a critical step to getting the best results from your worker.

Outsourcing can be a great tool to make more money doing less work. Make a list of all the tasks you perform and decide which of them you would prefer to outsource. Take it one step at a time and you'll find the right person for your needs. Free yourself to spend more time on the important and lucrative tasks. You'll get more enjoyment, and income!

Public Speaking

If you're looking for a way to significantly boost your income, public speaking might be the answer. Speaking fees of $40,000 or more aren't uncommon. The average professional speaker makes approximately $6,000 per speech! It might seem far-fetched if you've never given a paid speech, but it's easier than you think.

There are a variety of ways to earn a lot of money for your time, but most will fall into one of two broad categories:
1. **Doing something that most others can't.** These are the things with a high barrier to entry. This would include activities like playing professional sports or becoming a brain surgeon. It's not possible to simply start doing these things and expect to start earning a paycheck tomorrow.
2. **Doing things that others don't want to do.** Dealing with nuclear waste or living on an oil rig 100 miles out in the middle of nowhere would qualify here.

Public speaking falls into the latter category. Not many people enjoy public speaking, which is part of the reason professional speakers are paid so well.

Follow these tips to come up with a great speech and join the ranks of well-paid speakers:
1. **Learn how to give a good speech!** Perhaps the best solution to this step is joining Toastmasters International. They can have 20+ chapters in just one medium sized city.

The cost is minimal. Most chapters meet about 4 times per month, though some meet more and some less.

- You have the opportunity to speak at every meeting, and the members take turns leading the meetings.
- You receive immediate feedback and speeches are recorded.
- Consider joining multiple chapters to get more practice! Chapters meet on a variety of days at a variety of times. There's bound to be a day and time that work for you.
- There are also additional opportunities for learning other skills and networking with business leaders in your community.

2. **Figure out what you're going to talk about.** There are several different types of public speakers:

- Informational. These speakers educate and teach others about a specialized topic. It might be providing information about a piece of software or teaching something about bass fishing. Maybe it's a speech about Buddhism or an exciting African safari.
- Inspirational/motivational. Often these speakers relate stories of hardship, overcoming adversity, or achieving great things.
- Humorous. Everyone likes to laugh.
- It's important to figure out what your exact topic is going to be. What do you know that could be valuable to others? What fascinating things have you done or experienced? Are you great at making people laugh?

Brainstorm a few ideas and share them with your fellow Toastmasters.

3. **Create your speech.** Think about how long you want your talk to be. Are you interested in talking for an entire day? A professional speech can be as short as 30 minutes. A good plan might be to create a 2-hour speech and a shorter version of 30 minutes.

4. **Practice with a Toastmasters group.** Once you have your speech written and practiced several times, try it out on your new group of friends. You'll receive tons of expert feedback. Record your speech so you can critique yourself later and see your progress over time.

5. **Keep improving and practicing**. Take the constructive criticism to heart and keep improving your speech. When you've improved it, practice again with your Toastmasters group.

Marketing Yourself

Now that you have a great speech, it's time to find an audience. While many people, like Olympic medal winners and famous politicians, can start at the top of the pay scale, you might have to start closer to the bottom and work your way up.

There are many ways to find some work:
1. **Consider giving a free speech.** Many speakers started out giving free speeches. Consider what groups would like to hear your information and contact them. After one or two free speeches, you can probably start getting paid. It's very

common to find your first client from your audience. There are plenty of free opportunities to speak if you just ask.

2. **Sign up with a speaker's bureau**. These companies are like a clearinghouse for public speakers. Those that wish to hire a speaker can peruse the listings and pick out a speaker. The speaking bureau will normally take a cut of your fee, but they will also normally handle the logistics, scheduling, and collecting your fee.

3. **Set up your own website.** Put short video clips of your speech online. Let people see what you have to offer. Really take the time to put your best foot forward. Take advantage of YouTube, too.

   - Make it easy to connect with you. At the very least, have your phone and email on the front of your web page.
   - Learn how to fully utilize social media. Use every tool at your disposal.
   - Create a "speaking brief." This is similar to a resume. It should include a good photo, a paragraph mentioning your speech topics, your background, speaking experience, references, links to videos of your speeches, and your contact info.

4. **Be seen.** Be everywhere you can be. Get up on the stage at every opportunity. Comment on relevant blogs, write a guest post for a website, go to events, and meet as many people as possible. People need to know you and what you have to offer.

5. **Keep pushing.** After your early speeches are behind you, you might be charging $2,500. It could be $10,000 in a year. The key is to continue improving and asking for more money as you get more experience. Many times, the only difference between the $2,500 speaker and the $25,000 speaker is that he latter simply asks for more money.

6. **Build relationships**. Along the way you'll meet many people. Stay in regular contact. Make friends with these people. Word-of-mouth is always the best way to find new speaking engagements.

Even if you've never given a speech, you can become a professional speaker and do so successfully on a part-time basis. Just as you don't have to be the best auto mechanic to make a living, you don't have to be the world's greater public speaker either. Take the time to learn to speak well. It doesn't take long. Very few people do public speaking on a regular basis, so you can be better than 99% of the general population very quickly. Make a great speech, practice, and get out there. Market like your life depends on it. Many groups are constantly looking for good content. Let them know about yours! You might even decide to quit your day job! I've mentioned one person a few times already who makes thousands when he does public speaking. An when I say thousands I'm talking upwords of $50,000 for a single speech which may only last 45 minutes to an hour and could be a one time in a single day or 2 times over a weekend. Crazy right? Bet you'd love to make that kind of income from public speaking too you just have to get yourself out there and share what you know and are good at and you to could be the next speaking at an event making thousands like Pat Flynn and countless others.

Public Speaking 101:
The Benefits Of Speaking In Public And Learning How To Do So Successfully

Preparing A Great Speech

When you give a speech, whether it is a presentation at work or a talk in front of unfamiliar faces, the most important way to help ensure that you hit it out of the park is to prepare in advance. Even if it's a topic that you feel you know backwards and forwards, preparation is still a vital component to making a great speech.Research Your Topic Even if you know the topic well, research will give you confidence. You want your speech to rely on facts, not faulty memories. Double-check your speech for accuracy by conducting research. If you are new to the topic, research is even more essential to a successful speech. Research also makes you more comfortable with the material. The more you prepare beforehand, the more comfortable you'll feel as you deliver the speech. Thorough research makes your audience feel comfortable, allowing them to trust you as an authority. Should I Write the Speech or Just Make a Basic Outline? Is it more effective to deliver a speech from an outline, or to write it out and read it verbatim? Both options have their advantages and disadvantages. By writing the speech out, you can memorize it more easily. You can use repetition to your advantage and have the whole thing stored in your brain word for word. The downside is that you run the risk of sounding almost robotic. It won't sound natural. And if you have a copy of your speech on hand, you run the risk of reading it directly from the page, which is boring to those who hear it.

With an outline, you can still have your basic facts in front of you. This will also give you some flexibility. You can ad-lib a little and tweak some things, freeing you up so that you sound a bit more natural. The downside is that this makes it a little difficult to rehearse the speech since you don't have a concrete speech to work with. The best solution is to combine the best of both worlds into your approach. Write out a full speech that you can read, rehearse, and know well. When it comes to giving the speech, take only an outline with you. This will ensure that you don't just read it off the paper and, should you forget something, you can always glance down at your outline and refresh your memory.

Conqueing Your Stage Fright

One of the biggest obstacles many people face when they're about to speak in public is stage fright. Your heart starts to race, your palms are sweaty, and you get butterflies in your stomach. The few minutes before the speech can be surprisingly nerve wracking!

Even experienced actors still feel some stage fright before a big performance. The good news is that once you begin your speech, the nerves will subside when you're thoroughly prepared. There are ways to help combat stage fright so you can feel confident when you go out there to deliver your speech.

Read the Speech Aloud to Yourself

As mentioned in the previous section, reading the speech aloud to yourself can help you feel more comfortable with it. Reading your speech over and over will give you an opportunity to work the kinks out of the speech and make it better. You'll also get a feel for the flow and become comfortable delivering the material.

Rehearse in Front of a Small Group

One of the best ways to get comfortable talking in front of a large group is to start by becoming comfortable talking in front of a small group. If possible, get some friends and family together to sit down and listen to your speech. This will give you a group of friendly listeners that can provide feedback in a comfortable environment.

Your audience can give you suggestions on how to improve the presentation or your delivery. They can also help you get comfortable performing it in public. Since they are people you know, you'll feel more at ease in front of them and 'll be able to relax. The more comfortable you are ahead of time, the more comfortable you'll be when the time comes to step up in front of the crowd for real. Should I Visualize the Crowd in Their Underwear?

This is a common suggestion that is given to people who have stage fright. The idea is that in your mind, your audience will be more embarrassed than you are. This approach has a few drawbacks. Let's say you're delivering the speech, making a solid effort to make eye contact with several people in the crowd to engage them. You're nervous, so you start picturing them in their underwear. Your mind becomes distracted, and you begin to lose your place. All of a sudden you're stammering to remember the point you were making. Instead, pretend that they are not even there. Or pretend that the crowd is much smaller than it is by focusing on one person at a time. Ignore anything that adds to the pressure, such as cameras, lights, or sounds.

Psych Yourself Up

Before getting on stage in front of your audience, do what you can to get yourself pumped up psychologically. Listen to your favorite music beforehand, if possible. Calming music can decrease your nerves, distract you from the pressure, and even increase your memory retention. If you can't listen to music, hum your favorite tunes in your head or recite some positive affirmations. Different music affects people in different ways. Do you perform best when fired up? Then pick your favorite rock tunes that are upbeat. If you perform better when you're relaxed and calm, perhaps classical or instrumental music is best.

Knowledge is Power

As mentioned in the previous section, you'll be most confident to deliver a memorable speech if you know the material backwards and forwards. Nothing places thorough preparation beforehand! If you know what you're talking about, you'll be less nervous and your performance will be a winning one Knowing your stuff also has the added benefit of preventing you from constantly looking down. Also, if you have a copy of your speech in front of you, knowing it backwards and forwards will help keep you from just reading it directly off of the page.

Things To Remember As You're Giving The Speech

When delivering your presentation, what you say is very important, but remember that your nonverbal behavior often communicates more than what you say. Make an effort to control your body language and present the right impression to those watching your presentation.

The Importance of Eye Contact

As you step up to begin, you may briefly forget everything you prepared. It's usually a temporary effect, but it can lead to an over-reliance on your notes or speech. You'll want to make eye contact with the audience because it'll help to get them involved in what you're saying. It's okay to glance down periodically, but your focus should be on the crowd. Avoid looking awkward by knowing your speech well. That way, you can focus on maintaining eye contact with your audience without looking up and down constantly to refresh your memory. As a result, your audience will see you as an authority on the subject and trust what you have to say.

Move Your View Around the Room

When making eye contact with your audience, try to make sure that every section of the crowd gets attention. Rather than focusing your gaze on one person, try to go from section to section, picking a person at random and making eye contact.

Talk Rather Than Read

When you have your speech in front of you, it's very tempting to look down to read it. If you're an author and you're doing a public reading of a new work, you might be able to get away with this. Otherwise, talk to the crowd as if you're inviting them into a conversation about your subject matter. In order to connect with your audience, it's important that they can see your face. Therefore, try to look down at your notes seldom and only briefly. Holding the speech in front of your face is ineffective and will muffle your voice. Talk to your audience like you would a friend discussing your topic. Just think of it as a conversation!

The Benefits To Learning To Speak In Public

While speaking in public can be a daunting task, it comes with incredible personal and professional benefits. The pressure of giving a speech makes you more prepared for many different types of situations in which you must communicate effectively with others.

Impress Your Boss

If you are assigned a major presentation for work, you can take advantage of the opportunity to show your boss what a great employee you really are. By hitting the presentation out of the park, you can showcase your knowledge and work ethic. A great speech or presentation will really make you stand out from the crowd, which can lead to a raise or promotion.

Prove That You're a Real Go-Getter

One of the main traits of the office workplace is that many employees do the minimum amount of work required of them. A good presentation or speech will show the higher ups that you mean business and take work seriously.

Stand Out From the Rest of the Pack

By learning to speak in public, you can become a person who stands out from the rest of the workers in ability and initiative. By showing your bosses that you are willing to go above and beyond, putting a lot of effort and energy into your presentations, they will be more willing to bring your name up in discussions about promotions or raises. There are also benefits to your life outside of work that come with learning how to speak in public. For example, public speaking actually increases your confidence! If you're shy, delivering a powerful presentation on something you're passionate about can help you to move out of your comfort zone. If you can speak comfortably in front of a whole room of people, you can speak comfortably in front of one or two.

Conclusion

Public speaking can be an intimidating task for a lot of people. Take comfort in the fact that even actors and others who make a living speaking in front of large crowds suffer from some degree of nervousness before making a speech. By preparing yourself, you can help combat the anxiety by making sure you know what you want to say. This will help keep you from stammering to fill the silence and boost your confidence. Thorough research will help you to ingrain the information into your brain. It will also help you avoid reading your notes like a book. That way, you can more easily engage the audience and make a greater impact with eye contact. A "pre-game ritual" can help you to ease your nerves. Music can be a helpful tool. You can either listen to your iPod or hum your favorite tune in your head to ease the nerves.

During your speech, look around to every section of the audience so that each member of your audience is engaged. Try to move your eyes instead of your whole head so that your movement appears more natural and less forced. There are many benefits of learning to speak in public. Most of all, you gain valuable experience in leaving your comfort zone, rising to the challenge, and conquering your fears. Prepare well, trust in yourself, and make the most of the opportunity to present your ideas and persuade others. Face your fears of speaking in public and emerge triumphant!

Public Speaking 101: Worksheet

Multiple Choice
1. The best way to make a great speech or presentation sound natural is to:
    a. Research the topic thoroughly
    b. Wing it completely
    c. Go in with a vague idea of what you're going to talk about

2. You'll want to focus your attention on:
    a. The audience, so that they can feel connected
    b. The clock, so that you'll know when you're done
    c. Your speech, so that you don't forget what you're saying
    d. Whichever audience member you find most attractive

3. In order to ensure I don't forget what I'm going to say, I should:
    a. Write the speech the night before and glance over it the next day
    b. Memorize the data as well as my speech to make sure I know the material
    c. Make things up as I go along
    d. Let someone else do it

General Questions
1. What topic I will be discussing?

2. What are some resources (i.e. websites and books) that I can use for research?

3. What can I do to become more familiar with the subject matter?

4. What are some songs I can either listen to or play in my head to psych me up for my presentation?

Yes or No

1. Have I researched my topic?

    Y - N

2. Do I have all of the information I need?

    Y - N

3. Have I done a trial run or rehearsed?

    Y - N

4. Should I envision the crowd in their underwear?

    Y - N

True or False

1. I should read my speech to make sure I don't mess it up.

    T F

2. Eye contact is very important. Public speaking outside of work is pointless.   T F

3. Learning to speak in public can boost confidence.

    T F

4. You should focus on one section of your audience.

    T F

Answer key:

Multiple choice: 1.A 2.A 3.B True/False: 1.F 2.T 3.F 4.T 5.F

Public Speaking 101: Checklist

____ I've come up with my topic.

____ I have found several sources to cite in my speech.

____ I have gathered all of the information that I need.

____ I marked down all of my sources so I can credit them.

____ I have organized the information.

____ I have written my speech.

____ I have written a second draft.

____ I have written a third draft.

____ I believe that this is as good as I can possibly make it.

____ I have prepared note cards to keep the basic points on hand.

____ The cards are short and contain only a few details.

____ I have numbered the cards.

____ The cards are in sequential order.

____ I have read my speech aloud at least twice to myself.

____ The speech sounds natural.

____ I have timed the speech.

____ It falls within the time I have allotted.

____ I have recited my speech without a copy of it on hand.

____ I was able to recite my speech without stammering or blanking

____ I have rehearsed my speech in front of friends and family.

____ I have tested all props and technical items.

____ I made eye contact.

____ I received feedback on how to improve.

____ I used the suggestions to make my presentation bette

Selling Your Household Items Online? Read This First!

Are you interested in creating extra income by selling some of your household items online? Listing them on the internet can be a creative way to generate money, but it's important to do it safely.

Use these techniques to protect yourself and your family:

1. **Research sales websites carefully.** Each website has different policies for the types of items that can be listed. Pay attention to fees for using the website and selling an item. Shipping or delivery rules can also vary.
   - Niche websites that are geared toward specific audiences or markets can help you sell some items. Do you have a rare antique doll you want to sell? Consider using a website that only sells antiques or dolls. This may help you sell the item faster and find legitimate buyers.

2. **Post photos carefully.** As you post photos of your items online, avoid using pictures of yourself or family members.
   - Your children may look adorable playing with the toys you're selling, but as a safety precaution, it's wiser to avoid images of your family in the photos.
   - Avoid posting images of your home, other belongings, or pets as well. Criminals can track things easily, and any of these images can provide clues about you or your belongings.
   - e careful with the background you use in the photos because it can provide information about you or your

family. Find neutral backgrounds such as bare walls or clean tables.

3. **Find a safe spot for business transactions.** If selling your items online involves meeting the buyers in person, then seek out safe spots where you can meet.
   - It's popular to use public parking lots and other public locations to do business. However, you may also want to check with your local police department. Departments around the country are starting to create safe havens for online transactions.

4. **Choose safe payments.** If the website you selected allows for safe online transactions that don't require meeting the buyer, then you may want to consider this option. Some websites allow the use of an escrow service that protects you from fraud.
   - Online sales can be a target for scams, so it's important to carefully consider how you'll accept payments. You may not feel comfortable with checks, debit cards, or credit cards. Money orders and cashier's checks might be forged, even if they look identical to the real versions
   - Cash is one of the most popular payment methods for household items. You can make sure the money is real by going to an ATM with the buyer to withdraw it.

5. **Watch out for common scams**. The type of item you sell may attract specific scams. It's important to research them and be aware of the tactics.

6. **Notify friends or family about meetings.** If you plan to

meet the buyer in person, notify your friends or family first. They should be aware of the meeting location, time, and purpose. They can call and check in on you during the meeting.

- Better still, bring a friend or family member to the meeting for safety purposes.

Selling items online can help you increase your income and pay your bills. Be safe with your transactions, so everyone benefits.

Tips for Selling Items to Accumulate Extra Cash

Experiencing periods of financial strife has happened to almost everyone. When it happens, it can bring on feelings of worry and anxiety. But one way to make some quick money is to sell some belongings you don't use or no longer want. From big ticket items to clothing and tchotchkes, you might be surprised what you can
sell to thicken your wallet. As they say, "One man's trash is another man's treasure."

Follow these strategies to make the most from your sales:
1. **Consider selling almost everything**. Make a list of the items you'll sell room by room and jot down reasonable prices to ask. Don't worry; you won't miss them once they're gone.
   - Are your rooms over-stuffed with too much furniture? Sell your least favorite pieces.

- Sell that extra recliner in the back bedroom that's piled with junk. Sell the junk on it too!
- Consider selling your SUV that eats too much gas.
- You don't use your bread maker anymore? Sell it to someone that will.
- What about wrong size clothes or those you dislike? If you don't wear them, sell them.
- Remember to sell those long-unused items in your garage as well.

2. **Create ads.** For larger items worth more money, write quick ads to sell them.
   - 1997 Ford F250, automatic, good condition, $3,500
   - 60 Foot ladder for sale, $150
   - Nicole Miller strapless dress, $25
   - On Craigslist, you'll be given the opportunity to select how you prefer interested people contact you, either by phone number or e-mail. Also on Craigslist, you can upload a picture of the item for sale, which will help the item to sell more quickly.
   - In the event you're writing ads for your local newspaper, you'll be required to keep to a certain number of words, particularly if the newspaper offers free "For Sale" ads. Here are some samples of "For Sale" ads for the newspaper:
   - Sofa & chair, black leather, 3 tables, excellent condition. $325, 555-0100
   - Queen bed with white wicker headboard, great condition $300, 555-0100

- Pool table, regulation size, American Heritage Classic, $1,000, 555-0100

3. **Have a yard sale for the smaller items**. For your items that are too small for Craigslist or newspaper ads, put together a yard sale. If you don't have enough items for a sale on your own, get together with your neighbors to share in one.

4. **Gather your gold.** Look through your old jewelry and separate out pieces you don't like or wear anymore. Cufflinks, tie clasps, pierced earring backs, bracelets or the like can bring in some cold, hard cash. Take your items to the local gold exchange to see what you can get for them.

   - Follow safety protocol: avoid allowing anyone to leave the room with your jewelry. If a staff member at the gold exchange says the scale is in the back, go to another shop or state you'll not let the gold out of your sight. If the place is reputable, this will not be an issue as the scale will be located on the counter for all to observe.

5. **Collect cash in a large envelope**. Obtain a large envelope and label it "Sales Profits." Accumulate the money from your sales into it and then deposit the profits into your bank account. This way, you won't be tempted to just use up the cash as you receive it and you can designate it for whatever purpose you need.

Selling items you no longer want or need is a great way to pave the way for your new and improved financial life. Make your list, post ads, gather your gold, and get that envelope ready to save toward a bright, shiny financial life.

Increase Your Income With Craig's List

Craig's List (www.craigslist.org), is the online equivalent of the newspaper classifieds. Nearly every type of item and service under the sun is available there. The best part is that the site is free to view and post ads. Of course, there are a few premium advertising options that require a small fee, but it is not required.

The site is hugely popular, so there are opportunities to really make some money with a little bit of work. You may have heard of the high school student that traded his way from a used cell phone to a Porsche. This was all done on Craig's List, and he never spent a dime, he only traded items.

Here are several ways that you can make money with this great site:

1. **Sell your stuff.** This is the most obvious way. Take all that stuff in the closets, garage, attic, and basement and get it out of your life and out of your way. Someone out there wants it and would be willing to pay you for it.
   - If you have real junk that you want to get rid of, things like broken bikes, tree limbs, scrap metal, or similar items, you can usually find someone interested in hauling it away for free. Someone out there fixes bikes or wants wood or scrap metal. You're not making

money, but you're saving money by not paying someone to haul it away.

2. **Sell other people's stuff.** There are people that make a fulltime living from buying stuff at flea markets and yard sales and then selling those items on Craig's List. You need to know the going price for whatever item it is that you're buying. If you have a smart phone, it's easy to check prices.

   - When you find something that seems like a great deal, pull up the website on your phone and see what similar items are selling for. Be smart about your decisions. Check multiple ads.

   - If you're already visiting these sales anyway shopping for yourself, why not keep your eyes open for things that you can sell to make money? You can have a good time and make money simultaneously!

3. **Buy and sell stuff from Craig's List**. Many people scour the website for great deals, snatch them up, and then improve the item (clean, paint, or repair) or improve the quality of the ad and sell them back on Craig's List.

   - Sometimes it's simply a matter of patience. You might find a seller that is in a hurry to sell. Those sellers will usually take a lower price than a seller that has the option of waiting. Find those sellers.

   - This is no different than stock arbitrage. It's like you're in high finance. Imagine bragging to your friends!

4. **Pick up free items on Craig's List and sell them**. A common practice is to grab items from the Free section and then sell them. It helps to have a truck, because a lot of these are larger items, like furniture.
   - Again, improve the item quickly. This most likely means some paint or cleaning. Sell it and find some more stuff.

It pays to move quickly on the free items. Frequently, the owner of the item will simply leave it out by the curb and it's 'first-come first-serve'. Stay on top of the ads and be prepared to move quickly.

5. **Sell your services.** If there is something you can do well for someone else, and you have the time to do it, put your own ad on there. Can you build websites? Clean homes? Walk dogs? Do taxes?

Secrets of Making a Great Craig's List Ad
Follow these tips for writing an effective ad:
1. **Use a great headline**. Address your customer's problem. You don't have a lot of room to work with, but give the title some time and effort. Look at the other ads and notice those that stand out to you.
2. **Use pictures.** Ads with pictures are much more successful than those without images. People want to see what they're buying. If you're selling a service, some simple clip art related to the service makes your ad look more professional.

3. **Consider using HTML**. Even if you're not a programmer, there are lots of free programs on the Internet that will allow you to create a visually pleasing advertisement. Then you can simply cut and paste the code into Craig's List. Anyone can do it.

4. **Spend some time on the text of the ad.** To get some ideas, look at what some other people have done. Write like you know what you're talking about and be clear. You'll find that some people have one, long endless paragraph that's difficult to read – these serve as examples of what not to do.

   - Give them the critical information that you would want to know. For example, if you were to read an ad about a couch, you'd want to know the condition, color, style, and shape or size. You'd also want to see a picture of it. Include this same type of information in your ads and make it easy to find.

5. **Consider the best time to post it**. Many of the categories get a lot of postings each day. The postings that are near the top get a lot more views than the ones further down the page. The amount of traffic varies throughout the day as well. The smart tactic is to post your ad when there are likely to be a lot of people online and looking.

   - Early in the day can be good. About 9:00 or so in the morning is a good time. Everyone has made it to work but they're still not quite ready to really get busy. Many people sit at their desk at peruse the ads.

- Lunch time or just after lunch also makes a lot of sense. Many people eat lunch at their desk and get on the Internet. Others get online immediately after going out to lunch. This is another great time to post.
- The evening around 9:00 pm is another good time. The kids are in bed, and many people get online in the evening before going to bed themselves.

6. **You'll need multiple ads.** Craig's List currently only allows 3 ads to be posted per account per day. You can only get as many accounts as you have verifiable phone numbers. The other catch is that you can only post the same ad every 48 hours.

   - To create multiple ads that aren't picked up by their system, you don't need to change a lot from your first advertisement. You'll have to play around with it to see just how much. But you'll need 6 versions if you're going to post it 3 times per day.
   -

After 48 hours are past, you can simply start reposting your various ads. There is an option to do this on the website.

7. **Answer promptly.** The default method of making contact is via email. You can choose to include your phone number, but f you do, it's important to return calls as soon as possible. You don't want them running off to buy someone else's stuff!

8. **Be persistent.** Test different ads and keep posting them. It might take a week to sell something. It's just a matter of the right person seeing it. You never know when that will be.

Craig's List provides many opportunities to make money on the side. There is even the possibility of making a full-time income. Take a look at all your options and go for it! All of the methods require some work, but the money you earn per hour of work can be impressive. Do you think it would be all that difficult to find a couch for sale for $200 that you could then sell for $400? Or do you think you could pick up a free desk and sell it for $100? That's pretty easy. You would be shocked at how many people are making several hundred dollars or more each month. With some very part-time work, you could easily pay for a great vacation for the whole family each year. Happy posting!

Money for Your Junk:
A Guide to Selling on Facebook

Most of us simply have too much stuff. This extra stuff gets in the way, costs you time and money, and causes stress. If you think about the things that you really love and use regularly, you'll probably find that you have a lot more stuff than you really need, right? It's probably too late to take all of your extra possessions back to the store, but you can always sell them. While you might have sold items at a yard sale or on Craig's List, you probably haven't used Facebook to unload your junk. That's unfortunate considering how many people are on Facebook each day.

Use the following tips to leverage Facebook and sell your unwanted items:

1. **Find the active local sales groups**. Even fairly small areas will usually have a yard sale group or other similar group with a few thousand members or more!
   - Everyone knows how committed both yard sale lovers and Facebook people can be.
   - A lot of eyes will see your item within 24 hours.
   - The more people that see your item, the more likely you are to get rid of it quickly.
2. **Follow the rules.** Different groups have different rules. For example, some require pictures. Follow the rules and use them to your best advantage.
   - Some have rules about who has the first chance to purchase the item.
   - There are usually rules about when an item can be bumped back to the top of the list.
3. **Take good pictures.** Get a friend to help if you have trouble taking pictures. Be sure the pictures you post are in focus with good lighting.
   - Let buyers see what they need to by choosing a good angle for your photo.
4. **Post at just the right time**. Be smart about when you post your items. The ideal time to post is when people are perusing the listings, but not a lot of things are getting posted.
   - If you post your item when everyone else does, yours can get lost in the shuffle.
   - Try to take note of when people are claiming items and when items areposted.

5. **Write an accurate description** and take care of your own needs. The group may have a policy that whoever claims the item has 48 hours to take the item away. But if you want it gone today, put that in the posting.
    - It could be problematic if someone took 48 hours to show up and then decided against purchasing the item.
6. **Be available**. Those that are interested are bound to have questions. Keep your phone and computer handy and reply promptly to inquiries.
    - People will move on to other items if they can't get their questions answered in a timely fashion.
7. **Stay organized.** This is especially important if you have several items for sale. It can be helpful to keep a post-it note on each item. You can list the buyer's name, contact information, expected pick-up date, time of pick-up, and the price.

Most people never consider selling items on Facebook, but it can be a quick, easy, and free way to get rid of the items cluttering your life. Everyone could use a little extra money and more elbowroom. So clean out the garage, attic, and closets. Facebook is a hugely popular website with a very active user base. Your unnecessary items will be gone in a flash. Why not give it a try?

The Stay-At-Home Mom's Guide to Making Money With eBay

Being a stay-at-home mom isn't easy. There are meals to cook, dishes to wash, clothes to clean, kids to control, and whole host of other challenges to deal with. It can be quite nerve-racking. But sometimes, when the kids are at school and you have the house to yourself, you might feel a little restless. Does this sound a little bit too complicated for your tastes? Well, it's easier than you think. Making money via the internet doesn't require any particular set of technological skills. One of the easiest ways to make fast money is with eBay. All you need is a bank account and PayPal.

Follow these simple steps to create your own eBay business while taking care of your family:

1. **Decide which eBay business path fits your personal preferences.**There are several different types of businesses that can be created on eBay. For the sake of simplicity, it can be narrowed down to two options: sell items you already own or sell something from a different website.

   - The first option (sell items you already own) is a solution for fast cash. You would be surprised what people are willing to purchase through the internet. However, this will be a short-term business idea because eventually you'll run out of stuff to sell.

- The second option (sell something from a different website) is a more valid, long-term business idea. People all around the world have been using this business model to generate thousands - if not millions - of dollars in revenue.

2. **Find a product in demand**. The next step is to find a popular product that others will want to purchase. Think about what internet shoppers might want to buy.
    - If you check out various online marketplaces, you'll find that most of these websites have a section for the products that are selling like hot cakes.
    - Go to eBay and look at their popular searches. This shows what's in demand.
    - This step is a little tricky and requires some research. Many give up when they encounter this issue.

3. **Examine sellers and offer a better deal**. Chances are that others are selling the same product you're interested in. Stand out from the crowd and create a more attractive deal. Find a way to spice it up.
    - Consider including a free item in the package. This is often called "bundling" and it's a highly effective technique to smash the competition.
    - Reduce the price, but increase the shipping and handling fees.
    - Examine the reviews on other seller's products, take note of the complaints, and provide a better service.

It isn't difficult for a stay at home mom to make money with eBay, but some research is required. It's helpful to examine the competition, create attractive offers, write intriguing sales descriptions, and order products from different suppliers for a cheaper price. The e-commerce world can be tricky and competitive, but it can also be highly profitable. Selling on eBay is the perfect business for stay-at-home moms because it can be done at random times without leaving home. Sell what you want, work when you want, and your storefront is open 24/7 without the worries of running a website yourself! What could be better?

How To Use Abandoned Storage Units
To Augment Your Income

Can you make money with storage units like the folks on TV? Buying and selling stuff has been a respectable way to make a living since the beginning of human kind. Just because it's been around forever, though, doesn't always mean that it's easy. Just like anything else, there are some fundamental rules to follow for the best results. On the most basic level, you must acquire items that people actually want. You must also get these items at a price that permits you to make a profit when you sell them. If you can just accomplish these two things, you will be successful. One great place to find such items is at abandoned or foreclosed storage units. All you really need to get started is a way to haul the items back home and a few hundred dollars.

Acquiring the Merchandise

Fortunately for you, the US is full of packrats that can't let go of their excess stuff. Businesses and people will store this excess stuff and many eventually fall behind on their payments or simply decide that they don't want it anymore. The owners of the storage facilities essentially take control of the unit and auction the contents off to the highest bidder. These units can range from 25 square feet, with few items, up to several hundred square feet, with a whole treasure trove.

Use these strategies to successfully profit from these auctions:

1. **Find the auctions.** Do some Google searches and call all the storage facilities in your area. Ask when the next auction is scheduled. You'll find that the larger places have them regularly, and the smaller ones only hold them as needed. Be sure to call the smaller places back at least once a month.

    - They might advertise the auctions in a local paper. Find out what paper they use and keep your eyes open.
    - Some storage facilities actually just sell the contents of the unit to anyone that will bring the rent current. If that's the case, ask to be put on their list of potential buyers. Ask about the process. How do they choose between multiple buyers?

2. **Show up at the auctions**. Arrive a little early to figure out what's going on. Ideally, you'll have a pickup or some other type of large truck. Vans can be okay for most items. You can always rent a truck if needed.

    - A strong partner is nice to have because some of the items might be quite heavy. How is your back? A dolly or hand truck is nice to have, too.
    - A strong partner is nice to have because some of the items might be quite heavy. How is your back? A dolly or hand truck is nice to have, too.

3. **Inspect.** Different storage facilities have different rules. Typically, they'll open the door and give everyone a couple of minutes to inspect the unit from outside. You aren't

allowed inside. You might be able to see everything, but frequently things will be in boxes. You might get to see inside some of the boxes or you might not.

- Keep a tally on a pad of paper what you think the items are worth. You'll have to guess at some things. A smart phone and a quick check on eBay can be a big help.
- Set your maximum bid. This should be about 50% of what you think everything in the unit is worth. If you have a lot of doubt about the value of the items, don't bid. There's always another storage unit and another day.
- If you smell mildew or anything else that smells bad, it's probably best to pass on that unit. The same goes for obvious signs of water damage.

4. **Bid.** It might be a good idea to sit back and watch the bidding on the first couple of storage units. There is an art to bidding at auctions, so go slowly at first. Remember not to bid more than 50% of what it's worth.

- The auctions are usually live auctions but occasionally silent auctions are used. The pace is usually slower than most other auctions you've seen. The auctioneer will usually be the storage facility manager or owner.

5. **Winning,** sorting, and repairing. When you win an auction, you can usually settle up and take possession of your treasures immediately. You typically have 24 hours to get

everything out of there, so don't waste any time. It's time to start sorting.

- There is frequently a cleaning deposit that must be paid. It will be returned if the unit is completely cleaned out and swept before the 24 hours are up. Your refunded deposit might be mailed to you in the form of a check.
- There's almost always some stuff that's just worthless. Leave all the trash for now. You'll need to take it to the dump eventually, but first, get all the good stuff home. Any clean items in good shape that have no value can be donated to Goodwill or someplace similar.
- Start hauling the good stuff back home. An alternative is to rent a storage unit for a month and keep everything there. Just a month! Don't get lazy or you'll be in the same situation as the person who owned the stuff before you.
- Try out all of the electronics and other powered items. If it works, great! If it doesn't, try to figure out what it will take o get it working again.

6. **Sell,** sell, and sell. Get a good idea of what each item is worth. There are several places to check. These include craigslist.org, the newspaper, yard sales, eBay, and flea markets. Find the most lucrative places to sell your items.

- Remember your time, too. It might be better to sell something in the newspaper rather than spending all the time to go to a flea market. Only you know what your time is worth.

- Some full-time storage auction folks actually set up a small retail location to sell their items. It's worth considering if you decide to get really serious. Having a retail location entails another set of responsibilities and expenses as well, so consider these carefully in your plan.
- Some things will sell better in some places than others. Large common items probably won't sell well on eBay. Something that is easy to ship or uncommon will probably fare better in an online auction.
- A lot of little, inexpensive items are probably perfect for a yard sale or a flea market. Read up about flea markets – it's a whole world unto itself.

Storage unit auctions have become quite popular with the new TV shows that focus on this type of activity. You can be part of the excitement and make some extra money. Every once in a while, you're going to hit it big and find something in a box that's worth $1,000 or more! It might be cash, a coin collection or baseball cards. Sooner or later, you'll hit it big.

Find the auctions and check one out just for fun before you consider bidding. Remember that you'll need a way to transport the items home and might need some strong help. Bring a flashlight, hand truck, gloves, a pen, and paper. Figure out what the storage unit is likely to be worth and only bid up to 50% of that amount.

All that's left is to sell your items. Find the best place to sell your stuff and avoid taking too much time. Spending hours to make another $10 just isn't worth it. You can do this! Get started today and follow these guidelines to gain some experience and garner your first successes. As you learn what works best for you, you'll enjoy the extra income.

Becoming A Mobile Notary Public

If you're looking to start your own small business, you've probably been wracking your brain trying to come up with some low-cost options. As you know, commencing a business usually takes quite a bit of cash up-front to get things going. But there's one possibility for a business you might not have thought about: becoming a mobile notary public. Although you're probably familiar with notary publics in general, you most likely haven't heard of a "mobile" notary public. Read on to learn more about a new twist on an old profession that just might make you some easy money.

Whether you plan to earn some extra cash on the side or make it your full-time profession, developing a mobile notary public business can be done by following the information herein. Keep in mind you'll likely want to have available at least some time to make notary calls during business hours, 9 a.m. to 5 p.m., Monday through Friday.

What is a Notary Public?

A notary public is a licensed person who has completed training and a state exam regarding the statutes and duties of a notary. They can professionally witness signatures of individuals on official documents and issue official oaths. More specifically, many types of important papers require a notary's signature and stamped impression to verify the authenticity of the signatures. Depending on the state you live in, you'll most likely be required to complete some fairly brief training — 3 hours in several states.

Some states offer online courses in becoming a notary public while others have in-person classes that you must attend. Once you satisfactorily complete the training, you're required to pass an exam and apply for state licensure.

In most states, a notary must be "bonded." For example, notaries the state of Florida must be bonded for $7,500. This means that in the event you make an error in your work, the company who bonded you will pay the harmed customer for the error. In essence, the bond is similar to professional liability insurance in the event you make a mistake as a notary. The states of Florida, Maine, and South Carolina even allow notaries to conduct official wedding ceremonies that are "legal and binding," if they're performed only in the state that licensed you. Depending on your state, as a notary, you might also provide acknowledgements and affirmations or offer oaths and certify copies of original documents for your customers. Although you could probably locate quite a few notary publics in your area, you could be the first mobile notary public locally. This means you'll travel to the people, offices, and organizations that need notary services, which is a great selling feature for the business.

What You'll Need to Start Your Mobile Notary Business

As compared with other businesses, a notary public business won't require huge investments of time, energy, or money.

Take a look at what you'll need:

1. **Completion of your state's requirements to become a notary public**. Based on where you live, these requirements (as mentioned above) will most likely involve a brief educational course, passage of a state exam, your bond, and a license to be a notary in your state.

2. **A telephone where people can reach you**. Of course, you'll need a contact telephone number so your customers can get hold of you. You can use your home phone number or a cell number.

The advantage of using your cell phone is that you tend to have it with you at all times and you can access calls and messages quickly and easily.

3. **A dependable car.** Since you'll be traveling to most of your customers, you'll need a vehicle that runs well.

4. **Spiral notebook and pen**. Carry paper and pen to keep track of the miles you travel and the names and addresses of customers with a brief note including the date of what you did for them.

5. **Your seal stamp**. You'll be required to have a "stamper" that will make an imprint of your name and official seal on documents you notarize. The stamp also says you're an official notary in your state.

6. **A GPS**, although not a requirement, will help you find your way efficiently from place to place. Depending on how well you know the area where you live, a GPS could come in quite handy as a traveling notary.

7. **A log book,** if your state requires it. A log book or journal is your record of sensitive information regarding the people for whom you performed notary services. It's your record of what you did, who you did it for, what their legal address is, and how much you charged. Your state might require you to keep other relevant data in your log book.

   - Twenty of the 50 states in the U.S. require notaries to keep a log book. Those states also specify what must be done with the book upon your death or after you stop doing notary work.

   - Even if your state doesn't indicate you must keep a log book, it's a good idea to do so. Your journal will come in quite handy for you at tax time.

The key to being an efficient notary is to know well your own state's statutes regarding notary publics. You can also find several notary public associations online that will provide you with valuable insights and information into serving as an official notary public in your state.

Marketing Your Notary Public Business

Unlike other small businesses, there are special precautions you must take whenever it comes to advertising your mobile notary public business. Consult the legal statues for notaries in your state as they will be your guide on how to advertise your notary business in an ethical manner.

Think about how to get your name out there in front of as many people as possible. Some items for consideration when advertising are:

1. **Mention you're not an attorney in your advertising.** In many states, this is a requirement for notaries who aren't attorneys when marketing their services. Further, it's necessary to state you cannot provide legal advice nor can you accept any payment for it.

2. **Avoid translating the term**, "notary public" into any other language. In some states, (Florida, for one) it is actually illegal to do so.

3. **Refrain from showing your notary stamp in the advertisement.** Because your stamp is for use on legal documents only and must be paired with your own original (not copied) signature, using the stamp in advertising is illadvised.

4. **Ponder what types of notary services you wish to offer.** Focus in on your preferences.
   - For example, will you notarize real estate documents and transactions?
   - Will you perform wedding ceremonies if your state allows?
   - Are you willing to notarize wills, even if written in long-hand by a person?

- Know the direction you wish to go so you can focus your marketing on your potential customers.

5. **Know your state's maximum established fees** for each type of notarization before you advertise. For example, in the state of Florida, notaries cannot charge over $10 per signature that they notarize. Also in Florida, notaries can charge up to $25 to perform marriage ceremonies, but no more.

6. **Think about what you'll charge to travel to the customer.** In making your decision for the fees to charge, consider what your state's reimbursement mileage rates are. For example, if your state's reimbursement rate is 45 cents per mile, would it be reasonable to charge double that amount or even round it up to $1.00 per mile round-trip?

7. **How far will you travel to provide notary services**? Decide on your limits before getting your advertising plan together. You could say something like, "Will travel anywhere in the city limits of Timbuktu" or "Will come to your home or office anywhere in Jackson county."

8. **Set the days and hours you're willing to work**. Keep in mind that since you'll be traveling to and from your customers, your work day will begin a bit earlier and extend a bit later. For example, an advertised work day of 9:00 p.m. to 4:00 p.m. will allow you an hour at each end (morning and evening) to travel to and from your customers.

9. **Use the media that's best for you to get the word out.** You have many choices: from television advertising (most expensive) to printing your own flyers (least expensive). You an advertise through radio spots, put up a sign on your property (if allowed where you live), and put ads in local and area newsletters, newspapers, and magazines.

10. **Business cards could be your pathway to success**. Remember to keep plenty of business cards on hand. Use your business cards to "sprinkle" your name and contact information everywhere you go. For example, almost every restaurant and café has a bulletin board or some other type of way to display a business card for its customers.

- Tack up business cards on your grocery stores' boards. Leave them on the counter at your barber, hair dresser, cleaners, and car mechanic's garage. Give one or two to everyone you meet. Leave them in reception areas at doctor's offices.

- Keep in mind that business cards are relatively cheap to haveprinted at your local office supply stores like Staples, Office Max, and Office Depot. The more you have printed, the less you pay per card.

- Also, if you have a computer and printer, you can easily design and print your own cards at home at very little cost. All you have to do is purchase pre-perforated pages of business-size cards, also at the office supply store.

Growing Your Notary Public Business

Now that you understand all about how to establish and market your new mobile notary public business, you'll want to take steps to grow your business. Expanding your business to ensure ongoing work is necessary for your financial livelihood.

These techniques will keep business dollars rolling in:

1. **Find your niche**. For example, if you live in or near a senior community, maybe you could specialize in notarizing wills, both in attorney's offices and in your customer's homes.

2. **Establish relationships** with people in the community that regularly require notary services. Attorneys and business owners are people you should become acquainted with.

3. **Join your local Chamber of Commerce.** Most cities and towns have a group of business owners who get together monthly to share ideas and help one another expand their businesses. You'll become acquainted with many business leaders who will eventually start utilizing your services and telling others about them.

4. **Know your community.** When you know your community, you'll have steady business.

In terms of a small business start-up, a mobile notary public business may be the way to go. You get to be out and about all day, interact with people from all walks of life, and earn some money with few over-head costs. As a supplemental job to your full-time position or as your only career, consider becoming a mobile notary public to beef up your incoming dollars.

How To Mke Extra Money
As A Consultant

Maybe you already have a good job but you have some extra time and would like to put your skills to work outside of your regular job. Consulting in your spare time can be a great way to put some extra money in the bank for retirement, send the kids to college, pay down debt, or just have some extra spending money.

Becoming a consultant on the side isn't complicated, but there are several things to consider if you're going to be successful.

Gettting started

1. **Consider your risk**. The more high profile you are within your current company, the more likely you are to run into trouble if your current employer finds out. Tread carefully.
   - Especially if you already make 6-figures, it's a possibility that your employer will have the opinion that any extra time should be spent on your current job and not doing work for someone else.
   - Don't lose a good job so you can make another $200 a week!
2. **Take inventory of your skills and experience.** What are you really good at? Consultants are typically paid well for the time they work, so consider what you can do for someone that is worthy of a decent payday.
   - For example, if you're a quality manager for a large corporation, it makes sense that you could consult on

quality matters for smaller businesses that don't have the luxury of employing someone full-time with your expertise. It would save them money to pay you $3,000 for a few days of your time instead of having another employee.

- Are you a corporate accountant? Maybe you can do tax returns or give tax advice on a part-time basis.
- Are you a copywriter? There are lots of online opportunities for work. Be honest and assess your expertise as well as what the market needs.

3. **Market yourself.** Let the appropriate people know you're available. Consider whether or not you can safely market your services actively. If you're careful, you might be able to be very aggressive and open with your marketing.

- To get started, contact businesses and contacts you already have directly.
- Even better, hire someone from Craigslist to make the calls for you. There are a lot of great telemarketers out there that will work for a relatively small amount of money.
- There are also plenty of sites online where employers outsource jobs and you can bid on them, such as elance.com and odesk.com.

4. **Set your fees**. This will be a function of demand and supply. However, you should expect that your consulting work would pay 2-3 times or more than your current hourly rate. When you factor in the time and extra expenses for

marketing and other costs, this really should be your minimum.

- Your rates should be as high as you can set them and still get the amount of work you desire. If you're overwhelmed with people that want to hire you, that's a good sign to raise your fees.

5. **Manage your time.** Even if your boss knows what's going on, he's not likely to be happy if you're running out of meetings, late for work, or leaving early for your new clients. It's critical that your consulting work doesn't interfere with your current employment. Avoid giving the impression that you're dropping the ball in any way.

- Consider using your lunch hour to take or make any phone calls. Depending on your situation, it might be worthwhile to hire someone to take your calls. There are plenty of answering services that are quite inexpensive and very professional.
- Avoid using your company cell phone, computer, printer, copier, and other equipment or supplies for your side jobs. Technically, that's theft and will not bode well for your current job.

6. **Continue marketing**. Many consultants market until they get work and then they stop. You should still be prospecting for additional work even if you're busy. Momentum is difficult to re-establish after things go stagnant.

Becoming a part-time consultant is a great way to make some extra money! Avoid upsetting your current employer; you don't want to be forced to be a full-time consultant at a moment's notice! Assess your skills and the available market in your area. Once you get going, don't be afraid to hire outside help to assist with your marketing and handle the busy work. You're not likely to have the time to do it all yourself. Finally, be respectful of your current employer and their equipment. It's not for your personal use. Now go out there and take advantage of your unique expertise to make some money on the side. You'll enjoy your new status as a consultant!

Green Consulting

Green consulting is becoming a popular home business option because more companies want to be environmentally friendly. You can get certified and run this business from your home. The core focus is to make recommendations to companies about making their businesses eco-friendly. Green consultants can make $40,000+ a year and don't have huge expenses. If you're interested in this type of business, follow these steps to get certifications and clients.

Required Supplies
The supply list for a green consultant can vary based on the location and niche focus, but there are several key elements.

Consider these supplies as you build your business:
1. **Smartphone.** A reliable phone that will help you connect with clients and run your business is crucial.

2. **Computer**. A computer will enable you to efficiently connect with clients, invoice them, and produce reports.
3. **Transportation**. Whether you have your own car or use public transportation, you'll need to be able to get to your client's business.
   - Green consultants frequently set up in person appointments and visit the client's home or business to do their assessments.
4. **Word processing software.** Make your reports and invoices look professional. Google Docs is free.
5. **Spreadsheet software**. Making spreadsheets for your clients will put your information and recommendations into easy-toread charts tables. Again, you can use Google Docs.
6. **Comfortable desk and chair**. Even though you'll most likely be working from home, quality office furniture will cut down on fatigue and help put you into a business frame of mind when you're doing business.
7. **Tools and toolbox.** Depending on the level of consulting you do, you may need tools to check the green status of the business or home. These tools include devices to measure voltage, check for air leaks, and other equipment.
8. **Strong internet connection**. You may have to contact your clients online.
9. **Notebook and pens or pencils**. As you visit a client's home or business, you'll have to take notes and keep track of ideas.

10. **Online certification programs**. If you choose to get certified, there are convenient online certification programs for green consulting.

11. **Camera.** Many green consultants like to document the issues they see with photos. With a digital camera, you can easily share the photos with your clients.

12. **Invoicing software**. Invoicing software makes professional invoices and helps you keep track of your bills.

13. **Business cards.** Professional business cards are essential for connecting with new clients and asking for referrals.

14. **Briefcase,** purse, or portfolio. Look professional and have a place to carry your notepads, pens, tools, and other supplies.

A green consultant needs several tools to have a successful home business. Once you have these essential elements, you can add others as your business grows.

Getting Started

There are several crucial first steps to start your green consulting home business:

Consider these steps to get started:

1. **Evaluate your local area**. Is it a good fit for a green consulting business? Although some green consultants work exclusively online, most focus on their local area.
   - Are there plenty of homes and businesses that are interested in eco-friendly services?

- Do you see a need in the green industry that you can fill?
- If your city lacks interest in environmentally-friendly ideas, you'll have a harder time setting up a successful business in this area.

2. **Evaluate your ability to do consultations online.** Doing green consultations online is harder because you can't see the actual business and analyze its energy use.
   - However, some consultants are able to do this by having carefully crafted surveys and reports.
   - It's important to be comfortable with multiple programs and social networking sites to interact with clients online.
   - Think about how you'll present your services online to attract clients.

3. **What services will you offer**? Some green consultants only focus on homes while others only focus on businesses. A third category does both.
   - Who do you want to serve, and who is your ideal client for green consulting?
   - Will you focus on reducing energy costs and waste? Or, will you offer other ways to make their carbon footprint smaller?
   - What tools will you need to offer these services?

4. **Consider the tax implications**. A new home business can change your tax obligations. Your accountant can be immensely helpful.

5. **Check your local guidelines and laws for home businesses**. Some areas require you to register your home business and pay a fee. If you don't do this, you may face a fine and other issues.
6. **Check the green consulting competition**. Who is the competition in your area? What services do they offer?
7. **Get certified**. This may be one of the most important steps for your green consulting business. Many clients won't hire you if you don't have proof of green certification.
   - This type of certification shows that you have the training and skills to properly evaluate a business or home for energy savings and eco-friendliness.
   - A certification shows you're a serious professional who wants to succeed.
   - You can get certified online or take courses at a local college. Some technical and trade schools offer this certification.
   - √Many green consultants choose the online version because it's easier and faster. You can do the class at your own pace and schedule. Check for accredited and legitimate programs with good reviews.
8. **Pick a business name.** Consider a unique name that communicates your green consulting services.

By taking these initial steps, your business will be ready to grow and prosper.

Finding Customers

A successful green consulting business needs a steady stream of clients. Focusing on several types of clients usually gets the best response.

Consider these tips for finding customers:

1. Government offices. Although it's harder to get a contract as a small business owner, you still want to try to reach out to government offices. They may be interested in green consulting services. Try both local and bigger offices.

2. Nonprofit organizations. They may need green consulting help.

3. Local small businesses. Other small businesses may be interested in your services, and you could start referral programs with them.

4. Large corporations. Large corporations often try to be more eco-friendly for customers.

5. Individuals and home owners. You don't have to focus exclusively on businesses. Reach out to home owners who are interested in environmentally-friendly ideas and need help.

6. Construction companies. The popularity of green buildings and housing has made your consulting services in demand. Get in touch with construction companies and set up a mutual relationship. They frequently need green consultants to work with them.

7. Online businesses and individuals. This may be a more difficult route since you won't be able to visit their homes or offices, but you can still pursue it.

- ✓Provide online surveys, quizzes, and evaluations they can complete. Offer to examine the data and give customized reports that detail step-by-step instructions to make improvements.
8. Online job boards. You can find both virtual and local jobs and clients on these sites.
9. Social media. Sometimes companies and individuals post about their need for green consulting on social networks.

Finding clients may be an ongoing process until you have a good list of referrals. Diversify your efforts and look for clients in multiple places.

Marketing Your Business

The marketing aspects of a green consulting business are also important, with tactics that will attract eco-minded clients and businesses.

Try these marketing strategies:

1. Create a strong website. Use your website to show clients your green consulting services. You can also use it to share your ideas and blog.
   - As a home business, your website can become a virtual office.
2. Join green groups. Do you know of any local eco-friendly groups that meet on a regular basis? Green groups will often meet to discuss the community and how to help.
   - By joining this type of group, you'll be able to meet likeminded people and potentially connect with new

clients. You can learn more about the industry, discover new concepts, and grow your reputation.

- Offer to be a speaker at some of the meetings.

3. Use social media networking. Set up profiles on the big social media sites such as Facebook, Twitter, LinkedIn, and others. These profiles will help you connect with clients and reach out to other green consultants.

4. Advertise in home improvement magazines. Clients who read these types of magazines are often interested in getting green audits for their homes or businesses. You can target both online and print home improvement magazines.

5. Advertise online. Buy ads online in relevant places. You can use ads on social media too. Craft your ads to speak to your prospects and encourage them to hire you.

6. Advertise in newspapers. Both online and print newspapers are still an important marketing tool.

7. Partner with other businesses on the local level. Search out businesses that offer services that would complement your green services. Partnerships can benefit both of you.

8. Consider volunteering. A short-term volunteer project can get you recognition and more clients. Look for small, community projects that need green consulting. Find a good balance between volunteering and doing projects for profit.

- Volunteer for projects where the owners will give you a testimonial.

9. Try direct mail. Although it has decreased in popularity, targeted direct mail campaigns can help you.

10.   Blog. Setting up a blog and posting on it on a regular basis is also a good way to market your green consulting services.

- A blog helps establish you as an authority and expert on green services.
- It helps you stay higher in search results online and gives clients something new to see on your website.
- Blogging gives you the chance to explain green audits and consultations to potential clients who may be hesitant to try these services.

11.   Try cold calling. Getting on the phone with a potential customer can seal the deal. Create a script to follow as you make the calls, so it's less stressful.

12.   Use networking. Whether it's a government organization or other group, networking can help you get marketing leads.

13.   Do presentations and speaking engagements. This helps establish you as an authority on green consulting. Presentations will also help you reach a new audience interested in green living. You can meet new clients and create joint ventures.

14.   Focus on referrals. Referrals are easier than cold calls and bring you prospects that are more likely to work with you. Ask every client for referrals often: whenever you finish a job, on your invoices, and during regular communications.

15.   15.Send out a newsletter. A monthly newsletter to your clients is a great way to continue your relationship, provide new information, offer new services, and ask for referrals. Marketing is not an easy process, but it can help you secure an ongoing stream of clients. Maintain several marketing strategies that you can implement at the same time.

Conclusion

Green consulting can be a fun and profitable home business idea. You can work full-time or part-time in this business without large overhead costs. Getting certified in green consulting will provide important information that will help you do a great job and bring in more clients so you can enjoy a growing business. My cousin is a sustainability consultant and operates his own business as a second job on top of being a member of the Coast Guard. You can check out his services here: https://sustainablemgmt.net/ If you have questions feel free to contact him there and let him know Andrew - Consult A Blind Guy sent you. As Indigenous people we have a connection to our mother earth and know quite a bit about sustainability and environmental care.

There are tons of ways to go about preserving the natural resources and environment so our next 7 generations can have a liveable society where it's safe to drink the water and swim in the lakes, rivers and oceans, forests to go camping in and walking trails and etc. We can all do our part to make a sustainable environment for all of us and the future generation.

Make Money With Scrap Metal

Millions of dollars' worth of scrap metal are shipped from the U.S. to China on a daily basis. The scrap metal market is booming as emerging countries need to sustain their rapid industrialization and more developed countries produce tons of trash that can be recycled. The Chinese market is only a small portion of the scrap metal market. Huge quantities of metal are needed by a wide range of industries all over the world. You can find valuable metal in your home and community. Collecting and selling scrap metal allows you to generate an income on your own terms. All you need is some free time, a truck or trailer to haul the scrap metal you find, and some motivation. You can work whenever you want and make money by selling the scrap metal once you've collected enough.

Which Metals Are Valuable?
Recognizing metals and assessing their value will become easier as you gain more experience.

Familiarize yourself with these metals and their value before you begin looking for scrap metal:
1. Ferrous metals. These are easy to recognize because a magnet will stick to them. Ferrous metals aren't worth as much as non-ferrous metals, but it's possible to make money if you have large quantities.
   Ferrous metals include:

- Steel, which can rust and produces long yellow sparks when a grinder is used on the metal.
- Iron and cast iron, which produces short orange sparks under a grinder.

2. Non-ferrous metals. These metals are usually worth a lot more money than ferrous metals. The bulk of your money will come from non-ferrous metals.

   These are the non-ferrous metals you'll want to find:
   - Copper, a brown or reddish metal. Copper is easy to identify by its reddish, brown, or green color if the metal is not in good condition.
   - Aluminum, a white or silver metal that bends very easily.
   - Brass, a very heavy metal with a yellow color and a slight red tint in some areas. Brass is an alloy made with copper and zinc.

Where Can You Find Scrap Metal?

The best method to find scrap metals varies in view of where you live. It might take you a while to figure out how to consistently make good finds.

Try these tips to get started with finding scrap metal:

1. **There is plenty of metal to scrap around the average home.** Go through your belongings to get rid of things you no longer need and offer to do the same for friends and relatives.

   This is what to look for in and outside of your home:

- Plumbing pipes, door handles, and light and bathroom fixtures are often made with brass or other metals.
- Most household appliances, electronics, HVAC units, and replacement parts can be scrapped.
- Siding, roofing, gutters, and other items that can be found on the outside of your home may be made from aluminum.

2. **Offer to help local businesses get rid of bulky items** they no longer need and don't know how to recycle:
   - Steel companies and factories might have scrap metal that needs to be hauled or some equipment and machines they no longer use.
   - If you live in a rural area, contact local farms. Farmers might need help with getting rid of unwanted tools, equipment, or vehicles.
   - Construction companies often end up with unused materials. Some local construction companies might need help with getting rid of these materials.
   - Local thrift stores may have very inexpensive appliances or electronics you could scrap.
   - Charities often receive donations such as household ppliances and electronics. Most charities don't have any use for these items and might need your help with hauling bulky appliances.

3. **Networking** is another good way to find scrap metal. Everyone has junk they no longer need in their house, basement, or garage, and offering to haul it off is a valuable service.

- Advertise your haul-off service online. Use Craigslist, social media, local newspapers, and other classified sites to list your services. Networking is another good way to find scrap metal. Everyone has junk they no longer need in their house, basement, or garage, and offering to haul it off is a valuable service.
- Check the free section on Craigslist. You will probably come across people wanting to give away appliances and other items you could scrap because they no longer have any use or room for these items.
- Go around your neighborhood. Introduce yourself to your neighbors and let them know you can help them get rid of unwanted junk. Dumpster diving can be a good way to find items to scrap.
- Dumpster diving is legal but some cities and townships have local ordinances against this practice. Check with your local government before you decide to go dumpster diving.
- Hand out business cards. Local businesses and residents will call you again the next time they need help with getting rid of an old appliance.

Make Money With Insulated Copper Wire

Copper is one of the most valuable metals you can scrap and it is used to make cables in most appliances and electronics. It is definitely worth it to take the time to strip cables so you can sell the copper.

Look for these items to start collecting insulated copper wires:

1. Desktop computer towers, laptops, TVs, monitors, radios, DVD players, and VCRs.
2. Appliances such as refrigerators, ovens, dishwashers, washers, and dryers.
3. Smaller appliances like toasters, blenders, coffee makers, and fans.
4. Any small electronics that need to be charged, such as MP3 players, cameras, phones, or Gameboys.

Stripping cables is easy. Cut the wires or cables from the electronics or appliances and leave them in the sun. Heat will make the cables easier to strip, but it is unsafe to expose insulated copper wires to a direct source of heat. You can strip wires and cables by cutting around the copper with a razor or by using a tabletop wire stripper.

How To Sell Scrap Metal

Once you've figured out how to find and transport scrap metal, look into storing your findings. Some metals are valuable enough to attract the attention of burglars, which is why scrap metal should be stored in a safe place that can be locked. It's also best to protect scrap metal from humidity to prevent rust. Scrap yards and recycling centers are the best places to sell scrap metal. Most places will pay you by the pound and might even purchase appliances and electronics you did not strip since these items can sometimes be fixed and recycled. Getting paid by the pound means it is more interesting to focus on the more valuable metals, including copper, brass, and luminum. The prices offered for scrap metal can vary from one area to another and it might be worthwhile for you to drive a little further to sell what you collected.

Do your best to build a good relationship with the owners or local junk yards, scrap yards, and recycling centers. Find out what kind of items and metals are the most valuable to them.

A Word To The Wise

Collecting scrap metal to sell to local junk yards is a good way to generate an additional income in your free time. However, it's important to stay safe.

Use these techniques to protect yourself:

1. Always wear gloves when handling metal. Edges can be sharp and rusty. Wear gloves when stripping cables and wires too.
2. Avoid looking for scrap metal on private property, abandoned houses, or abandoned factories.
3. It is illegal to pick up trash from the curb. If you see something valuable, ask permission first.

4. Don't throw away scrap metal that is worthless to you. Take it to a recycling center or a junk yard to ensure it is properly disposed of or recycled.

5. Ask for a receipt or for written permission when collecting scrap metal. The scrap yard owner might ask about the origin of the items you bring. This is especially important if you are hauling construction materials or equipment that came from a factory, since there have been many cases of thieves stealing this type of items to scrap them.

6. Be honest with the people who want to get rid of unwanted junk. Charge them if you won't be able to scrap the items, but let them know you can make a profit off scrap metal. Think about offering a small compensation if you feel that offering to haul off an item for free isn't enough.

Conclusion

Hauling and selling scrap metal can be physically demanding, but this activity is an ideal way to generate an additional income if you have a truck or a trailer and aren't afraid of hard work. It's important to learn to recognize the metals that are worth hauling and to identify the objects you'll be able to sell. Recognizing valuable metals, appliances, and other objects will become much easier as you gain experience. Besides making money, you'll be helping local residents and businesses get rid of unwanted junk. And since the scrap metal you sell will be recycled, this activity is a great way to help preserve the environment. I have been scrapping metal for a long time, I use some of the metals I scrap for crafting, and working into useable pieces. For example: I use copper wires to melt down and create decorative bullion pieces and depending on the wire thickness use it for dreamcatcher webbing. I use scrap steel to make knives and other blades. And I use some of it to create artistic pieces entirely out of metal.

These are just some of the ways I use the scrap metal and I know there are other artist's who will purchase scrap metal for their projects as well. So the possibilities of scrapping metal dont just end at the scrap yard or recycling plant. There are people out there who will buy it directly from you as well.

Create And Sell Mobile Apps

The phone app industry was expected to reach $77+ billion by 2017 from 268 billion downloads it is now well over that. You don't need a very big piece of that pie in order to boost your income significantly! You might have considered creating your own phone app, but decided that you lacked the necessary programing experience. If so, there's good news:

- Some of the programming languages are very easy to learn.
- There are platforms that will permit you to create your own phone app without programming at all.

If the idea of performing a task once and then selling your work potentially millions of times appeals to you, creating and selling phone apps might be an ideal opportunity for you.

This guide will show you the crucial steps involved in creating and selling your own mobile apps. Let's get started!

Choose A Device Platform

Are you going to make an app for the iPhone or for Android devices? It's an important decision, as the programming languages are different.

Consider these differences:

- iPhone and iPad apps are likely to result in more income. Apple has done a great job of creating an active marketplace for app developers. The average app will earn the creator $4,000.
- An Android-based app will likely sell 50% more, but the revenue earned per sale is significantly smaller. You can expect to earn roughly $1,125 for an Android app.
- There are apps for Windows-based phones, but the market is presently too small to be worth your time. Keep your eyes open, though.
- Of course, this assumes your app is "average". You could earn less or much more!

Decide The Type Of App

Take the time to look at the various app marketplaces. You'll undoubtedly be amazed by the variety available. Take note of which apps are the most popular.

Limit yourself to these two broad categories:

1. Apps that entertain. These include the various games and other non-productive apps that people use to take a break from reality.
   - Do you have an idea that others would find entertaining? Consider the gaming apps you already own. Are there any that you could improve upon? Many apps are almost enjoyable, but there's something missing. Can you add that missing ingredient?
2. Apps that solve a problem. You could create an app that keeps track of a household budget or finds the cheapest skim milk in town.
   - Brainstorm for ideas. Again, are there any apps that you could improve upon? Do you have an idea for something that's never been done?

Keep in mind that many of the most popular apps have been quite simple. Your app doesn't have to be sophisticated to be successful. At one time, pet rocks and smiley face t-shirts were all the rage. Avoid believing that humans have evolved dramatically in the last 40 years. You can create a simple app that will boost your income.

Create The App

As stated earlier, Android and Apple have their own app programming languages. There's no reason to believe that you can't learn to program quickly. Fortunately, there are options available, even if you'd rather not take the programming plunge.

There are 3 general ways to create a mobile application:

1. Apple recently released a language named Swift. Swift is extremely easy to learn for beginners. A quick search will reveal countless free resources that will have you programming in no time.

2. The corresponding programming language for Android is Corona. While the official language of Android apps is Java, Corona provides a much easier experience for new programmers. The language was developed specifically for building apps. There are also numerous free resources to get you up and running with Corona.
   - Also, be sure to investigate the Android Studio at developer.andoid.com.

3. Skip learning a programming language. Several appbuilding platforms don't require any programming at all! Here are few of the more popular options:
   - Zoho Creator. You can create up to three apps free. If you can click and drag, you can build an app.
   - Zengine. This platform specializes in database management apps for businesses. If you're creative, you could use this platform to your benefit.
   - Appery. This platform also utilizes click and drag elements. There is a free option available.Good Barber. Despite the unusual name, Good Barber is a very popular app builder. The minimum plan is $16/month.
   - This is just a small sampling. There are many more!

When was the last time you learned something new? Maybe you're a programming wizard and you just don't know it! Whether you want to learn how to write code or not, you can create an app.

Selling And Marketing The App

Where you choose to sell your app will depend on whether you chose to create an Apple or Android app. If you created an Apple-based app, you'll need to sell it on the Apple store. If you haven't already, create an Apple Developer account at https://developer.apple.com Follow the instructions for uploading your app. An Android app can be sold at http://developer.android.com/develop/index.html Both accounts also provide a lot of information on app development. There are also several other locations online that sell and even market mobile apps. Do a quick search and spend some time researching the options.

If you'd like to try your hand at marketing your app, there are many options:

1. **Create a website dedicated to your app.** Explain to the world all the great things your app can do. Be sure to create a link so your customers can buy it.

2. **Use social media** to share news about your product. Put all those social media accounts to good use. Tweet, post, and announce to your heart's content.

3. **Make a YouTube video**. Videos continue to become more and more popular. Many potential customers would rather watch a video than reading text.
4. **Contact app review sites**. There are thousands. Contact several and pitch your app to them.
5. **Offer a promotional price**. Consider pricing your app at a low cost, or even free, for a limited time.

Once you have your app completed, it's time to sell it. There are only a couple of primary platforms to sell your app, but there are many ways to market it yourself. Many app developers claim that the marketing is the most essential part.

Conclusion

Creating and selling a mobile app is well within your capabilities. Come up with a great idea and bring that idea to life. There are so many tools available, it's not necessary to be a trained programmer. Many of the most successful apps have been very simple, but clever. Boost your income by taking advantage of the constantly expanding app market.

Setting Up A Part-Time Office Cleaning Business

How would you like to start a part-time business that doesn't require much money to get started or have many overhead costs? A part-time office cleaning business can be a great way to get started as an entrepreneur and also has the added benefit of being tremendously scalable. With this type of business, you can ultimately grow extremely large and make a lucrative income.

Follow these steps to get your office cleaning business up and running:

1. **Decide what type of businesses to target**. There are many issues to consider. Would you like to clean large office buildings or small? Would you prefer to service small businesses? Schools?

   - If you're taking on this business alone, with no other employees, you're likely going to have to start small. This can be a good thing. It will provide you with time to learn the business and become successful. You'll learn how to deal with clients, what supplies you'll need, and how to manage your finances.

   - As you get more experienced and earn the funds to hire additional employees, you can target larger buildings.

   - Also consider the hours you're available. Assuming you already have a full-time job, you'll need to work around your other work schedule.

   - Keep in mind that most businesses won't want you there during their normal business hours, so you'll probably have to clean at night.

   - Think about how much work you can handle. Start small until you have a good idea of how much extra workload you can add to your routines.

2. **Name your business**. Since your clients are professionals, you'll probably want to name your business something that

sounds professional. If you want to keep your business local, you might incorporate your city name into your business name. Avoid trying to be cute. You want the give the project a professional image.

3. **Get your business license and a bank account**. Different states have different rules and laws about business licenses. You may only have to get a DBA (doing business as) name, which is usually very inexpensive. However, getting your business registered as a limited liability corporation will limit your liability should something happen.

   - If you can afford an attorney, it might be a wise investment at this point. What would happen if you or your employee knocked a client's computer off a desk?
   - It would be best to get a separate business account at your bank. Mixing personal and business funds can be an issue, especially at tax time. What if something happens and your single account gets frozen due to business issues? You wouldn't be able to access your personal funds either.
   - Shop around for the best deals. Some bank accounts have higher minimum balance requirements and higher fees.

4. **Find liability insurance**. Most commercial clients will require you to have insurance. Most businesses will ask to see your insurance certificate and may even have a minimum amount of coverage they require. $500,000 worth of coverage will be enough in most instances.

- Your local insurance agent should be able to provide you with the advice and coverage you require. Liability coverage is not expensive.
- If you have employees, a bond is a good idea. A bond primarily protects you if an employee steals from your client. Bonds are inexpensive and offer good protection from unscrupulous employees.

5. **Set your rates**. Determining what you're going to charge your clients for cleaning services is the last step to complete before you actually begin operating your business. There are a couple things to consider:
   - What is the competition charging? With a few phone calls and a little research, you can determine a good average rate for your area. It might be smart to set your rates a little lower until you build up a sufficient client base.
   - What hourly rate do you want to earn? When you have an interested potential client, consider how many hours a job is likely to take and set your fee accordingly. Remember to consider the cost of travel and supplies!

6. **Advertise**. Advertising and marketing are always important, especially when first starting a business. You can't be hired if nobody even knows that your business exists. Consider some of the following options:
   - Phone calls/mail/flyers/brochures. These are all direct contact methods. Flyers are inexpensive to create and can be inexpensive to distribute if you do it yourself.

Consider faxing your information to potential clients. Brochures are also inexpensive in significant quantities. The cheapest option is to just pick up the phone.

- Website. Every business should have a website. With WordPress, anyone can put up a good looking website in short order. Visit wordpress.org for details.
- Newspapers and magazines. Print media formats can be good advertising tools, but they can also be expensive. The effectiveness can depend a lot on the local area.
- Online advertising. Advertising online can be inexpensive or even free. There are a variety of places to advertise online. It would be great to link your advertisement back to your webpage.
- Business cards, car magnets, or other forms. Do everything you can to get your business out in front of people by giving them your contact information.

7. **Give Estimates**. Anyone who contacts you should be offered a free estimate. Always be on time and dress professionally.

- Use a tape measure to determine room size. You'll quickly learn how long it takes to vacuum, sweep, or mop a articular size room.
- Find out exactly what your client wants cleaned. If possible, find out what they liked or disliked about the previous cleaning service. Use this information wisely.
- Complete your bid within a few days. You should

include a cover letter, your bid sheet, copy of your insurance, and several business cards. They might pass your card on to another business owner.

8. **Start cleaning**! Ensure you get high quality cleaning supplies, but also watch the cost. There is bound to be at least one janitorial supply company in your local area. Also consider green cleaning products, as they don't emit harmful fumes. Do a great job, but manage your time well.

   - After the initial cleaning, ask your client to review the work and offer feedback. It's much easier (in most cases) to keep a client than it is to find a new one. Strive to make each client happy.
   - If you have employees, review the quality of their work on a regular basis and make your expectations and those of the business owner you are cleaning for very clear

9. **Grow** your business, cautiously. Expanding your business can be exciting, but be careful. Sometimes costs can quickly get out of control. Managing multiple clients and employees can be time consuming as well. Continue to add clients and employees at a rate you can handle.

10. **Know when to cut a client loose**. Not all clients are good clients. For every 10 clients, 2 will probably be more trouble than they're worth. It's not worth spending all your time managing those two clients and their issues. Simply let them go and find two better clients. Don't be afraid to cull your duds. The same goes for your employees.

Setting up your own part-time cleaning business is something anyone can do. It requires a minimum amount of money and knowledge to get started. The best advice is to start small and then scale-up as you gain the expertise to grow efficiently and intelligently. A cleaning business can provide a great supplemental income and it also has the potential to grow into a full-time business where it could become your sole income.

Get Paid to Clean Up Real Estate Properties

Although the economy is providing us all with a bit of a rough, unpredictable ride, the good news is that the housing industry is undergoing a gradual process of bouncing back. Luckily, this good news about the housing industry also opens up some interesting ways for you to earn money.

Consider these options:

1. Clean out trashed houses and properties. Start a side business during your off-work hours to clean out bank-owned houses or homes purchased by investors who want to flip them. Be specific about what you'll do.
   - For example, you could advertise that you'll remove all trash in the home, down to the walls and floors. Your job would be to carry out all the debris, load it into your truck, and take it to the dump. You can charge per property or by the hour.

- Prior to bidding or accepting the job, meet with the owner at the property for a walk-through. This way, you'll see exactly what you'd be dealing with so you can name a price you're comfortable with. Before you know it, banks or contractors will be calling you for your services.

2. Take care of the lawns of properties for sale. Contact the realtors or banks to let them know you're skilled in lawn maintenance and have the necessary tools to keep up their properties.
    - Particularly if the properties are in your own neighborhood, you stand to make some decent cash without traveling too far from home.
3. Phone local building contractors and offer your "gopher" services on the weekend.Offering to pick up needed tools, building supplies, and even lunch for over-worked builders on their weekend workdays could grow to some pretty lucrative occasional work.
4. Paint the interior or exterior of homes for sale.If you enjoy painting, why not sell that service to banks or home "flippers?"
5. Perform the final cleaning prior to going on the market. Final cleaning may include scrubbing floors, polishing wood floors, vacuuming carpets, scouring sinks, and shining up countertops. Nearly anyone can do this. Plus, it's very rewarding.
6. Poll your prospects and offer your services. Contact bank representatives, realtors, and property owners to inquire

what kind of work they need done on their properties. Give them your name and number and have them call you with their needs.

- When you demonstrate you're eager and ready to go to work, someone may very likely take you up on your offer. Show your motivation.

7. Apply for work at banks or other lenders. If you have stellar office skills, consider checking to see if local financial institutions require additional assistance to process paperwork and make phone calls on short sales, bankruptcy properties, and the like.

Use your creative nature to put the current housing recovery to good use. You have the power to fill your bank account with extra dollars right now. Think of every step from property clean-up to putting up real estate for sale. You'll be surprised at the money you can make!

How To Find And Flip Your First Property

It's exciting watching those programs on television where the investor goes out, purchases a property and flips it for a fast $10k + profit. Is it possible to do that yourself? Is it a scam or is it a viable way to make some money? Can you really do it without any money or credit like you hear on those 2:00 am infomercials? It is possible, but you must do a lot of things that make the average person uncomfortable. That's not to say you have to do anything unethical; simply that the activities involved are not pleasant for most folks.

Like any business you need a couple of things:
- Inventory
- Customers

And these two things will be accumulated through marketing and prospecting. Real estate investing is largely a marketing business.

The Basic Process

In a nutshell, you need to find someone that is willing to sell their house at a deep discount, typically at no more than 60% of the retail value. Then you need to find someone else to buy it from you at 70% of retail value.

Your first question is probably, "Who would sell me their $100,000 house for $60,000?" Have you ever had an old car you didn't really use anymore? Maybe it didn't even run anymore. The car just took up space in your driveway or on the side of the house. Eventually, you would reach the point where you'd had enough. You just wanted the thing gone, regardless of what you could sell it for.

Like your car, some houses aren't providing any value to their owners, and these owners would be willing to give you a deal. Other owners are just looking for some cash and will also come way down on the price if you can close quickly. So such owners are out there, but it may take a lot of work to find them.

Your second question is probably, "Why would I sell that house for only $70,000?" The short answer is because you can sell it quickly for cash. Especially if you're trying to put together deals without any money or credit, time is critical.

Finding a House to Buy

We're looking for a house that fits certain criteria. In most cases, your best buyers will be rehabbers that will either resell the property or rent it out. As with any business, you need to figure out what your customers want. In most cases, this will be houses with 3 bedrooms in decent, but not really nice areas (in the case of properties that will be rented). Houses that will be resold can certainly be of any size, and higher price ranges are acceptable.

In general, you'll look for properties that are 70-100% of the median home price for the area. So, if the middle-of-the-line house in the area is $100k, you're going to be looking at houses that would sell for $70-100k after they're repaired.

Here are some ways to find the owners that are willing to sell their house at a deep discount:

1. Bandit Signs. These are those 12x18 or 18x24 signs you see hung on telephone poles all over the place. Check out the legality in your area. You see them all the time because they work.
2. Craigslist. Call all the ads for properties that are for sale or rent. If you call enough people, someone will be thrilled to give you a great deal.
3. Ads: Put your own ads in Craigslist. The newspaper is fine, too, if you have the funds.
4. Abandoned Houses: Even some nice neighborhoods occasionally have abandoned homes in them. Frequently,

the owners are out of state. Track them down and send them a letter or give them a call.

What Do You Say to These Owners?
It's perfectly fine if you're not some slick salesman. The people you're looking for are looking for relief and they'll take it wherever they can get it. Your basic message should be, "I can give you cash for your house very quickly, but I'm only going to be able to give you about half of what your house is worth."Expect that it will take approximately 30 phone calls with sellers to find a property that fits your qualifications. Out of those sellers, the number will be much greater to actually get a deal. You could easily make 100 or more calls before you make a deal. But consider that many telemarketers are expected to make 400+ calls each day at their jobs. All in all, it's not a lot of work for a good payday. How Much Do You Offer?
The basic formula is: 70% ARV – Repairs – Your Fee
ARV = after repair value; this is the retail value of a home in great shape. You can get the home's value from a real estate agent or by doing some legwork yourself. You can get free estimates for repairs from contractors.

Selling the House
Now that you have the house under contract, your job is to find someone to take it off your hands at closing. There are two basic ways to get paid:
1. **Assign the Contrac**t. You can assign your rights to the house to another person for a fee. This is the easiest and

cheapest way to get your money. The only potential issue is that your buyer will know how much money you're making.

2. **Do a Double Closing**. In this case, you're reselling the house to your buyer during the same closing as you buy the house. This keeps everything more confidential, but there are two sets of closing costs: one set from buying the house and one set from selling the house.

Finding a buyer is usually quite easy. Once again, you can advertise with bandit signs and classified ads. Your message should be something along the lines of, "3 bedroom house for sale. 40% off. Cash only." The other method is to contact people that are likely to have the cash to buy a house quickly. So doctors, lawyers, and other investors are likely prospects. Also contact people with house-for-rent ads; these are going to be people that buy the type of house you're selling. A common method to build a list of possible buyers: Find your buyers first. This is actually very smart, since it's not always easy to sell the house as quickly as you need to once you've got it under contract. You would simply do all of the activities above, but whenever someone calls you, you simply say, "I'm sorry, but that house already sold. I might have some others coming up, though. If you give me your name and number, I'll let you know the next time I have something available." When you call the owners of rental properties, just tell them what you're doing and ask them what kinds of properties they're looking for. You can then call them back when you have a property to sell.

Where Do You Go From Here?

There's not enough information in this report to run out and flip a house, but the main structure is here. You'll also need to further educate yourself about a couple of things:

1. Know your market. It's important for your own success to become an expert on your local market.
   - Find an area of town that has many of the types of houses that will work for flipping.
   - Take a Saturday and look at every house for sale. Learn what they're selling for.
   - You should eventually become so familiar with your market that you know facts like a house on one block in good shape is worth $72,000 and the same house 3 blocks over is worth $81,000.

2. Know the players. It's amazing how many real estate investors buy and sell deals to/from other investors. It's common to find more deals than you handle. Other times you can't find a buyer, but another investor can.

3. Have courage. It's not easy, at first, for most people to call up someone and offer them 50% of what their house is worth. A lot of people will be upset with you. Some will hang up. Some will be verbally abusive. That's okay. They're not the people that need your help. Just call the next person and keep on moving.

4. Keep learning. Get as much knowledge as you can about repair costs. Learn how to do a quick, but knowledgeable inspection of a house. Learn about the closing process. Learn how to do a quick title search.

Budding real estate investors are notorious for believing they need more knowledge before they can do a deal. The truth is one day of educating yourself is more than sufficient to get out there and start making some money. Don't let fear stop you. That $5k-10k payday might be less than 30 days away.

How To Wholesale Real Estate
In Your Spare Time

Wholesaling real estate can be a great part-time activity. You can easily make another $25k-$50k per year. It's relatively simple, but you have to work it hard. In a nutshell, you put houses under contract for less than 70% of their retail value and then sell the contract to investors and renovators at 70%. They then sell or rent the house on the retail market. You can make money without ever owning the house and without needing money or good credit.

Here are few definitions you'll need to know before we get started:

- MLS = Multiple-listing service. This is the database that real estate agents use to list houses. Investigate how you can gain access yourself. There's always a way. At the very least, you'll need a friendly real estate agent person to help you. There is a ton of information in the MLS that will be invaluable.
- ARV = After-repair value. This is the retail value of a home after it has received any needed repairs.

- Comps = Comparables. These are the sales prices of nearby houses that are similar in size and quality. You can get these from your local real estate agent. You can also find the information from the local government, depending on your state. In some states, the information is only available on the MLS.

Now let's move on to the good stuff.

Find Your Buyers First

Ideally, you're going to spend your time finding the properties and not spend your time trying to sell them. The best way to accomplish this is to find your buyers first. You will frequently hear that if you have a great deal, it's easy to sell it. That's not always true!

Try these ideas to compile a buyers list before you start making offers:

1. Find buyers on the MLS that have paid cash. Call your friendly realtor and ask them for a list of houses that have been bought in the last 2 months for cash. From those listings, it's a simple matter to find the buyers.
    - Check out the county clerk's office or the local tax records. It will depend on your state, but there is a simple way to find these folks if you ask.
    - Once you've found them, give them a call and say, "Hi, I'm a real estate wholesaler. I was wondering if you're actively buying properties." Then ask what types of

properties they're looking for. Get their phone number and email address – you'll need it later.

2. Run a fake ad. This is a common tactic. Put an ad on www.craigslist.org that says something like this: 3 bdrm / 2 bath. 50 cents on the dollar. Must sell. Cash only. Nice house.

   - The types of investors that you're looking will call so fast your head will spin. Let them know that the house already sold but you'll let them know the next time you have something. Get their name, phone, and email.

3. Call 'houses for rent' ads. The owners of these rental houses are prefect buyers for your properties. Call the ads and ask them if they are looking for houses to buy. Again, find out what they want and get their phone and email address.

4. Contact title companies. Title companies know everyone. While they might not be willing to give you names, they will certainly pass on your name to the appropriate people.

5. Join the local real estate club. Every city has at least one. Join and talk to people. Find out who actively buys or rehabs and then get in contact with them.

Now you have 5 ways to find buyers. Keep in mind that you only really need 1 or 2 good buyers, though it never hurts to have more.

When you have a property to sell, shoot-off an email with all the relevant details of the property (bcc everyone). With a good buyers list, you should be able to sell a property in a few days, at most. Don't be bashful about approaching these people.

When you approach the right people, they will be overjoyed that you found them.

Finding the Properties & Sellers

The types of properties you're going to be looking for will depend on your buyers. You just go out and find whatever it is they want. Typically though, the most common properties will be from 50% of the median home price to the median home price in your area.

So if your median home price is $120,000, you'll be looking at properties that would sell (in good shape) for $60k to $100k. Keep in mind that what you're really looking for are the right owners. These are owners that are either forced to sell or owners that just desperately want to get rid of a property.

These owners could be:

- In serious financial difficulty. Some people need to sell immediately and really need your help.
- Out of state owners. Sometimes people move out of state and leave a home behind. Owning the home becomes too expensive or too much hassle. They may have inherited the hose and just want it out of their lives.
- Disgruntled landlords. Some landlords just want out and they want out today.

The trick is to find these owners. Here are few ideas:

1. Hang bandit signs in suitable neighborhoods. These are the type of signs we're talking about: dirtcheapsigns.com/

yard_signs. All you need is a sign that says "We Buy Houses" and your phone number. Hang them up on telephone poles or mount them on stakes.

2. Run ads on craigslist.org. Run an ad stating that you buy houses for cash and can close quickly. Keep running it over and over.

3. Call, email, and/or send a postcard to local realtors and attorneys. Again, let them know that you can close quickly for cash. Offer a finder's fee.

4. Look at bankruptcy and foreclosure filings. Contact these folks and make an offer on their house.

5. Find owners of abandoned properties. Every time you see an abandoned property, track down the owners and ask them if they'd like to sell. A great person to ask is the local mail carrier for that neighborhood. They see all the houses and know who isn't getting any mail. Offer some money for leads that pan out.

Negotiate

Usually, you don't have to do a lot of negotiating, just to stick to your numbers. Keep in mind that you want to have your first offer rejected. If they say 'yes,' you'll always wonder how low they would've been willing to go! You'll need to find comps to determine the market value of the house. Repair values can be determined by getting some free estimates from contractors. Your highest offer should be: (65% × ARV) - repairs. So a house that is worth $120k in great shape, but needs $10k in repairs would have a high offer of $68,000. That's 0.65 × $120,000 = $78,000 - $10,000 = $68,000. Your starting offer should be no more than: (50% × ARV) - repairs. In our example, that would be $50,000. You might be asking yourself, "Who in the world is going to sell me their house for half-price?" The answer is: not many people, but there will be some. You just have to keep asking. You won't really understand until you do your first deal. The right owner will be so happy for your help that they are likely to be crying while they are thanking you. Then you'll understand.

Close & Sell
Once you have an offer accepted, you need to get busy:
1. Immediately start selling the house. Take pictures, get the comps together, and send off an email to all your buyers with all the details they need.
2. Immediately contact a title company to start the title work. If there is a problem with the property, you want to find out ASAP.
3. Get your money! Ideally, you'll 'assign' the contract to your buyer. This simply means that you assign all your rights in that contract to your buyer. In exchange for that assignment, your buyer gives you money.
   - Typically, you should get the difference between the contract price and (70% x ARV) - repairs. Investors should be willing to give you 70%. So the better price you negotiate, the more money you're going to make.
   - To clarify, a house worth $100k ARV that needs no repairs, should earn you $10k if you got it under contract for $60k. $100k x 70% = $70k. 70k-60k=10k.

Understand that you're not likely to get paid until closing. Most investors won't give you the money unless everything works out, which is fair.

4. Repeat!

Keys to Success
Once you have an offer accepted, you need to get really busy:

1. **Realize that it's a numbers game.** You will get told 'no' a lot. It's not unheard of for a beginner to have to make 100 offers or more to get one 'yes'. In time, you'll learn which homes and owners are more likely to result in a signed contract. Don't let all the rejection get you down. Someone will be happy to sell his house to you.

2. **Never stop marketing**. Each day, try to do something to market your business. This type of investing is almost entirely a marketing business. Never forget that.

3. **Get the proper forms**. There are tons of legal forms available online. You also should be able to get forms from your real estate investing club. Depending on your state, an attorney might be a good idea.

Conclusion

Being a real estate wholesaler is tough, but doable. Investigate the details on your own. There are a lot of great articles online that can fill in the gaps, but don't get too carried away reading and learning. The part that makes you money is taking action. Stick to your numbers and you can't go wrong. Good Luck!

Let Your House Pay For Itself

One of the best strategies to boost your incoming dollars is to creatively think of ways to reduce your home mortgage or monthly rental payment. Your monthly mortgage or rental amount is likely the largest recurring expense you have.

So, utilizing your home to make some extra dollars is a wise thing to do. Consider these suggestions to accumulate money from your home:

1. Take in a roommate or renter. If you have a larger house or condo that has at least one extra bedroom, you could rent out one of the bedrooms to a student or single working person.
    * Even if you charged them $75-$100 a week for the bedroom, including a shelf in the refrigerator and kitchen privileges, you'd end up with roughly $300-$400 extra a month. You can apply those dollars toward your house payment.
    * You'd shave costs off of your monthly mortgage. Plus, you'd be helping the other person.
2. Rent out your home occasionally. Another way to earn with your home is to rent out your house to others for short stints, like vacations, holidays, and special events. It's possible for you to get enough cash on a regular basis to pay your mortgage at least some of the time whenever you rent out your home a few times a year.

- If you live in a tourist town, renting your home out during the high tourist season for three or four weeks a year could provide you with a nice tidy bundle to apply toward your home loan.
- Perhaps you live in a community that has a large sporting complex that holds many state or national events or where people come to see the natural landscapes and fall colors.
- You could stay with friends and family for just a few short weeks a year while renting out your home for as much as $1,500-$2,000 a week to those who wish to see the sporting events or enjoy the colorful foliage in the fall.
- If you prefer, when you go on vacation, rent out your home to someone who wants to vacation in your town and then use the cash to cover your vacation costs. Websites like Vacation Rentals by Owners (VRBO) make it easy for you to list your home for the exact period of time you wish to make it available for rental.

3. Renovate your home to include a small apartment unit. If live in a two-story home or a home with a basement, you may have a virtual gold mine. Do some renovations to include a small living area, kitchenette, bathroom, and bedroom.
   - If you have a large upstairs area, it may be easier than you think to hook two or three of the rooms together and have a kitchen installed. Voila! You now have a

small apartment that you could rent out for several hundred dollars a month.

- The same goes for a finished basement. You could make a studio apartment with open living, dining, and kitchen area with a bedroom area installed behind one wall.
- Even though both of these plans would involve you doing a lot of the work (tearing out walls, painting, and the like) and then paying upfront for the renovations you're unable to do yourself (wiring, plumbing, and cabinet installation), you stand to make hundreds monthly once you rent out the space.

4. Purchase a multi-unit property. Another way to let your home pay for itself is to buy a multi-unit property like a duplex or triplex. You could live in in one unit and rent out the other(s). Then, use the rent from the other units' tenants to pay your entire mortgage payment on the property each month.

- Owning and living in a multi-unit property allows you to live "rent-free" while you build up equity in the property.
- You'll also learn how to become a landlord while banking some extra bucks.
- In fact, you may even have extra money left over from the tenants' rent payments after paying your monthly mortgage payments. Then, you can use that income to invest in more real estate, which then pays for itself with its own renters, too.

- Or you might want to use the extra income to start "flipping homes"—buying bank-owned or short sale properties to fix up and sell.
- However you decide to use it, the multi-unit property purchase plan is great for getting you the cash for investing in your first real estate deal, regardless of what you do with it after you buy it. Plus, you'll have the opportunity to "stick your toe" into the waters of becoming a landlord and managing a real estate investment.
- Ultimately, your home will be paying for itself when you buy and live in a multi-unit property.

t's exciting to think about how your home could be the key to your future financial freedom. Take some time to explore all the ways you might be able to let your home pay for itself. When the money starts coming in, you'll be glad you did.

Special Factors To Consider Whern You Plan To Boost Your Income With Your Home

As you're mulling over the above strategies to let your house pay for itself, keep in mind these tidbits of information:

1. Extra money each month. With some of the above suggestions, even though you may not make enough to pay every monthly mortgage payment, you'll surely bring in the extra money to pay a portion of your mortgage payments or pay down your principal to pay off the mortgage more quickly.

2. **Invest in an attorney**. Another factor to consider is meeting with a real estate attorney to help you draw up a contractual agreement form to use with renters to ensure you understand one another. Spelling out the specific aspects of your arrangements in advance can help prevent troublesome situations later.

3. Keep an open mind. When it comes to earning money from your house, it's a good idea to ponder doing things that you wouldn't have considered in the past. For example, you may have trouble imagining taking in a stranger to rent one of your bedrooms.

   - However, you could use word of mouth with friends and neighbors to find a trusted college student or young professional who's just starting out. If you do end up trying it out (renting out a room), you may be pleasantly surprised to see how simple it is to adjust to sharing your home with another person.

   - The added income could really take the pressure off paying a high mortgage payment. Allow yourself to try some new ways to boost your income. Who knows where you could go financially after you develop an additional stream of steady income?

4. **A cautionary note. It's important to carry the necessary liability insurance and include the extra income in your taxes if you decide to undertake some of these suggestions. Check with your city's coding and zoning officials or an attorney with questions.**

It may be hard to imagine that your home could actually be paying for itself. But as you can see, it is possible. With some work on your part, you can make hundreds of extra dollars monthly. Using your home to gain more income can get you out of a financial jam. Join the thousands of people who enjoy extra income from their homes. Your financially abundant future is waiting.

How To Make $500 Fast In Offline Marketing

Offline marketing is all the buzz now and it's not surprising. There are a lot of small businesses that don't really know how to market their businesses effectively online. Your local dry cleaner or cosmetic dentist probably knows less about online marketing than you think. Even if you're not a computer whiz, it's likely you know enough to provide a valuable service. While it can be a competitive field, it's not that difficult to make some real money quickly.

Here are several ideas that can help you make money as fast as today:

1. **Target smaller businesses**. Businesses with 10 or fewer employees are able to make decisions quickly. Larger businesses are more likely to want to hire someone with demonstrated experience and expertise or need to have meetings to reach a conclusion to use your services.

2. **Target businesses that are already advertising in some way**. You don't want to have to convince someone about the importance of advertising. You want someone that's already advertising in some fashion. A few good places to find such businesses are:

   - The Yellow Pages. Yellow Pages ads are quite expensive. Any business with an actual ad as opposed to just the standard listing is a good candidate.
   - Groupon. Go to their website and search around. Any company with a Groupon deal is already willing to spend money to advertise.
   - Val-Pak. These usually come in the mail, but there is also a website you can you use to find prospects. The minimum charge to a company for advertising with Val-Pak is around $1,000. These companies see the value of advertising and are willing to spend money on marketing.

3. **Offer a specific service at first**. Become known as the gal that makes YouTube videos or the guy that creates mobile websites. Find something that interests you or that you're already good at. Consider these services for inspiration:

   - Make videos of the business and distribute them to online video sharing services.
   - Create websites or mobile versions of their websites.
   - Set up a blog for the company. Offer to make weekly posts.
   - Write press releases and submit them to online press release services.

- Manage search engine pay-per-click advertising campaigns.
- Design Facebook pages.
- Handle their social site marketing on Facebook, Twitter, Instagram, or similar sites.
- Build their list of customers and prospects and send coupons, ads, or newsletters by using an autoresponder service like Aweber.
- Once you've been hired for one service, you can always come back and sell them additional services later.

4. **Contact the businesses offline.** Many offline marketers want to find customers online, since a lot of computer people can be a little shy socially. It's much quicker to approach them directly. These ideas make it easier:

- Phone. The phone gets much easier with practice. Have a script and just make those calls. There are plenty of scripts available online. A neat trick is to call when you know the business will be closed and simply leave a message! When someone calls you back, you know they're pretty serious

- Flyers or pamphlets. Print up some simple flyers or pamphlets. Pass them out to business owners, saying something like, "I've started a new business and I'm just getting out in the neighborhood to get the word out." Give them your flyer.

- Direct mail. There are a lot of services, including the U.S. Postal Service, which will print and mail postcards and brochures for you. All you really need is a mailing list.

- Combine all of these ideas. Give them a phone call and then a week later, send a postcard. A few days later, stop by with a brochure or flyer. Where most offline marketing wannabes make their mistake is simply giving up too soon. Most people will not hire you on the first contact. It might take five!

5. **Market daily.** You'll generally spend more time marketing than actually 'working'. Doing the actual work for the clients is the easy part. Set a goal each day for what you want to accomplish.

- You'll find that it takes about an hour to make 20-25 afterhours phone calls when you include the answering machine time. How many phone calls are you going to make each day?
- If you go to strip malls, you can hand out a lot of flyers in an hour. Do you know where all of your local strip malls are located? Office parks can be another good location to get a lot done in a hurry.
- Strive to send out some mail each day.
- Have a spreadsheet to keep track of who you've contacted. Make a note of the date and the method. Don't beat a dead horse – five contacts and then they're out!

6. **Utilize your friends and family**. Posting a notice on your Facebook page might be all you need to find someone that

knows of a good client. You might even find a good client among your friends and family.

- All your message needs to say is, "Hey everybody, I'm starting an offline marketing business to help small business owners advertise their businesses effectively online. If you know of anyone that needs help in this area, please let me know. Thanks!"
- Remember to include the contacts in your phone and email account(s). Send off a message to everyone you know and let them know that you're in business.

7. **Ask for referrals**. Small business owners tend to know other small business owners. Don't be afraid to ask for referrals when you're talking to them. This is especially true after you've done some work for them.

8. **Expand** your business. You can easily take on an unlimited number of clients and add more services if you outsource some of your tasks.

With outsourcing, you could just focus on your marketing and let others do the actual work of the services you're offering! Find others to do the work at places like http://fiverr.com and http://warriorforum.com You could even outsource a lot of your marketing. Simply pay a commission that still leaves you in profit for each sale. A lot of work-at-home telemarketers work on commission and could make many contacts for you in a short period of time. Making $500 or more, quickly, is really quite simple. Get together some basic marketing materials and get them out there to as many suitable people as possible. In a good, solid day, you could make 100 phone calls, pass out 100 flyers, and contact everyone in your phone or email account. The yellow pages and Val-Pak will keep you busy for a long, long time with a never-ending supply of potential clients. If you'll limit your search to smaller companies that are already advertising, you're halfway home. The only other requirement is to never stop marketing. Hit each potential client five times. If you stay busy and are aggressive in your efforts, $1,000 each week can be a realistic goal!

Selling Your Photos Online

Many of us love to take photographs. We'll take a picture any place, any time. It can be a fun and creative way to spend time. Wouldn't it be great to be able to make money doing something you're already willing to do for free? If you have a hard drive overflowing with images, you might be sitting on a goldmine. There are several ways to make money online with your photos. Pictures you've already taken, as well as the pictures you take in the future, can all be a potential source of income. Many people need great photographs for content, and they're willing to pay to use them.

Try turning your photos into profit with these online strategies:
1. **Create a portfolio website and sell advertising space**. Google AdWords is probably the most common example of this strategy. While people are looking at your beautiful photographs, they will also be presented with

advertisements from Google. Anytime someone clicks on one of these ads, you will receive money.

2. **Post your photos to a stock website**. There are many stock photography websites. Just set up an account and begin uploading your photos. When someone falls in love with one of your photographs, they frequently have the option to purchase it outright or to merely license it.
   - The options vary from website to website. If you desire, you have the ability to maintain ownership of your photographs and stick to providing licensing rights.
   - Some of the more popular stock websites are Shutterstock, iStockphoto, and Fotalia.

3. **Use your images to create products**. You could put your photos on coffee mugs, calendars, greeting cards, or t-shirts. You could even sell physical copies of your photographs. All you need is a website to get started.
   - There are several businesses online that will do the actual printing for you. You just make the designs and your chosen printer will put them on whatever products you want to offer.

4. **Put your photographs on Flickr.** This is a great way to show off your work to others. It's not unusual for someone to offer to purchase your photos. Be sure to watermark your photos so they can't be used until you've been paid.
   - There are several software packages that will allow you to apply a watermark to your photographs. Adobe Photoshop, Watermarker.com, WinWatermark.com,

PlumAmazing.com, and Digimarc.com are a few of the options available

Pricing

How much is a photograph worth? It depends.
It might be just a few cents. Some websites give you the option of choosing a price for your photographs.

There are several factors that determine the pricing structure:

1. **Are your photos exclusive** to the website? Many stock photo sites will pay higher commissions if you agree to only post a photograph to their website. The difference can be as high as 200% for exclusivity.
2. **The size of the photo**. Many websites provide the option of purchasing different size photos. The larger the photo, the greater the cost.
3. **How many times it's been sold**. Some websites increase the price after the photo has been purchased a certain number times. Popular photos are simply worth more money.

Getting paid is a snap. Most stock photo sites have a minimum payout level, usually $100. You can be paid via several methods once you've reached the payout minimum. Paypal, check, and bank transfer are the usual options.

What Types Of Images Are Popular?

Photos of you and your friends probably wouldn't sell well. You an't just post any old photograph on most websites. The photos are reviewed and can be rejected if they don't think there is a market for your photo. Think about the types of photographs that appeal to or are useful to a large number of people. Landscape photos are always popular. Simple photos on white backgrounds are also popular. Remember that many people like to use Photoshop. A photograph of a Porsche on a white background can easily be moved to another background by the purchaser.

How To Sell More Photographs

There are a lot of people out there trying to do the same thing, sell photos. How can you get your photos noticed and purchased instead of the next guy's?

Increase the visibility of your photographs and sell more with these strategies:

1. Give the people what they want. Many sites specialize in certain types of photos. In time, you'll be able to figure out which types of photos sell well. You can then develop a portfolio around what people are buying.
2. **Link to your photos** on social media. This is also a great way for your friends and family to see your work and spread the word.
3. **Edit your photos**. Unless you're using raw photos, your camera is processing the photograph for you. It determines

the best tint, contrast, and more. You can likely do better for various effects!

4. **Get feedback**. When your photos are rejected, you'll usually be told why. Take that information to heart and do better next time.

5. **Take a photography class.** Improving the quality of your photos is sure to increase your sales. If you're attempting to make a profit from your photography, the class should be tax-deductible.

6. **Purchase better equipment.** While it's possible to take nice pictures with a $50 compact camera, a $1,000 camera has far more options and capability. Consider taking some of your earnings and upgrading your equipment.

7. **Tag your photos**. When people are searching for a photo like yours, be sure they can find it! Use relevant keywords to tag your photos

8. **Consider offering a few photos for free.** This can be a good way to get people familiar with your work. Charge them the next time around.

It's possible to make a good second income from your photography hobby. But to really make a reliable income will take consistent work. Build up your portfolio and you'll be able to generate a consistent passive income. Imagine how great it would be to sell your photographs while you sleep!

It's even possible to parlay your exposure into photography gigs. Selling to private clients can be especially lucrative. You might get hired by someone local to take photographs or hired by someone online to provide specific types of photos. If you love to take photos, why not see if you can make some extra money from your hobby. Having a good time and boosting your income can be the best of both worlds.

Make Money With YouTube

You may have wondered how to make money on YouTube. Now is the time to learn so you too can become an expert at it and make the money that you deserve. You can have fun while you're making money on YouTube. It's a great way to make your own videos and promote them to the world while you're making money. Read on to find out just how you can become your own YouTube professional with a bankbook to show it. Some creator's have reached six figures and even seven figure incomes from doing YouTube.

What Is YouTube?

YouTube is owned by Google. An they put Google Adsense ads on your videos and Google will pay you for page views or clickthroughs on the ads. It takes many thousands of page views to make money, so you'll want to promote your YouTube channel everywhere you can to reach the required 1000 subscribers and 4000 watch hours for the YouTube partner program.

Another way to make money at YouTube is by putting ads for your own website or products to channel more customers your way. Or, you can include ads for products for which you are an affiliate and earn commissions when folks buy through your affiliate link.

Ideas For Videos

At YouTube, the most successful people show others how to do something that they don't know how to do themselves, such as playing games online. Also, there's a huge audience of people who enjoy watching someone open and use brand name, items.

Consider these ideas for your videos:

- Art. Art is a great subject to do on YouTube. Show the creative process of making your masterpiece from beginning to end.
- Music. Another great way to highlight your talents is with music.
- Woodworking. Show your expertise at making something out of wood.
- Auto mechanics. Anything to do with keeping up with a car is a great way to make money on YouTube. Be specific so people can fix their own vehicles.Martial Arts. Protection is a key reason for success in life. If you're an expert, show what you know in the martial arts field.
- Martial Arts. Protection is a key reason for success in life. If you're an expert, show what you know in the martial arts field.
- Dancing. Most people want to learn how to dance, but can't find the courage. Show them how on YouTube.
- Travel. Show videos of the places you've visited or lived in.

- Tattoos. Ensure the video is clean enough to see the details. Dancing. Most people want to learn how to dance, but can't find the courage. Show them how on YouTube.
- Makeup. Makeup artists do a great job making money on YouTube. Have a special niche that you can fill.
- Video Games. Help others learn how to play video games.

Other Interests. What are you an expert at? Use what you know to make a detailed video and allow it to make you money.

Getting Started
Be serious about what you're doing and have fun too.

Follow these steps to get started:
1. Ensure your computer and video camera are in good working order. You'll get higher quality videos.
2. Gather your supplies. Get everything that you need in order to make your video.
3. Go to the YouTube website and create your account. They have instructions for how to make your account.
4. Think about who would like what you're filming. Who's your audience? Keep them in mind when you're showing them what they can do on your video.
5. Film your video. If you don't feel confident about filming, have someone else film it for you.
6. Promote your video to family, friends, and neighbors. Tell everyone you know so they take a look at your video.

7. Use your own blog. Make your own blog and share your video there, too.
8. Use social media sites to promote your video. Use Facebook, Twitter, and other social and video-sharing sites to help you promote your video to the world.

Equipment and Supplies

You want to have a computer that is in good working order. It's a good idea to have a camera attached to your computer or a phone camera that you can work with on a regular basis. You may already have your equipment and supplies so you can just begin shooting your videos and making money right away

Things To Consider
These tips will give you a great edge over what others are doing in the YouTube arena:

- Have a great imagination. Be creative with your video.
- Be meticulous. Make the highest quality video that you can. Improve over time no need to be perfect when you start out.
- Take the project seriously. Making money on YouTube is a serious business, even if you are having fun.
- Know that you must get the word out. Understand that it's your job to get the word out about what you're doing.
- Create another video as soon as you can. Once you get one video up, make another, and another, and be consistent. Continue adding videos to your YouTube

channel. The more the merrier – and the more money you'll make!

YouTube is a great way to make money in your spare time, and can be very lucrative once you build an audience. Remember to be positive, have fun, and be smart about what you're doing. You may find that you have quite a knack for bringing interesting ideas to others with video. This is just some quick tips, if you want more in-depth info and ideas check out my channel on http://youtube.com/c/consultablindguy I have a free course for beginners and videos on more ways to make money online and offline. I have been on YouTube since it's founding in 2005 and have multiple channels. You can also check out some of my friends who can also show you plenty of their tips, tricks, and strategies as well. Like Dan Currier- Creator Fundamentals, Nick Nimmin & Dee Nimmin, Pat Flynn, David Foster and plenty of others. Hope to see you in the community, we're all happy to answer your questions.

Make Money Writing Kindle E-Books

Writing and selling Kindle eBooks on Amazon.com has become a very popular way to earn extra money. At the high end, there are authors that routinely make over $100,000 per month. If you've always wanted a source of income that can conform to your hectic schedule, writing eBooks is an option. Anyone can write an eBook. You don't need the approval or support of a traditional publisher. There's no upfront cost involved. Amazon will simply take a percentage of your sales. You won't make big bucks right out the gate but you will make a decent amount the more sales you get and depending on the program features you choose, and how many books you have available. Many aspiring writers are intimidated to get started, but this is unnecessary. You've been communicating all of your life. Only now you're going to communicate your thoughts and ideas via writing.

Tips for writing your first eBook

1. Write what sells. If you're writing fiction, you can choose just about any topic. However, some topics are more popular than others. For instance, anything about zombies has been quite popular lately. If you're interested in writing non-fiction, investigate what's currently selling well.

   - Anything to do with relationships, health, and money is perpetually popular. There are many categories within these three broad topics. For example, dating, marriage, divorce, weight-loss, dieting, investing, and making money are all popular topics.
   - Inform. We all have things that make us want to know more.
   - Solve a common problem. Find a need that matches your expertise and start writing.

2. Know your audience before you begin. Who would be interested in your eBook and how much would they be willing to pay? If your target audience is over 65, you might find that audience is a little bit less internet savvy and less likely to find your eBook.

- A book written for teenagers might require a different voice than one written for business owners. You'll find more success if your writing style closely matches your target audience.

3. Can the information be found for free elsewhere? With all the blogs and other websites available online, there's a lot of great information available for free. That's okay, but you'll need to provide something "above and beyond" to make your eBook a worthwhile purchase.
   - While the information might be available for free, you could compile it into a more useful and readable format. You might be able to present a fresh perspective on the topic. What benefit will you be providing?

4. Create a writing schedule. Nearly all writers state that they'd never get anything done if they waited for inspiration to strike. A schedule is important if you want to complete your eBook in a reasonable amount of time.
   - You'll likely learn through trial and error that you write better at certain times of the day. Some authors find writing to be easier in the morning or the late evening. Others prefer the middle of the day.
   - Some environments work better for some than others. Do you require total privacy or silence? Or would you rather write in a coffee shop or at the park?
   - Set a schedule and stick to it. Thirty minutes per day will probably result in higher compliance and productivity than a single marathon session.

5. Keep writing and edit later. It can be a mistake to write a page and then stop for editing and formatting. Once you start writing, keep going! Do one task at a time. Set aside a separate time for these other activities.

6. Save, save, save. Sooner or later, you're certain to lose a large chunk of writing due to a power failure or simple oversight if you don't save your work often. Word-processing programs have auto-save features. Use them.
   - Save your work in multiple locations. That means your hard drive and another location. It can be a USB drive, external drive, online storage, or even a copy that you email to yourself at the end of each writing session. It ould a shame to lose 200 pages of work due to a hard drive failure.

7. Ensure the formatting is acceptable. You'll find many reviews of Kindle books that complain about the formatting. After you've uploaded your eBook, check the formatting. Spend the time to ensure your work looks as good as possible.

After your eBook is completed, it will be necessary to carefully edit and format your work. It's advisable to first edit the book yourself and then enlist the services of another. Experienced and inexpensive editors can be found on any of the freelancing sites. You might even have a friend that's qualified.

Marketing Your Book

Many authors claim that writing is the easy part, and the marketing is the real work. Even the best eBook can languish if no one knows it exists. Marketing doesn't come easy for many writers, but it's a necessary part of the process. Avoid the mistake of waiting until after your book is completed to being your marketing efforts. A marketing campaign requires time to be effective.

Tell the world about your eBook:

1. **Create and maintain a blog.** It would be challenging to find a successful eBook author without a blog. A website is very simple to build with Word Press. You can even build a site for free by using one of the free blog-hosting websites. Wordpress.com and blogger.com are two of many examples.

2. **Price your book appropriately.** Amazon takes a share of your sales, but the percentage varies with the price. Look at your competition and the commission rate. Find a price that works for you.

3. **Consider giving a few copies away for free**. People swarm to free items, and eBooks are included in this phenomenon. Your readers will tell their friends, and you could win future customers.

4. **Get reviews**. Give away review copies to relevant websites and organizations. One positive review from a recognized expert can make all the difference. Enough positive reviews from anonymous sources are also powerful marketing tools.

5. **Take advantage of social media**. Open and use social media accounts for both yourself and your blog. Inform everyone in your world that you have an eBook available

for sale. It's just as important to let everyone know before it's finished. Pick a release date and start advertising.

6. **Make a video. Talk about your book and provide a link to purchase it**. Share the video through your blog and social media accounts.

7. **Continue editing.** Invariably, your readers will find errors and point out mistakes. Take advantage of this free help! Amazon makes it easy to edit your work and reload it. Your readers will appreciate your responsiveness. One advantage of eBooks is the ability to go back and make corrections after your work has been released.

Marketing your eBook is hard work. Many experts recommend spending at least as much time marketing as you do writing. Create and maintain a marketing schedule. Consistently spending time each day on your marketing efforts will prove to be the most effective strategy. Even if you don't consider yourself a gifted writer, it's very possible to boost your income by writing, marketing, and selling Kindle eBooks. Many eBook writers are even earning full-time incomes from their work. Keep in mind that writing is only one part of the process. Marketing your work is just as important.

Consider Kindle for extra income. It might just be the solution you're looking for. If you want more info on top of this check out my friend Dale L. Roberts on YouTube and social media at Self-Publishing with Dale. He's a best selling author and advocate of self publishing.

Power Washing Service

Offering power washing, or pressure washing, services can be a good source of extra income. Many will welcome your services as they do their spring cleaning or get their homes and yards ready for sale or summer barbeques. Retail stores, banks, office buildings, and other establishments regularly use power washing to keep their outdoor areas spruced up for their customers. These clients can be very lucrative, providing you with repeat business several times per year.

What Is A Powerwasher?

A power washer is a machine that sprays water under pressure to clean driveways, sidewalks, sides of houses or other buildings, and more. Power washers can often remove stains, dirt, and mildew left behind by other cleaning methods, so outdoor areas look clean and refreshed.

Services You Can Offer

You can provide your clients an array of services.
Consider these different ways that you can make money with your power washer:

- **Driveways** – Quickly remove stains and other types of debris.
- **Patios** – Get rid of the dirt from winter storms or spruce up a patio for outdoor parties.

- **Gutter**s – You can clean the gutters of a home or one-story business when you have the extension or telescope wand accessory for your pressure washer. This will allow you to get the inside and outside of the gutters as clean as possible, even removing leaves that have become stuck over time.
- **Outdoor Furnitur**e – Cleaning outdoor furniture is a breeze with a power washer. For best results, keep the pressurized water quickly moving across the furniture so it doesn't damage it.
- **Grills** – Get the grime off of barbeque grills in preparation for parties or to clean them before covering them for the winter. The power washer makes it easy.
- **Decks** –It won't take you much time to make small or large decks look great.
- **Siding** – Make the siding of homes and other buildings look like new again with a power wash clean.
- **Sidewalks** – A power washer is excellent for cleaning off sidewalks. The dirt and grime that gets embedded in them over time darkens the cement. Your pressure washer can easily clean and brighten the concrete.
- **Boats** – A power washer is perfect for cleaning boats.
- Vehicles – Cleaning vehicles is also a breeze with your pressure washer.

Getting Started

Starting your power washer business will be an exciting adventure.

Follow these steps to get started:

1. Check for license or certificate requirements. Some areas require a business license or registration with the local water supply company.

2. Make space in your home to accommodate your business. You'll probably want to store your equipment in your garage. Set up your home office with a desk and filing cabinet. Keep all important papers, contracts, and receipts related to your business together in your filing cabinet from the outset.

3. Develop a list of services that you'll offer to your clients. Determine your prices with some research into what local companies are charging for similar services.

4. Acquire promotional materials. Have business cards and flyers printed or make them yourself on your computer. Be sure to include all your contact information.

5. Make a contact list. Include friends, family, neighbors, and local businesses that might be interested in your services.

6. Buy a pressure washer and supplies. Get the proper equipment for the types of services that you're offering. Shop around for the best prices.

7. Learn how to use your equipment. Using a power washer will take some time to get used to. Read the directions thoroughly and practice your technique.

Equipment And Supplies

Prices for power washers will depend on several different factors. The size, shape, and model that you decide to purchase will determine your price. An average price for a pressure washer is $120. An extra washer will run another $15.

Accessories

These accessories will make your job easier, give you a great edge, and allow you to offer more services:

- **A good long washer**. A 50 foot washer is the size that most people get. There are 25 foot washers for smaller jobs, and it will be handy to have one of each for the ultimate performance.
- **Wand**. The wand is the part that goes on the end of the washer in order to clean certain surfaces.
- **Gutter cleaner**. The gutter cleaner will come in handy for you. You'll be able to get the gutters uncluttered so they rain properly.
- **Dirt blaster**. The dirt blaster goes on the end of the wand and rotates to clean surfaces better.
- **Telescope or extension wand**. The telescope or extension wand will allow you to clean surfaces that are located higher up on the house or business that you're cleaning. It's a good idea to have one of these so that you'll be able to get the most use out of your power washer.
- **Rotating nozzles**. Rotating nozzles allow you to clean surfaces quickly. When there are two nozzles rotating at a time, you'll be able to clean bigger surfaces.

Tips For Using A Pressure Washer

You'll want to get the surfaces for your clients as clean as possible without causing damage.

For best results, follow these tips:

1. **Test**. Always test-spray a part of the surface that you're cleaning. There are several different sized washers, and testing will allow you to find the one that will work the best for your situation.

2. **Spray from the bottom up** on vertical surfaces. Rinse from the top of the surface down for the maximum cleaning effect

3. **Use a wider nozzle**. The smaller one may damage the surface area of what you are trying to clean. Test. Always test-spray a part of the surface that you're cleaning. There are several different sized washers, and testing will allow you to find the one that will work the best for your situation.

4. **Keep the washer moving**. Because of the pressure, the water can cut into the surface if you keep it in one spot.

5. **Keep your distance**. To avoid damaging the surface you're cleaning, position yourself a short distance away and hold the power washer nozzle at an angle from the surface.

6. **Store your equipment properly**. For greater safety, efficiency, and to keep your pressure washer and accessories working properly, it's important to follow the directions when putting away your equipment.

A Few Words Of Caution

Remember that a power washer is a machine. It has to be used properly in order to operate correctly. Children should not be permitted to use it nor be around it because they can be injured. Cleaning the power washer properly is also necessary, so it's important to pay attention to the information that is given with the model you purchase. This can make a huge difference in how it continues to operate. Take care of it well and it will last a long time for you.

Tips For Success
1. Ask for referrals before you leave. An opportune time to ask for referrals is right after you finish a job and the customer sees your excellent results.
2. Leave your business card. Always leave your business card so that clients can contact you for repeat business and also recommend you to others. Word of mouth is an excellent way to acquire more business.
3. Market your business online and offline. Make use of very venue you can to let others know about your services.
   - Use Wordpress software – free at wordpress.org – to put up an attractive website with your contact information, services, before-and-after pictures of some of your jobs, and good reviews from your customers.
   - Use social media sites like Facebook, Twitter, and Instagram to spread the word about your services and let your customers and clients know when you're running specials.

- Arrange with business owners to leave your flyers at local businesses frequented by those who might be interested in your services.
- Call or visit local businesses and chat with the owners about how nice you can make their outdoor areas look. Make a portfolio of before-and-after pictures of some of your jobs and take it with you to show the owners what you can do for them.

4. Contract your services for repeat business. Get local businesses to sign a contract for you to come several times a year. Make some premium packages for those who want the very best. You'll show professionalism, pride in your business, and increase your profits.

5. Schedule clients appropriately. Line up your clients so that you can complete their jobs in a reasonable amount of time. Avoid overbooking yourself because you want to ensure that you keep your clients happy

If working outdoors appeals to you, you just might want to try setting up a power washing business. You'll make money from both homeowners and business owners from offering these valuable services.

How To Start Your Own Part-Time Landscaping Business

Landscaping can be the perfect part-time business. Lawn care can even be a year-round source of income, if you live in the certain climates. Those that live in cooler climates might consider adding a snow removal service in the winter months.

The late fall period can be a good time to offer leaf removal services. While landscaping isn't a complicated endeavor, having a plan before getting started can make your life and business venture much easier.

Research

Before starting your landscaping business, it's important to do some research. When you do the appropriate research before starting your business, the odds for success are greater and the number of surprises can be greatly reduced.

Consider these items when researching the viability of your landscaping business:

1. What services are being offered by your competitors? Take a look at what's being offered in your area. Can you offer something different than competing companies? Are there required services that would be difficult for you to offer?
2. How much is your competition charging? If you can't readily find out how much your competition is charging, call some of your competitors and ask for some quotes for various services.
3. How do other companies present themselves? Are they professional in appearance with new trucks and logos on all their vehicles? Or is the competition primarily a single person with a rusted pick-up truck from the 1970's?
4. How are other companies marketing? Consider how other companies are making themselves known to potential clients. What is your plan?

5. How can you be better? After gathering all of that information, find ways that you can make enhancements. Could you be more professional in appearance? Could you offer more reliable service? What about better rates or additional services?

Research is an important part of starting any business. If you're exactly like the other companies, it will be difficult to be successful.

Planning Stage

Now that you know your marketplace, it's time to make a plan. Your plan doesn't have to be perfect, and odds are that it won't be. But you have to start somewhere. Strive to make your operation better over time as you gain more experience.

Consider these factors when deciding how to profitably meet the needs of the marketplace:

1. Figure out how much money you are able to invest. Landscaping doesn't require a great outlay of funds to get started, but it's important to assess your financial situation. Do your best to avoid taking on any unnecessary debt.

2. Get the proper equipment. A vehicle, lawnmower, trimmer, fertilizer spreader, shovel, rake, and wheelbarrow will take care of most of your needs. If you're short on funds, a lawnmower and trimmer are enough to get started.
   - Find a mower that has the option to bag the clippings. Most modern mulching mowers do a great job without

the need for a bag, but some customers will want the clippings to be taken away.

- Be sure the trimmer is gas-powered rather than electric. Some customers would prefer to not supply the electricity. Electric trimmers are also limited by the length of your extension cord. They also have less power and are slower. And time is money!
- Many great, used items can be found for sale in the various classified ads found online, like at craigslist.org, and in your local publications. It's not unusual to find free items, too.

3. Think about how you want to organize your business. If you're just mowing a few lawns, you might consider not formalizing your business at all. A sole-proprietorship can be a viable option for small operations, especially if you have limited assets.

- A limited-liability corporation will be the best option for most. Your personal assets are protected from any legal actions resulting from your business operations. This will cost a few hundred dollars to get started, however.
- Consult a local attorney for advice in how to structure your business.

4. Consider how you want to be paid. Getting paid is the most important part. It's relatively easy these days to accept debit and credit cards with a smart phone. There are many good options. The easier you can make it for customers to pay you, the more likely you are to get paid.

- If possible, avoid any co-mingling of business and personal funds. Again, if you're just mowing a few lawns, putting your earnings into your personal bank account is unlikely to be an issue.

- However, realize that it's possible to have the bank account you use for business purposes to be frozen in the event of any legal issues. For that reason, separate bank accounts are probably a good idea.

- Companies like PayPal make it easy to set up recurring payments. This can be great because you minimize the amount of time you spend collecting your fees. However, be aware that these online companies typically charge high-fees for their services.

- Remember to provide an invoice for your clients. Invoice forms can be found in your local office supply stores. There are many free forms available online, as well.

5. Figure out how to advertise. Advertising is a critical part of any business. Some forms of advertising are expensive, but many are free or at least very affordable. It's perfectly acceptable to start with the lower-cost forms before moving up to the more expensive options.

   - It can be surprisingly difficult to rank in the search engines for local search terms. A little research into search engine optimization can really pay off.

   - Print up some flyers and go door-to-door. Copies are inexpensive, so all it really takes is your time and energy.

- Phone book advertising is getting less effective every year, but it can still work with the older generation. Be aware that Yellow Pages advertising is expensive.
- There are many free, online advertising opportunities. Craigslist is one of the most well-known.
- Post flyers on telephone poles and in other public areas such as grocery store bulletin boards. However, be careful of local ordinances.

6. Start making money! Answer inquiries from potential customers, schedule the work, and start earning some money.
- Respond to potential customers as quickly as possible. Few things shout 'unprofessional' more than not answering your phone and not responding to calls and emails in a timely fashion.
- Be professional. Make an effort to sound and appear professional. Landscaping has a relatively low barrier to entry. It's important to do what you can to rise above the competition.
- Be on time. If you say you'll mow a lawn or plant a tree at 2:00 pm on Thursday, make every effort to abide by that schedule.
- Ensure you get paid. Many service providers struggle to get paid, even your local dentist. Those that sell goods get paid at the time of the sale. Service providers typically get paid after the service has already been provided.

- After customers already have the service they want, they lack the motivation to pay. Be diligent with your collection efforts.
- Ask for referrals. This is the cheapest advertising around. It doesn't require time or money. There's no better endorsement than word of mouth.
- Regularly assess your operation and seek ways to make your business even better.

Starting and running a part-time landscaping business is a viable idea. Avoid diving in headfirst without first performing the necessary research. Stand out: try to do things better than your competition and offer services that they don't. Landscaping can be a lucrative part-time business that can be expanded to full-time once a suitable customer base is in place. If you enjoy the outdoors, consider spending more time outside, making money in your landscaping business.

Make Money At The Farmer's Market

Bringing in extra money to bump up your bottom line requires putting your creativity to work. If you can open your mind wide to the possibilities that might exist in your backyard or even within your skillset, you'll be amazed at the enjoyable and unexpected ways you can make money. A pathway to more green that you may not have thought about is becoming an active participant in your local farmer's markets. This guide will help you realize the possibilities that farmer's markets can bring in terms of financial success.

What To Look For During Your Next Farmer's Market

This weekend, attend your farmer's market. Instead of just running through to pick up produce for the week, take your time examining what you see and what's going on there.

1. Observe. What are people selling? Of course, the standard fruits and vegetables are available. But what else? Maybe there are freshly-cut herbs, pretty baskets of assorted soaps, and even some small hand-crafted tools for the kitchen, like whisks or cleaning brushes. You might want to jot down the array of products available for sale.

2. Notice how vendors are displaying their products. This one is particularly important because it lends some info about what type of overhead costs you may generate to display your own wares and products.

   - Are they simply laid out on a fold-out table? Is there a decorative table cloth? How are the items for sale packaged? Are fresh herbs tied with decorative ribbon, simply spread out so people can pick up how much they want, or banded with a rubber band? Is there package wrapping to consider?

   - Look for simple, no-frills, yet attractive ways that products are displayed. Which product displays attract you? Make notes.

3. Ask yourself, "What's missing?" Now that you have a good idea of what's for sale, ponder what types of products you and others might like to purchase from the farmer's market.

4. Look for signs or pamphlets about who's in charge. Usually, there's someone you can talk to about how to become involved in the farmer's market. If there's a phone number or name of the organizers posted, write it down. It may be the local town's business association or chamber of commerce. Get down that info so you can call them later with your questions.

   - This information may also be found in the newspaper article that advertises the market.

What Could You Make To Sell At The Farmer's Market?

When you get home, take a look at things you're good at and what you do that earns kudos from others. Your next income stream might also flow from something you love to do.

1. What are you good at? Maybe you love to try different soup recipes. Why not buy up some quart-size Mason jars and sell your freshly-made and jarred soups at the farmer's market?

2. When do you get compliments from others? If people rave over your five-ingredient homemade bread, maybe it's time to start a cottage industry baking and selling loaves of it.

   - Perhaps your garden isn't all that large but you love to get fresh produce and make your own salsas and jellies. With a case or two of pint-sized wide mouthed jars, you'd be all set for next week's market. Stick with simple, natural ingredients to make things easy for you. Plus, customers love the idea of buying something that's homemade.

3. What do you love to do? Of course, you can sell fruits and vegetable from your own garden, and maybe even sell small plants, like a strawberry pot already planted with strawberry plants or an herb pot full of growing herb plants for kitchens.

   - Perhaps you think there's nothing more fun than making home-made soaps and tying them up in stacks of two or three to give to friends for birthdays and holiday gifts. You love seeing all the pretty colors and smelling all the fragrances and the idea of others using soaps you made yourself. Plus, it's easy and fun to do on a Sunday afternoon.

Inspiring Ideas For Farmer's Market Profit

Just to get your creative juices flowing, consider some of these suggestions for what you could sell at the farmer's market. Bringing in more cash can be an enjoyable process.

1. Wood-crafted items. Maybe your grandpa taught you how o make small carvings from wood. You like to do it but you ever know what to do with all the left-over creations. Selling them at the farmer's market is your answer.
2. Knitted, crocheted, or sewn items. Many people love the idea of given a hand-crafted gift to others or even treating themselves to something extravagant from time to time.
   - Consider making washcloths, dishcloths, dishtowels, potholders, hats, purses, change purses, small gift bags, water bottle carriers, grocery store totes, baby

blankets, booties, and sweaters, coasters, placemats, cell phone socks, or an item you create.

3. Baked foods. Who doesn't love a fresh-baked treat to take home with them or present as a special gift to someone? Think about small wrapped clusters of cookies or candies, baked cakes, muffins, cinnamon rolls, and the like. If your forte is making such goodies, this could be the way to go.

4. Jarred gifts. If you think you lack skills in hand-crafting hobbies and you're not much of a baker, why not consider buying some Mason jars and layering ingredients for cookies, bars, bean soups, or even cocoa mixes into the jar? If you don't already have recipes for such items, look on the internet to find them. Tailor the recipe to make it your own.

   - Print up a decorative label and instructions on how to mix up or cook the food and tie a decorative square or round of fabric over the top of the jar. Voila! You've got an interesting, enticing, and money-making product to sell.

It's All About The Presentation

After you decide on what you're willing to make to sell at farmer's markets, decide how you can attractively display and present your items to entice prospective customers to your table at the market.

1. How can you make your table pretty? Maybe all you'll need is a one-color plastic tablecloth.

2. Think of color themes. Limit color selections on your table and packaging to no more than three to avoid looking "too busy."

3. Consider how you'll package your product. If it's fresh herbs, you may not need much but some light rubber bands and big baskets to display your bunched sprigs. If you're selling homemade noodles using your grandma's recipe, how will you inexpensively package them to look appetizing?

4. Include typed-up directions for anything that requires the customer to blend, mix, or put together a food item. Don't forget to put your contact information somewhere on the product.

FINAL STEPS TO BECOME A FARMER'S MARKET VENDOR

Contact the organizers of the market by phone or in person when you go to the farmer's market. Tell them you have a product you'd like to sell.

1. Ask if you're required to have a business license to sell your products at the market. Find out where you can apply for and obtain such a license.

2. Tell the organizers about what you plan to sell and listen to any feedback they offer. Although they might not restrict you from selling your fresh herbs from your backyard herb garden, they may tell you they already have two regular vendors who sell them.

Don't be concerned if you're told, "We've never sold that before." Bringing fresh ideas can be a welcome addition for market and make you some nice cash at the same time. Consider it an adventure to boost your income by trying your hand at the local farmer's market. Wouldn't it be great to have an additional income stream to pad your bank account?

Make Money Planning Parties

If you're looking for a rewarding way to make some extra money, consider starting a party planning service. Many people are unsure of their ability to plan parties, so they look for expert assistance. A party planner helps to create memories by offering the perfect party experience. It's a very rewarding and challenging job!

If you're organized and like the idea of creating memorable events, becoming a part-time party planner might be a great option.

Like most small businesses, a party planning service is scalable to provide a full-time income after you get some experience. There are many things to consider if you're interested in this exciting way to bring in some extra money.

Assess Your Suitability

Successful party planners can come in all shapes and sizes. The most important characteristics are organization and adaptability.

1. Organizational skills are pivotal. The devil is in the details. There are so many pieces that must come together to have a successful party.
2. Expect the Unexpected. Since there are so many moving parts, you must have the ability to deal with the inevitable hiccups. It's almost guaranteed that something unexpected will happen. The ability to adapt and overcome is critical.

Get Experience
If you've never planned a significant party or event, seek out some experience. Consider volunteering if necessary. You'll learn so many things:

- How to create a party budget
- Which local vendors are good for flowers, food, decorations, and music
- Where to find the best deals on invitations and other printed supplies
- How to manage the logistics of sending invitations and receiving R.S.V.Ps
- How to decorate for an event
- How to plan and deal with catering
- Creating fun activities
- Billing
- And many other things!

Getting this experience is important to your success. There are also books available that can help to fill in the gaps.

Choose A Specialty

If you're in a large metropolitan area, you can specialize in particular types of events. The less populated the area, the more you'll have to branch into many types of parties to find enough work. Consider your interests and the likelihood of finding a sufficient number of clients.

- Birthdays: Adult or children Anniversaries
- Bar/bat Mitzvahs
- Family reunions
- Cocktail
- Dinner
- Retirement
- Graduations
- Holiday
- Engagement parties or wedding showers

Get Organized

If there was ever a profession that requires organization, party **planner is it!**

Do everything you can to stay organized and on top of things:

1. Make a list of suppliers and vendors. Include at least two vendors for each thing you might need. It will depend on the types of parties you're planning, but your list might include things like live music, florists, clowns, magicians, venues, and caterers.
2. Create or purchase the necessary forms. You're likely to need budget forms, contracts, and invoices to get started.

A checklist for all the supplies and services you'll need for a particular party will be helpful, too.

3. Create your marketing materials. As with most businesses, marketing is critical. It's quite inexpensive to create or purchase the brochures, fliers, and business cards you'll need. See what your competitors are doing and try to make yours stand out from the crowd.

4. Determine your rates. It's easy to choose your rates. Call around and ask for some quotes for various types of parties to price your services appropriately.

Create A Web Presence

There is no less expensive way to reach so many people. If creating your own website is simply not your style, many highly skilled and inexpensive website builders advertise online. Also, the free Wordpress software at wordpress.org provides an easy way to put up an effective website very quickly, even without tech skills.

1. Make use of social media. Every presence you create on the web helps. Get a Facebook and Twitter account and keep them updated about events and specials.

2. Post local ads. There are several places to post classified ads online for free. One of the most popular is craigslist.org. Create a regular schedule to renew your ads.

3. Write articles related to parties and party planning. Ask if you can make a guest post on the websites of your vendors and other party planning contacts. Be sure to include a link back to your website.

- Invite your vendors to write a guest post about their specialty on your **website.**

Marketing Plan

Usually, the most challenging part of starting a new business is finding your first couple of clients. After your business has some momentum, you'll be able to rely more heavily on referrals.

1. Tell everyone you know. You know a lot of people. If you let everyone know about your new venture and ask them to tell everyone they know, you're likely to find at least one client.
2. Have brochures available. Send extra brochures to your vendors. They can refer their clients to you.
3. Consider a press release. You can post press releases online at many sites. Let your local media know of your new business in town. Put an original spin on your business and you could attract the local media to conduct an interview about your business – the best kind of free publicity!
4. Hang fliers in appropriate locations. Again, this will be dependent on the types of clients you're seeking. Find places where your targeted clients can be found on a regular basis.

It's critical to test how well your marketing is working. Whenever a potential client calls, ask how they found you. Always ask for referrals. Consider offering a bonus for every new client that someone brings to you.

Continuously Improve Your Process

Your first few parties are likely to have a few challenges, but that's to be expected! Before long, you'll be a pro and able to demand the best fees.

After a party, ask yourself what you could have done better:

- Did you handle your client well?
- Was your organization adequate?
- How was the food?
- Did you have challenges with collecting your fee?
- Did you get any referrals?

View each experience as an opportunity to learn. If you continue to work on bettering your skills and streamlining your processes, it's nearly impossible to not become successful! Becoming a party planner is similar to starting many other types of small businesses. It can be challenging to get started. Your marketing and the quality of service you provide will make all the difference. Get all the experience you can and learn something from every event. Planning parties can be a satisfying and lucrative way to boost your income.

Unique Ways to Make Money on a College Campus

Most college students have one thing in common: a lack of money. While you might think your only options are to work fast food, retail, or in the college bookstore, you're missing out on other huge opportunities. College is a unique place with a unique population. With some creativity and a little work, you can find a way to make some real money quickly and easily.

Let's look at a few possibilities:

1. Do laundry for others. Offer to do laundry for others. Either use their detergent or charge enough to make it worthwhile to use your own. Aside from throwing the clothes in the washer and dryer, there's really no work or time involved. Study while you wait.

2. Clean. Many dorm rooms are filthy; everyone is used to mom cleaning up after them. For a small fee, you could sweep and pick up. This can be a lucrative service for a few minutes of work. Don't forget to talk to the fraternities and sororities. They need all the help they can get.

3. Tutor. Tutoring can be a great way to pay the bills. Everyone has a subject in which he excels. Find someone that needs your expertise and charge him for it.

4. Be a designated driver. Offer to give inebriated students a ride home from parties and bars. Charging three people $5-10 apiece comes out to a nice chunk of change for 20 minutes of work. You're also providing a valuable service and potentially saving lives.

5. Write a blog about your school. If you can write well, you might be able to create a blog that becomes popular on campus. All you have to do is monetize it by selling products on it or charging for advertising and you can potentially make money in your sleep.

6. Recycle.College students go through a lot of cans and bottles. If you can figure out a clever way to collect them, all you have to do is drive them to the recycling center and pick up your check.

7. Be a personal trainer.Lots of students want to stay or get into shape, but not all know how to use the equipment at the student recreation center. You could be a personal trainer and make some easy money.

8. Deliver newspapers.Anewspaper route can be pretty good money for the amount of time it takes. If you're a morning person, this might be a great job and it fits in well with school.

9. Be a model.College art programs are always looking for models, and in most cases, you can keep your clothes on. All you have to do is sit still for an extended period of time. ,

10.   Sell your notes.If you take excellent notes, considering starting a little business where you sell your notes to your fellow students. You might even consider sitting in on some of the larger classes, even if you're not enrolled. A larger classmeans more potential customers.

11.   Help students move. Students are always struggling to move to school or back home. You could offer to help carry stuff either to or from the moving truck. It can pay well and you'll get some exercise, too.

These are just a few of the many possibilities available to you. The key to being a successful entrepreneur is to notice what people need and then provide it to them in a way that makes financial sense for both of you. A college campus has a lot of unique opportunities; take advantage of them.

Setting Up Your Own Tutoring Business

Tutoring can be a great part-time business if you're looking to really boost your income. Starting your own tutoring business can be a simple endeavor and the start-up costs can be minimal. It's a great business if you want to start small, but still have the option of expanding your operation over time. Though it's a relatively simple business, you're likely to be more successful if you take the time to do a little research and put your plans down on paper.

These 7 steps will serve you well as you start to build your tutoring business:

1. Decide which subjects you want to teach. There are several factors that will help you choose subjects to tutor that fit with your skill set.
   - Is there enough demand? You might be a great artist, but the demand for art tutors is practically non-existent, so you're not likely to get many clients if this is your area of choice.
   - It's important to find subjects with enough demand for tutoring to sustain your business. Subjects like math and English seem to have a never-ending supply of students requiring assistance.

- Consider whether or not you have the necessary knowledge. If you struggle with basic math yourself, it's unlikely you'll be a suitable calculus tutor.

2. What age group will you tutor? Consider which age groups will be best served by your experience, knowledge, and temperament. Younger children and teenagers both present their own unique challenges.
3. Decide on the geographical area you'll serve. You'll likely want to provide tutoring services close to your home, but it might be much more lucrative if you're willing to drive to other parts of town.
    - If your intention is to work out of your home or to meet students at a single location, such as the public library, consider how far the average student is willing to travel.
    - Thirty minutes tends to be about the maximum most will drive.
    - Pull out a map and draw a rough radius around the equivalent to a 30-minute drive in order to zero in on your tutoring area.
    - If you're willing to drive to your students, then consider how long of a trip you're willing to take. Remember to take the time and cost of your transportation into account. This will probably have a big impact on the fees you charge.

4. Determine your pricing structure. Pricing is a very important decision that will require a moderate amount of market research.

- Tutoring rates vary dramatically depending on the subject, student, and your geographic location. Your level of expertise can also play a huge part. Some tutors might charge as low as $10 per hour, but in larger cities, $200 per hour isn't unheard of.

- After determining your target age group, subject, and geographic area, finding a competitive tutoring rate is quite simple.

- Look at the prices being charged by comparable tutors. Take a look at their advertisements or website. You can even call and inquire about prices. You'll quickly get a good idea of the average rate other tutors are charging.

- Remember that your pricing accomplishes two goals. Pricing sends a message about the quality and value of your services, as well as having a significant effect on the amount of money you'll be able to earn.

- If you charge a low rate, you'll probably have plenty of students. But you're also likely to earn less money in the long run. This may also cause you to have insufficient funds to do any meaningful advertising.

- A low price may lead parents to think that your services are of lower quality.

- Pricing too high can leave you short of clients. A high price is fine, if you can show that your services deserve a premium price. You might have to show a track record of success first!

- In most cases, the best rate will be somewhere near the average fee being charged for tutoring. The market is currently supporting this price-point and your students are likely to be somewhat insensitive to price. This can allow you to raise your rates after proving your worth.

5. Market and promote your business. Marketing might be the most important factor in determining your initial success with your tutoring business. At first, others won't know who you are. It's up to you to figure out how to overcome that obstacle.

   - Consider how your students, or more likely their parents, search for a tutor. They are likely to either approach the student's teacher or guidance counselor for a recommendation or look online.

   - Contact the schools in your area and let them know about your tutoring services. You can easily find the names of the appropriate educators to contact on the school's website.

   - A handwritten note with a simple flyer or brochure can be a quick and simple way to reach potential customers.

   - Think about other places students and their parents spend time. It might be the local library, community center, sporting venues, or even the local grocery store. Hang flyers in those locations with your contact information.

- Tell everyone you know about your tutoring business. The time you spend on Facebook might finally pay off. Let the world know about what you're offering.
- Create a website. With Wordpress, it's very easy for ayone to create a great looking site. For a domain name, see if there's one available that matches the term someone would likely search for. For example, www.miamimathtutor.com would be a great domain name if you lived in that area.
- Use Craigslist. Many people turn to Craigslist, whether they're looking for a new stove, a place to live, or a tutor.
- Use the numerous online directories to list your website and services.
- Eventually, you'll be able to rely on word-of-mouth to secure additional clients.

6. Get organized. You'll want to keep all your relevant records and paperwork organized. This includes your session notes and progress reports.

- For your own sake, have a consistent billing system. It's up to you whether you want the student to pay before or after the session. But it's helpful to pick one or the other and be consistent.
- Sending a bill will result in you having to spend a lot of ime on collection efforts. Another useful method is to be paid ahead for the next 5-10 tutoring sessions.

- Keep track of your revenue and expenses. You'll have to pay taxes, and staying up to date is much easier than rying to recreate the past from memory. Keep all your receipts along with accurate records. This would include any gas expenses, your mileage, and any materials you purchase.

7. Enhance your business. As you're operating your tutoring service, ask yourself how you can make your business better and more profitable. There are likely to be challenges along the way, whether it's scheduling, difficult parents, or the students themselves. Find solutions that limit future challenges.

    - Set aside a few minutes each week and brainstorm ways you can take your business to the next level. You'll be surprised by how many great ideas you can come up with if you reflect on your business on a regular basis.

A tutoring business can be a great way to supplement your income. With enough clients, you might even be able to turn your tutoring business into a full-time income! There are many people desperately seeking tutoring services. Most adults that are still struggling can trace the source back to challenges in high school or college. Successfully navigating the educational system can have a profound effect on later success in life. Helping others successfully get through school can make you incredibly valuable. Few people have the opportunity to influence someone's life as much as a teacher or tutor! Get your business started, aggressively market your services, and collect the monetary rewards. It's a great way to boost your income while also helping others.

Introduction To FOREX Trading

Forex trading is all the rage, for good reason: it is possible for the average person to make a tremendous amount of money. This is largely because Forex trading offers an incredible amount of leverage, as much as 400:1. Let's take a look at Forex trading for the complete beginner and see if this is a viable wealth vehicle for you.

What is Forex?
Forex (FOReign EXchange) is the foreign currency market. It is actually the largest financial market in the world. The turnover is over $2.5 trillion per day, that's more than 100x the Nasdaq turnover rate! So with Forex trading, you're not investing in companies, like with the stock market. Instead, you're purchasing another country's currency in the anticipation that it will increase in value relative to another.

The Advantages of Forex Trading
There are many advantages to investing in the Foreign Exchange, including:
1. High Liquidity. You're simply trading cash for cash at the current exchange rate. Cash is about as liquid as an investment can be.

2. Easy Access. The foreign exchange market is open 24 hours a day, 7 days a week. This can be an incredible advantage. In the stock market, if something happens after the close of the trading, you can't act upon it until the next trading day. By then the market will adjust for the news.

   - The foreign exchange market is always open, and if you're quick enough, you can beat any market adjustments you see coming with investments that will benefit you.

3. Two-Way Market.Currencies are always traded in pairs. You always sell one currency to buy the other.

   - For example, you may sell US dollars to purchase Euros. This is the position you would take if you believed the value of the euro will rise against the value of the US dollar (this is considered to be "selling short").

   - If you believed the value of Euros will fall relative to the US dollar, you would sell Euros and buy dollars ("selling long").

   - So there is the opportunity to make money from both the rise and fall of a currency. In the first case, if the Euro rises or the dollar falls, you would make money.

4. Leverage. Forex accounts have anywhere from 50:1 to 400:1 leverage. This means you could control $100,000 with as little as $250. Wow!

Forex Definitions

Market Order: This is simply the execution of your decision to purchase a currency. You have made an order to purchase a currency at the current exchange rates.

Entry Order: While a market order is made at the current exchange rate, an entry order is only executed if the exchange rate reaches a value that you have specified.

Stop-Loss Order: This is a mechanism to limit your losses (or gains). You can specify that your position will be liquidated once your losses (or gains) have reached a certain threshold. For example, you could specify that you want to sell once you've lost $1,500.

Bid: This is the price at which you can buy.

Ask: This is the price at which you can sell.

Pip: This is the last decimal of the exchange rate. This is true for all currencies, except the Yen, which is the second to last decimal.

Margin: This is the minimum amount you need to purchase, as trades come in sets called lots. For example, the margin of one lot of a currency pair might be $200. This is the amount of money you are actually risking.

Lot: A lot is 100,000 units of the first currency. So a USD/GBP lot would be worth $100,000. The reverse pairing would be worth 100,000 GPB.

Currency Pairs and Trading Principles

Whenever you look at the quotes on the Forex market, you will see the items listed as pairs, such as USD/EUR. This would indicate the exchange rate for selling US dollars and buying Euros. So the USD/GBP exchange rate might be 0.6409, meaning that for every US dollar you would get 0.6409 British pounds. The opposite pairing would be 1.5603 .The first currency quoted is referred to as the 'base currency'; the second currency is considered to be the 'quote currency'. You may also hear this referred to as the 'foreign' or 'counter' currency.

Pips and Spreads

A pip is the smallest amount by which the price quote can change. If the USD/GPB bid is quoted at 0.6409 and it changes to 0.6411, the price is said to have moved up '2 pips'.

Just as with the stock market, there is a spread; the spread is where the brokers make their money. That is why the bid (the price you can buy at) and the ask (the price you can sell at) are never the same. So, if the USD/GPB price is 0.6409, the bid price might be 0.6411, and the ask price might be 0.6407. The broker would keep the 0.02, whether you buy or sell.

Note that a 2 or 3-pip spread is very common on the major currencies.

Trading Accounts

Just as you need a brokerage account to trade stocks, you will need a brokerage account to trade in currencies. There is no shortage of Forex brokerage houses available.

There are 3 basic types of accounts for those that wish to trade without professional guidance:

1. Standard Account. This account allows you to trade in full-size lots – 100,000 units. You will typically need $10,000 or more in your account to be able to open this type of account, though it is frequently recommended that the trader have at least $100,000. Standard accounts are only recommended for experienced traders.
2. Mini Account. The trade sizes are 1/10 of a standard lot or 10,000 units. These are recommended for accounts of $10,000 – $100,000.
3. Micro Account. Micro accounts are 1/100 of a standard account, or 1,000 units. These are recommended for accounts of $1,000 – $10,000.

The real difference in these accounts is the amount of leverage the trader has. In the standard accounts, the leverage is either 50:1 or 100:1. In the mini/micro accounts, the leverage is frequently 200:1 or even 400:1. This means that to purchase 1 lot with USD as the base currency (100,000 units) in a standard account would be $2,000. With a micro account, it could be $500. While leverage is great, it can also destroy your account quickly. The margin calls come much more quickly at higher leverage, since your account loses money much more quickly.

While the profits are much greater, the risk is much greater as well.

Practice Accounts

Many brokerages provide practice accounts that allow you to make trades without actually risking any money or making any. It's a great way to learn Forex trading, but does have one potential downfall. When you're trading with a practice account, it's easy to develop a tendency to take a lot more risk than you would if you were using real money. This can be especially bad if you do extremely well with your practice account, as you might then be too bold when you move on to a real account. Emotion also comes into play much less with practice accounts; after all, you're not really risking anything. Even so, it's still wise to use a practice account for a while until you understand the basics well enough before risking any real money. It will do you the most good if you take the account seriously as if it is real money and use it to work on real-life strategies as you learn the ins and outs of Forex trading. Forex trading offers a lot of opportunities, even to those with relatively small amounts of money. Real success comes from discipline and understanding the factors that can make currency values rise and fall. Now that you have a basic understanding of how Forex trading works, you can develop your skills in this area by researching currency behavior and utilizing a practice account.

It will take some time and effort to become comfortable in your skills, but once you learn some profitable techniques, the world of currency exchange can be your playground.

Make A Second Income
With A Pickup Truck

If you're looking for a flexible, second income, the lowly pickup truck might be the solution. Just about everyone needs a pickup truck at one time or another, but there are many people that don't own one. It's incredibly common to hear someone lament, "I wish I could use a pickup truck for 2 hours." When there is a need to be filled, a moneymaking opportunity exists!

Finding The Right Truck

You don't own one yourself? There's an endless supply of pickup trucks for sale for relatively little money. It might be possible to borrow a truck from a friend, neighbor, or family member until you can afford your own. Craigslist is a good place to start looking. A suitable pickup can be found for under $1,000.

Look for a truck with the following features:

1. A full-size bed: A truck with an 8-foot bed will naturally hold a greater variety of things than a smaller truck with a 6-foot bed. For example, many couches are longer than 6 feet in length. Many building supplies are 8-feet in length.
   - A full-size bed will permit you to take on more jobs.
2. It should be in rough enough shape that you won't mind scratching it up. If you have a brand new truck, be warned. Carrying things in the bed on a regular basis will create a

lot of wear and tear over time. There are so many older trucks available for relatively little money, there's no reason to ruin your newer truck.

3. It should be reliable. You don't want a truck that requires a lot of repairs, unless you're getting a good enough deal at a super price. A second income is more feasible if the potential pitfalls are kept to a minimum.

   - If necessary, find a qualified mechanic to check it over for you before making your purchase.

Trucks are plentiful and inexpensive. A little browsing will result in a suitable truck at a great price.

Types Of Work

You have a truck, but what are you going to do with it? There are more opportunities to make money with a pickup than you might think. Consider all the times you've used a truck or wished you had access to one.

There are many things that can be done to earn extra money with a pickup truck:

1. Help move furniture and appliances. While stores have delivery available for these items, many people prefer to purchase used items from private owners. The challenge lies in getting those larger items back home. This is where you come in. This is the most obvious type of work, but there are many other ways to earn extra money.

   - Most established moving companies charge at least $200 to move an appliance a few miles. You could easily charge $50 for an hour of your time.

- It might be worthwhile to invest in an inexpensive dolly and have a helping hand available for those heavier items. You might consider only providing transportation and leave the lifting and moving to the other parties.

2. Delivering firewood, sand, gravel, or any other similar material. Many sellers of these items charge two rates: one that includes delivery, and one that doesn't. It's possible to undercut the material provider and still make some worthwhile money in the process.
   - When moving material that can be bounced or blown out of the truck bed, like sand or gravel, be sure to use a tarp to keep your cargo where it belongs.

3. Delivering yard sale / garage sale items. Sellers of bigger items at these types of sales often take a hit on the selling price. There are many folks that would love to purchase a recliner or clothes dryer that simply don't have a way to get those items back home.
   - Find these sales in the classifieds and contact the owners about providing a moving service. You could charge a small flat rate plus mileage.
   - Drive around the sales in your area and pass out fliers advertising your service.

4. Haul away trash, junk, and other unwanted items. Many people have items they'd like to throw away, but the trash collectors refuse to take. These are often bigger items or building materials. Most local dumps charge a minimal amount for a pick-up truckload.

- It's not uncommon to find people that want a garage, attic, basement, or even an entire house cleaned out. In many cases, these are people that inherited a home or purchased one that was foreclosed on.
- This type of work not only yields a fee for your removal services, but the items can also be sold.
- Remember that many items can be recycled. This can be especially lucrative in the case of scrap metals.

Those are just a few ideas. Spend some time brainstorming a few of your own. Think about what services people in your area might need. That's usually the best place to start.

Finding Clients
A simple plan:
1. Advertise: In many cases, you'll be able to find plenty of work just by posting an ad online advertising your services. The key is to do it daily. You might also consider posting fliers in places that might get appropriate foot traffic. Laundromats and libraries might be good starting points.
   - A simple one-page website can also be a good idea and provides credibility.
2. Look for service requests. The classifieds frequently have requests for the very services you're providing. Spend a few minutes each day taking a look.
3. Know your pricing. Call around to a few others who provide similar service. Ask for quotes to perform the very services you plan to offer. Price your services accordingly.

- Also, ask yourself what you can do to separate yourself from the pack.

The lowly pickup truck is a great tool for making good money in your spare time. Not only are the hours and pay great, but you can also deduct your mileage on your taxes. The US rate for 2014 is now up to $0.56 per mile! Used pickup trucks are plentiful and inexpensive. With a little time and effort, you can create a worthwhile second income with your truck.

Driving With Uber And Lyft

People hailing taxis from the curb are a common sight in any big city around the world. However, such a sight could soon be a thing of the past, thanks to apps like Uber and Lyft. These apps hire drivers as independent contractors and connect users in need of a ride with the nearest available driver.

Uber has been around since 2009 and is already available in 69 countries around the world and in 10,000 cities. Its main competitor, Lyft, has been around since 2012 and is available in 644 cities around the U.S. & 12 cities in Canada as of 2021

These services have been receiving a lot of attention from the media lately and their success shows no signs of letting off. Uber announced it would launch a food delivery service based on the same principle in 2015 called Uber eats. When you become a driver for Uber or Lyft, it's possible to earn more than what a taxi driver makes. Plus, it's an ideal way to supplement your main source of income since you can work flexible hours.

How Does It Work?

Uber and Lyft are based on a very simple principle. Users input their location and their desired destination. They are matched with a driver who is in the area, and the driver is prompted to accept the ride. Once the driver accepts, the passenger receives information about the estimated pick up time and the car's license plate. Drivers and passengers can communicate through the app in case the passenger has to cancel or more information is needed to find the pickup location. Lyft and Uber offer different categories of vehicles to choose from. Most users choose the basic service offered, namely riding in an economy vehicle. Payments are processed through the apps. Lyft users can tip their driver and toll fees are automatically added to what the passenger pays. Passengers also rate their driver through the app once they have been dropped off.

What Do You Need To Get Started?

There are a few requirements you have to meet in order to become an independent contractor for these companies. First, ensure that Uber or Lyft is available in your area by checking their websites.

If one of these companies operates in your area, see if you can meet these requirements:

1. A reliable vehicle. Uber lets you sign up as long as your vehicle is in good working order. Lyft requires that you own

a 2000 to 2005 model car or newer, depending on your city.

2. Age and background. You have to be 21 or older and pass a background check for both services. Lyft also performs a check through the DMV to ensure you have a good driving record.

3. Driver's license. You need a valid driver's license to become an independent contractor for either service.
   - Uber also requires you to have a commercial driver license. Getting one of these licenses costs between $100 and $300 or more depending on where you live.
   - Lyft only requires you to have a regular license, but it is likely a commercial license will be required in the near future.

4. Personal auto insurance. You don't need additional coverage, since these companies will provide you with additional coverage for what your policy doesn't cover.

5. Good driving and people skills. The passengers you pick up will rate you through the app. Receiving good ratings from your passengers is important, since passengers who give you under three stars will not be matched with you again. Low ratings decrease the number of rides you could potentially get.

6. Smartphone. You also need a Smartphone so that you can access these apps to check the rides that have been assigned to you.

How Much Can You Make?

The average hourly income for an Uber driver is just under $20. However, this rate varies a lot by location and hours worked. Uber charges passengers a base fare for each ride. The additional fees are calculated based on a per-mile or a per minute rate, depending on the city. There are additional fees, referred to as "surge pricing," when there is a high demand for a vehicle, like during rush hour.

Earnings vary a lot from one city to another. For instance, the average hourly rate for a New York City Uber driver is $30, while Chicago drivers make around $16 an hour. The amount of time you're willing to commit to working for Uber will also influence your hourly rate, since drivers who work more hours tend to earn a higher hourly rate. It is possible to earn between $25 and $35 per hour with Lyft. Hourly rates vary from one city to another because Lyft uses different methods to charge passengers. In cities like Orlando, Madison, Ann Arbor, or Austin, passengers are shown a suggested amount. They can choose what they want to pay, which means you'll earn more if you provide your passengers with a great experience. If you drive for Lyft in New York City, Chicago, Atlanta, or Denver, your passengers will have to pay a base fare and additional fees, based on time or distance. Just like Uber, Lyft charges more when there is a high demand for cars. Passengers have the option of tipping their driver on top of the regular fare.

How To Maximize Your Earnings

Driving for Uber or Lyft can turn into a full-time gig if you take the job seriously and look for ways to get the most out of the time you spend driving.

This is how you can earn more with these services:

1. Compare different shifts. Since you are an independent contractor, you get to choose when you work. Take advantage of this and try driving during different shifts. Keep track of how much downtime there is between rides, how much time it takes you on average to go pick up a passenger, and how much they tip.
   - Focus on the shifts where you tend to earn more. You should be able to earn more by driving during weekend nights or rush hour due to the additional fees. This varies from one city to another, so you'll have to figure out which shifts are the most profitable in your area.
2. Choose profitable areas. Location has a lot to do with what you can earn since these apps are especially popular with young professionals and college students. You should be able to earn more by primarily working in neighborhoods where the night life attracts young people.
3. Provide a great experience for your passengers. The quality of the service you offer influences what you earn, especially if you drive for Lyft. Always be polite and professional towards your passengers and do your best to be on time.

4. Try driving for both services at the same time. Indicate that you are available on Uber and on Lyft to decrease down time between rides.

Becoming an independent driver for Uber or Lyft is a great way to supplement your income. The hours are flexible and you can easily get started as long as you have a reliable vehicle. You can even turn this into a full-time gig if you're located in a city where there's a high demand for these services. The downside is that these services are not available in every city yet. If Uber and Lyft are not available where you live, consider commuting to the nearest large city or wait for these apps to launch in your area.

Limo Service

A limo service can be a great way to boost your income. It's a business that's relatively inexpensive to start, but can provide excellent income, even on a part-time basis. It can also be expanded to full-time. You can also manage your limo service with your part-time efforts, yet provide full-time service by hiring others to do the driving. This isn't the easiest business to start, however. There are a few more barriers to entry than most part-time income boosters, but these barriers are all manageable.

What Do You Need To Get Started?
1. Limousine. While a brand new limo can be quite expensive, most companies that produce limousines have lease programs. Try to get a feel for the type of limo that's

popular in your area. That way you'll avoid leasing a more expensive vehicle than you really need.

- Many used limousines are surprisingly inexpensive. Be sure to have a mechanic inspect any vehicle you're considering purchasing. Also, ensure that the style isn't out of date for your expected clients.

2. Insurance. Your business will require auto insurance, including collision if you lease or get a loan to purchase your limousine. It would also be wise to get liability insurance to protect your personal and business assets from any lawsuits or injuries.

3. Create your business entity. While it is certainly possible to own a limousine service as a sole proprietorship, your personal assets will be at risk. Since you'll be providing a service that involves driving customers, there's a potential risk for someone to get hurt.

- A limited liability corporation probably makes the most sense, but it would be wise to consult an attorney for the best option for your situation.

4. Contract. When your company is hired to provide services, a contract will be necessary. The contract will stipulate the period of time the service is to be provided. It will also cover the fee, expected mileage, and what happens if service must be provided beyond the agreed upon timeframe. The limits of your services and liabilities will also be covered.

5. GPS and Maps. It's important to know where you're going, the shortest route, and to be able to quickly find alternate routes should construction or an accident create a delay.

6. Website. Nearly every business would be well served to have a website. More people use the Internet than use the phone book. Look at the websites other limo services are using and create something appropriate or hire someone to make your website for you. This should only be a small expense.

7. Driver. If you already have another job, you can still drive around your work schedule. In fact, you might choose to be the only driver and run your limo business part-time. Regardless of who is driving, the driver is expected to be clean, neat, prompt, courteous, and professional.

   - In most states, the driver will need a special driver's license to legally drive paying customers. In most cases, this simply involves a written test and a small fee.

It does require a few things to get started, but that also helps to limit the amount of competition. Avoid feeling overwhelmed and just tackle each item one at a time.

Marketing

The lifeblood of any small business is marketing. It's vital to have an aggressive marketing campaign that fits your budget. Before doing anything else, it would be worthwhile to develop a marketing plan.

1. **Set a budget**. Determining your budget helps to determine the other aspects of your marketing plan. How much can you afford to spend to get your business off the ground? See where other limo services are spending their marketing dollars.

2. **Consider your schedule**. Is your business going to run seven days a week? Just the weekends? Just evenings? Determining your schedule will help to address the next point.

3. **Consider your clientele**. If you're only going to run your limo service on the weekends, your customers are more likely to be weddings, proms, and groups going out for the evening.

   - During the daytime, Monday-Friday, business clients would likely be your largest source of work.
   - It only makes sense to gear your marketing toward your clients. This will not only determine the type of marketing, but also the mood of your marketing.
   - Those going out for a Saturday night on the town are probably looking for a fun service that includes a limo with a TV, a great sound system, and a mini-bar. Business clients will be looking for a more refined, business-type atmosphere. Emphasize the aspects of your service that your clients will want.

4. **Determine where and how you'll market your business**. There are numerous marketing options, from free to very expensive.

- The free (or nearly free options) include your website, Facebook, Twitter, Craigslist, and other social media or classified services. These can be powerful tools to get your business out in front of potential clients. They're also excellent ways to feed information and news to potential and existing clients.
- More expensive options are also available. Radio and televisions are viable options, but it might be best to wait until some money is coming in before spending thousands of dollars on these marketing tools.
- Around prom season, consider advertising at local high schools and where high school students congregate. Facebook and Instagram are perfect places for reaching this segment of the market.
- To attract business clients, consider advertising directly to local businesses that regularly deal with out of town clients. Use brochures as a marketing tool. Professional brochures can be ordered very inexpensively online.

5. **Review your result**s. One of the critical keys to effective marketing is to analyze your results. Make it a habit to ask your clients how they found your service. If certain marketing efforts aren't producing results, think about modifying that part of your marketing or drop it altogether. Beef up your efforts that are producing results.

Give your marketing plan the effort it deserves. A poorly run limo service with great marketing can probably survive. A well run service with horrible marketing is certain to fail.

A Few Final Tips

1. Focus on repeat business. It's easier to be successful if you don't have to keep finding new clients. Keep an up-to-date client list and stay in touch!
2. Focus on your client's experience. Be on time. Be professional. Your driver(s) should act the part.
3. Ask your clients for suggestions to improve your service. Most people are too polite or bashful to give constructive criticism, but a few will oblige. Take the information you receive to heart.
4. Fully research your competition. Call around to the other local limo services and see what others are charging. Set your rates to be competitive. Consider actually hiring one of more of your competitors to see how their services are run. Ask yourself what you can do better.

Starting a limo service is something nearly anyone can do. It can be a fun and interesting way to earn some extra money. It's also a business that can be expanded to any size. There are national limo companies. There's no reason yours can't be one, too!

Renting Out Your Car

In the wake of the great recession, a new industry has popped up, an industry known as peer-to-peer sharing. What is peer-to-peer sharing? If a person needs something, they can rent it from someone who already has it rather than going out and buying the item themselves. For example, people are renting out things like power tools, bicycles, storage space, and some are even renting out their backyards as campsites. Renting out your car is becoming especially lucrative. Discover how you can make extra money in the peer-to-peer sharing industry by renting out your car.

Getting Started

To do something like this completely on your own would be quite difficult. You would have all of the challenges of starting a new business, such as filing a business name, getting the necessary licensing in your area, setting up payment processing, getting the proper insurance, and more. The good news is that you don't have to do any of those things because there are a few companies that have already taken care of all of that. These companies put those who need to rent a car together with those who would like to rent out their vehicle. So you can make extra money without having to actually start a new business.

These popular websites enable you to offer your car for rent:

- RelayRides.com
- GetAround.com
- JustShareIt.com

Use this process to get started:

1. Create an account at one or more of these car-sharing websites. After you create your account, put in your car's details: the make, model, and year of the car along with its mileage.
   - Upload a few photos of your vehicle.
   - Update your calendar to let potential renters know when your vehicle will be available.
2. After you've set everything up, you'll start receiving requests. The requests will be submitted to the website and the website will in turn pass the request along to you.
   - You'll also have the option to contact the renter if you have any questions.
3. Meet the renter. When they come to pick up the keys, you can check their license and make a note about the current mileage and amount of fuel in the vehicle.
4. When your car is returned, inspect it to ensure everything is in good condition.
   - You can log onto the website and rate the renter so that other vehicle owners can have information about the people who may rent their vehicles.

Then, your vehicle is ready to be rented to the next person.

What Are The Risks?

You may have some concerns about renting your car to a total stranger. What if the person who rents your car gets into an accident? What if they smoke and the car smells like an ashtray? What if they leave food wrappers, greasy fingerprints, and potato chip crumbs all over the vehicle?

Luckily, by going through one of the websites listed above, you are protected:

1. They prescreen the renters. They must meet the eligibility criteria before they are allowed to rent vehicles.
   - All drivers must possess a current, valid driver's license.
   - They must be at least 21 years of age.
   - They must also have a driving history that doesn't show any major violations and no more than two minor violations in the last three years or one minor violation in the last year.
2. These websites carry a $1 million liability insurance policy. You are protected against any claims from third parties for injuries or property damage. Any physical damage to your car up to the cash value of your vehicle is also covered.
   - The insurance also includes comprehensive coverage that protects your vehicle from fire, theft, and vandalism.
   - If someone leaves food and trash all over your car or stinks it up with cigarette smoke or pet hair, contact the company within 24 hours of receiving your vehicle

back and the renter will be charged a fee to have your car cleaned and detailed.

How Much Money Can You Make?

The amount of money you can make by renting your vehicle out through these websites varies according to a number of different factors.

Consider these points:

1. You get to set the rates. You can set them by the hour, day, or week. But if you want your vehicle to be rented, your rates will have to be in line with those of similar vehicles.
   - The amount you can expect to receive will depend on the age, make, and model of your vehicle. For example, a 2007 Toyota Tercel won't command as much money as a 2014 Tesla Roadster.
   - Generally speaking, you may be able to get anywhere from $10 to $50 per hour for your vehicle, depending on these factors.
2. Rent out your car as often as you can. Your income will also depend on how often you make your vehicle available to rent.
3. Your portion of the rental income varies with the website. The amount of money you make will also depend on which website you sign up with.
   - For example, GetAround.com takes a 40% commission to cover their costs and provide them with a profit, leaving you 60% of the gross revenue.

- RelayRides.com keeps just 25% and gives you75% of the rental price.

Scaling Things Up

If you wanted to kick things up a notch and earn even more money, there are a couple of ways to do it:

1. Make your car available more often. You may have to ride a bike or invest in some other mode of transportation so that you can get around when your personal vehicle is rented out.

2. Acquire additional vehicles to make available for rent. One RelayRides.com user expects to make about $40,000 per year because he has three vehicles that he rents out.

It may seem a little odd to hand the keys of your car to a total stranger. But with the prescreening that these companies do and the $1 million insurance policy protecting you and your vehicle, there's not much to worry about. This is a pretty easy way to put some extra money in your pocket. Even if you just make an extra $400 or $500 per month, you'll make that money without doing very much work because the peer-to-peer rental companies take care of most of the heavy lifting for you. So if you have a vehicle sitting in your driveway, you might want to consider putting it to work, earning you some extra cash.

Local Courier Service

Starting your own local courier service can be a good way to boost your income. If you already have a vehicle or bicycle, then the startup costs are small. A local courier service can bring you an estimated $17,000 to $30,000 a year. Local businesses can hire you to transport or pick up and deliver documents, packages, and other items. This type of business allows you to offer customers flexible hours and delivery options based on your own schedule.

Supplies

A successful local courier service requires several essential items. You may be able to find used items to save money as you build your courier business. In addition, you may be able to borrow a car or bike from a friend or family member. Your creativity will benefit you in collecting the things you need.

Consider these supplies as you build your business:

1. Car or bike. You'll need a reliable vehicle or bicycle to pick up and deliver packages from customers and businesses.
2. Comfortable shoes. Although you'll be using your car or bike for most of your transportation needs, you'll still need good shoes that offer comfort and support. Couriers often have to walk long distances to deliver packages inside buildings.
3. Smartphone. You'll need a reliable phone, so businesses and customers can reach you. It may be a good idea to

invest in a Smartphone because you'll be on the road and away from landlines.

4. Planner. Electronic or paper planners can help you stay on top of your schedule. You'll know immediately where you can fit any new requests into your schedule.

5. Mileage tracker. You can deduct your mileage as a business expense, so you want to keep careful track of it.

6. GPS device. You may want to get GPS apps for your phone or a separate GPS device. Unless you know every inch of your city, the GPS will come in especially handy.

7. Software for couriers. There are specific software programs designed for couriers to help keep track of your business.

8. Handset and earpiece for your phone. You don't want to become a distracted driver, but you still want to answer important calls from your clients. A handset and earpiece can help you achieve this.

9. Insurance. Car insurance is a must if you're using your car. Other types of insurance, such as liability insurance, will likely also be required. Check the requirements in your locale.

10. Decals and signs for your bike or car. You can attach decals or signs that show your business information.

11. Business cards. They're an essential part of the courier service business.

12. Reliable pens. You'll need to carry pens for package recipients to sign delivery papers.

13. Messenger bag. Acquire a sturdy bag to hold envelopes and other small items.

14.   Cart. If you decide to transport heavier boxes and other items, you'll also need a strong cart to help you carry them.

Your initial supply list doesn't have to be long, but you do need several essential items. Your courier business can continue to expand over time, so you can purchase additional supplies later.

Getting Started

A local courier service can be a profitable and fun business. You'll enjoy your best results if you follow some important steps right from the beginning.

Consider these steps to get started:

1. Check on legal matters. Before you spend your time building a local courier service, ensure that your area allows for this type of business.
   - You may be required to obtain a business license and specific insurance.
   - You also need car insurance for the vehicle you'll use for business purposes. Your location may require commercial insurance, so check with your agent and company.You may also need to get a federal tax identification number. An accountant or tax lawyer can help you set up your business with a format that will work best for you while complying with all the local requirements.

2. Check out the competition. Spend some time visiting with other local couriers to find out what courier services and rates work well for your area. It can be enlightening to see how they handle the day-to-day operations of a courier service.

3. Find a creative name. Whether you use your imagination or a business name generator online, you'll need a unique name for your local courier service. Keep copyright and trademark laws in mind, so you don't pick a name that infringes on someone else.

4. Figure out your transportation and schedule. If you share a car with family, ensure your schedule works with the rest of your family's vehicle needs.
   - It's crucial to figure out your transportation and schedule before you start advertising because it affects the type of businesses you attract.

5. Find a niche. You may find it easier to start the courier service with a niche and become well-known in the circles of the industry you target. This way, you can be a big fish in a small sea instead of a small, unknown fish in a big sea.
   - After doing research on local businesses, you may want to narrow down your list of potential customers to medical or law offices. You can also focus on restaurants or other food service customers. You may want to target florists, banks, accountants, or caterers. Pick a niche and go for it!

6. Create a business plan. Establish clear goals for your local courier service.

Your initial steps matter as you begin your local courier service. You'll want to pay attention to local laws and regulations about couriers and small businesses and be compliant from the very start.

Finding Customers

Customers are the key to a successful local courier service. Target customers who are interested in working with a local provider.

You can find customers in many ways:

1. Consider picking up medical or hazardous items. This category always needs couriers, but you may need training and certification or special licensing.
   - You'll have to take special precautions with these items, but you can build a successful business.
2. Offer more than package delivery. Go beyond the typical package delivery and pick up services. Can you pick up specific items from a store and deliver them to their ustomers? Perhaps you could take care of everyone's lunch coffee orders. What about delivering and picking up someone's dry cleaning or taking on other errands?
3. Consider more flexible times. Early in the morning or late at night could bring in some extra business.
4. Create a website. Post details about the services you offer.
5. Expand your delivery area. How far can you drive for a customer? You may be able to find more customers by expanding your delivery area.

6. Focus on customers that need consistent deliveries. Customers who need regular deliveries will provide you with a constant stream of revenue.
    - These customers will be the core of your business. Repeat customers help build your reputation and give you a predictable income.

It's possible to build a long list of customers for your local courier service. You'll have enough business to keep you busy every day and to expand your services.

Marketing Your Business

Marketing is a crucial part of all successful local courier services. You're competing with large brands such as FedEx and UPS, so you'll have to target customers and find unique ways to build your business. Offer services that make you stand out from other couriers.

Consider these marketing tips:

1. Offer discounts for referrals or long-term business relationships. Customers love discounts, and referrals will help you grow.
2. Create a press release. Publish your press release online or in magazines and newspapers. Introduce your business and offer discounts for your grand opening.
3. Give away notepads, pens, or sticky notes. Include your courier business information on these materials.

- Individuals and businesses love free office supplies, so they'll gladly accept free notepads, pens, or sticky notes.
- Give long-term customers coffee mugs, flash drives, and other higher value gifts. They should still have your local courier service information printed on them. These items can serve as the perfect reminders of your business.

4. Network with local businesses. Do your local government agencies or small business associations offer networking events? Be sure to attend these events to network with potential customers and market your local courier service.

5. Don't be afraid of the competition. In some cases, you may want to network with other small courier businesses.
- If you work in different niches, you may not be competing directly with each other.
- Other courier businesses can offer valuable tips and advice to help you. They may also be willing to share customers if they're overwhelmed with work.

6. Pay for local advertising. Where can you advertise your local service?
- Billboards can be a good way to advertise a courier service. You can also pay for ads in local papers, magazines, or run online ads that are only shown to people in your locale.

7. Advertise your business on your car or bike. Purchase decals or magnetic signs with information about your local

courier service. Each time you are out working others will see your business ads.

8. Attend local fairs and other small business events. Do you know of any fairs or conferences that target small businesses?

- These events are a good place to meet businesses that may need couriers.
- Conferences can help you learn more about marketing and find new strategies to reach your customers.

9. onsider advertising on Craigslist and other online sites. Websites that allow you to place ads can help you find new courier customers.

10. Consider television ads. If you have the budget for it, television ads in your local area can help you reach new customers.

11. Consider online video ads. Create video ads online and post them on YouTube and other sites. If you make creative videos, your business name can go viral and reach many people online.

12. .Consider working with a charity. If you find a cause you're passionate about, it can also help your business. By working with a charity, you can get local news coverage.

- Local charities may also need help with packages or other items. For example, during the holiday season, many charities reach out to the poor and disadvantaged with gifts. You can help deliver these gifts for free.

13. Consider printing coupons in local coupon books. Does your city have local coupon books that offer discounts for using certain businesses? Join this offer and provide coupons.

14. Advertise in the phone book. Although it's not as popular as t used to be, the phone book is still used by many people. You can also place discount coupons for your courier service in the phone book.

Marketing is an essential part of your courier business plan. Create a clear marketing plan that includes advertising and networking.

Conclusion

Building a local courier service takes time and effort, but you'll be in control of your own income. The potential for growth is large for courier services. Businesses are in constant need of help and reach out to others for assistance with deliveries, errands, and other services. Find a target market, develop long-term relationships with clients that need regular deliveries, and you'll be on your way to a successful and prosperous courier service.

How to Use Social Media to Find Your Next Job

Social media is all the rage. Twitter, Facebook, LinkedIn, YouTube, and more seem to be everywhere. In social media like these, we get constant updates about the relevant and not-so-relevant aspects of everyone's lives.

Here, we'll consider a practical application of social media: finding your next job. Social media gives you great tools for sharing information electronically with a potentially very large audience.

Try these strategies to help you land a great job:
1. Focus your attention on people instead of companies. For instance, if you're interested in a particular company, look at blogs and on Facebook for people who work there. You're likely to also see the other people they know. Maybe you share an acquaintance or two. You can submit resumes to them, ask for advice, and get more contacts.
   - You'll want to be subtle; people are unlikely to be happy about being bombarded with job requests on their own time. By starting out with a few non-intrusive messages, you should be able to make in-roads toward your goal.
2. Start your own blog. By putting out content that showcases your knowledge and expertise, people will begin to see you as an expert. Blogs are easy to start, and many websites will host yours for free. Other than the work involved, it's free advertising for your skills.
3. Use Twitter. It's becoming common to hear stories of people getting laid off, sending out a few Tweets proclaiming their new unfortunate job status, and ultimately finding a new position as a result of their Tweets.

- With Twitter, word spreads quickly.
- Companies are beginning to use this tool as well, for this same reason. Recruiters use Twitter to announce positions and give updates.
- Here's a quick Twitter tutorial:
- Go to Twitter.com and fill out your profile completely, including a professional photo of yourself.
- Follow everyone you know. Also follow everyone who seems like they might be able to help you find a position.
- Tweet away.

4. Take advantage of video. In addition to more usual social media tools, video is becoming increasingly relevant. Upload a video resume to YouTube and let the world know what you can do and what you're looking for. Check out other video resumes to get a feel for how it's done.
   - When creating a video, keep brevity in mind. Explain your background; describe what you're looking for and why you'd be the best person for the job. Take your time and get it right - you can rerecord as often needed.

5. Consider Paid Advertising on Social Media. Also, consider Google AdWords and Facebook advertising to put the word out that you're in job-search mode. To do this, you'll need to make a landing page with your

resume. Adding a blog, video resume, and any publications you authored would be helpful as well. Social media is here to stay, so you might as well use it for something constructive. Finding employment is never enjoyable, but utilizing social media can really make a difference. Never before has the average person had so much capability to reach so many people. Craft your message and get it out there every way you can think of.

Seasonal Part-Time Jobs

When you run through suggestions of things to do to increase your income, you might find yourself at the end of the list with no real solution. However, the one point you can count on is that if you're willing to work extra time, you'll be able to boost your income.

The fact is that boosting your yearly income doesn't necessarily mean working more all year long. Instead, you can take additional, temporary part-time positions to bring in extra cash. Consider these ideas or think of your own to work short-term, seasonal part-time jobs:

1. Deliver phone books. This is a fantastic seasonal job. You choose your own hours and use your own vehicle to drop off phone books to people. Once the phone books are all delivered, you're done until next year's books come off the press. This seasonal, part-time job is about as flexible as you can get.

2. Work retail during Christmas-shopping season. Usually in late October or November and spanning through January, retailers look for dependable, hard-working extra help for the holiday season. Establish a relationship with the same retailer year after year.

   - You might even get a slight bump-up in pay every couple of seasons you work. Not to mention a discount on your own holiday purchases. This seasonal work will really pay off.

3. Shovel snow. Start your own side business of shoveling walks and drive-ways when it snows. If you drive a truck, consider purchasing a snow-blower or plow which will make you very decent money quickly and with less physical exertion when the white stuff comes down.

   - Once your neighbors see you out and about with your shovel or snow-blower, they'll be calling you over to take care of their snow. If you enjoy being physically active, you'll love this seasonal money-maker.

4. Mow lawns. If you love being outdoors in spring and summer, why not boost your income mowing lawns? Another job you can do in your own neighborhood, mowing lawns is a consistent job each year. Plus, there's a little flexibility in terms of scheduling this work around your full-time job.

   - Depending on the type of lawn mower you have, you'll get plenty of physical activity. And you can earn $20 to $50 or more, depending on the size of the lawn. But remember, when fall rolls around, this seasonal job is done.

5. Clean vacation properties. In the event you live in a community that enjoys a vacation season that floods your community with visitors, find work helping landlords and vacation property owners prepare homes and condos for vacationers. Once the season is over, you've earned your extra income until same time, next year.

6. House-sit. Speaking of vacations and vacationers, have you ever considered house-sitting as a seasonal or part-time job?

   - The upfront investment is low. You'll need some flyers or business cards that you make on your own computer for practically nothing. Then, you'll need transportation and a bit of organization to keep notes and keys for homes of people who're on vacation.
   - When you become a house-sitter, you might stay over in a vacationer's empty home to deter thefts while the owners are gone.
   - Some owners may not require you to stay over and just ask that you spend evenings in their homes so it appears someone is there. Keep the newspapers cleared away, lawns mowed or snow cleared, and a vehicle in the driveway occasionally.
   - Set your own rates to do house-sitting and earn additional income.

7. Be a tutor. Depending on your education and your level of comfort in working one on one with others, being a tutor is

a lucrative parttime job. What you'll find about tutoring is that some students will require tutoring during the school year or a month or two before exam time. Other students will need help through the summer.

- So technically, you could choose the season you want to do tutoring. Tutoring has its advantages: you'll earn $15-30+ per hour, you're indoors out of the weather and you get to make a difference in someone's life. What a great way to increase your income!

8. Help people clean out garages, sheds and closets. Believe it or not, there's quite a market doing this type of work. It's not exactly housecleaning. But you do help people, sort, organize, discard, donate, and re-organize these challenging spaces in their homes.

- You'll need a strong back, a free supply of cardboard boxes from your local grocery, work gloves, and plenty of garbage bags. Throw in some organizational skills and you've got a easonal, part-time job.

- Spring and summer are probably the best seasons to do this type of work. The jobs you get by word of mouth doing these ypes of tasks for pay will astound you.

- Do an estimate on each job separately before starting the work. List out what you understand your customer wants you to do so you can estimate the time and effort it will take. You'll be amazed at how much people are willing to pay to clean out, pack up and get rid of their junk. Plus, it brings in great seasonal income for you. A great solution to boosting your Income is taking on one of these seasonal part-time jobs!

Sources Of Temporary Income
While You're Looking For A Permanent Job

Have you been affected by the down economy? Are you struggling to make ends meet? While you may feel hard-pressed to find a job, there are many options that can pay your bills in the interim. Check out these suggestions and then see if you can brainstorm additional ideas of your own.

1. Get a part-time job. This is the first idea that may pop into your mind when you think of sources of temporary income.
   - Jobs that pay tips have the possibility of paying very well!
2. Freelance. Do you have skills that people need? Can you design websites? Good with graphics? A master with PowerPoint? Can you write decent articles quickly?
   - You may be able to find enough work to keep you pretty busy and might make more money than you would think.
   - Shop your services around; if you have some skills, someone needs them and will pay you for them. Look at freelance.com and elance.com for an idea of what's out there. Many other sites exist, too.
3. Fiverr.com has possibilities. Fiverr.com is a website that allows anyone to post a product or service that costs $5. The website takes $1, so your profit is really $4.

- If you can think of something that doesn't take a lot of time, you can make some decent spending money.
- There are also several other websites similar to Fiverr.com that allow you to charge up to $25 for quick services or products. A Google search for "Fiverr Clones" should call up several for you to consider.

4. Buy a storage unit at an auction. Or more correctly, purchase the contents of a storage unit. This practice can be hit or miss, but many people make a living from purchasing the contents of abandoned storage units and selling what you find.
   - Sell the junk at a garage sale and the good stuff on eBay. With a little luck, that $200 storage unit could be worth $10,000 or more.

5. Clean out the garage and attic. Some of the stuff you might see as junk, other people collect. Some items you never use, others may actually need. Unload the stuff you don't need or use anymore, and make some cash.
   - You can sell your unused items at a garage sale or on eBay.
   - Old toys, baseball cards, tools, and more can all be worth a surprising amount of money to the right buyer.

6. Consider the tasks most people don't like to do. Someone might be thrilled to pay you to cut their grass or walk their dog. In fact, you can make several hundred dollars in a weekend by maintaining a few customers' lawns. Here are some other examples:
   - No one likes to shovel snow off of their driveway.

- You could run errands or go shopping for someone. Just think about all the annoyances in the world and you'll be ble to find some work.

7. Sign-up with a temporary service. Most of the positions are unskilled, but there are some professional positions available and the money can be decent. Some jobs are just a day or two, but many are semi-permanent, and may even lead to full-time employment.

8. Buy garage sale items and re-sell for a profit. Spending Fridays and Saturdays snapping up bargains from garage sales and selling them at Flea Markets or on eBay can be very lucrative. This is also a profession that provides a full-time living with part-time hours for many folks.

9. Try landscaping. Landscaping has become a profitable hobby or full-time living for many. If you have a way with plants and an eye for design, you can charge a pretty penny for doing some landscaping and make some hefty profits.

10. Make money from your hobby. You can build furniture or decorative items, arts and crafts, create personalized scrapbooks, home-made gifts of all kinds, and so on.
    - If you don't have a hobby like this, the skills for many of them are easily learned and enjoyable as well.
    - Sell your items at flea markets, on Etsy.com or eBay, or spread the word through friends.

Being between jobs doesn't mean you have to do without income. You may have to swallow your pride with some of the solutions, but being without a job certainly doesn't have to be the end of the world. The ideas above are just a starting point and they can get you thinking about your options. As an added bonus, by earning any sort of temporary income, you'll be coming into contact with people who may be able to help you find a permanent position!

Questions to Ask Yourself Before Accepting a Job Offer

When times are challenging, it's easy to tell yourself that you'll take any job you can get. However, it's generally wise to be prudent. Accepting a job offer can alter the course of your life. You may have to move to a new city and adapt to a new work environment. Your future is also at stake. An unwise decision can be harmful to your finances, career, and happiness.

Ask yourself these important questions before accepting a job offer:

1. Can I be happy here? This is a very general question that takes all factors into consideration. It can also be a gut-level decision. There are companies that just "feel right" for some unknown reason. Others just feel wrong. Ask yourself if the overall culture and feel of the company are a good match for your preferences, needs, and personality.

2. Where is the company going? Even companies headed for bankruptcy can have positions to fill. Educate yourself on the past and projected future for the company. Is it in a dying industry? Is the company suffering financial

problems? What are the prospects for the company over the next 10-20 years?

3. Is my pay fair for the job description and my abilities? This is the most important factor for many job seekers. While money isn't everything, it's the primary reason 99% of us work.

   - Most jobs pay fairly, but this isn't always true. You should know what you're worth and what the market is willing to pay. Is your job offer in linewith the industry? Is the salary sufficient to meet your financial obligations?

4. Do I have room to grow? Smaller companies and departments can have limited opportunities for growth. This might be fine if you're a younger, single professional with the ability to move every three years. It might not be as feasible if you have school-age children that need more stability to thrive

5. Are the benefits adequate? Avoid only considering the salary. How much is the medical insurance? How good is the coverage? Is the 401(k) program attractive?

   - How much vacation will you receive? How many years will it take to earn another week of vacation? Consider all of the benefits before signing on the bottom line.

6. Do I like my supervisor? A new job can be great in every other way, but a bad boss can make your life miserable. The best managers are clear in their directions and grow their employees for the next level. Ensure that you can work effectively with your new boss.

7. Do I like my coworkers? There are few positions that don't require interacting with your coworkers. Ask to meet with the people that you'd be working with on a daily basis. Does it seem like a place with friendly, helpful people? You should already have a feel for the Human Resources department, too.

8. Will I enjoy living in this area? $50,000 a year might be enough to live like a king in rural Iowa, but you might find yourself struggling in Southern California. How do you feel about the climate and the people? Is there enough to do? If you love the city, living in the country might be difficult.

A new job offer is an exciting event. Few things can change your life more than a new job. Proceed cautiously and avoid focusing solely on the salary. There are many other factors to consider. Ask yourself the important questions before signing on the dotted line.

Conclusion

I hope that you have found this book helpful in finding ways for you to boost your income whether it's as a part-time job, your own business, or a way for you just to supplement your current income. I have personal experience in many of the ways listed and hope that these possibilities are beneficial to you on your journey ahead. Feel free to check out my YouTube channel http://youtube.com/c/consultablindguy Where I discuss all of these possibilities, I also have a course for beginner content creators for FREE. As well as a course for for sale for advancing your knowledge and skills with content creation. So definitely check them out. You can also find information on my website at https://consultablindguy.com

Feel free to reach out to me there in the comments or email me at andrew@consultablindguy.com These 100+ businesses are just some of the many opportunities out there for you do make an income from home, or start a business of your own. There are many more I will be covering in the future. If you would like to stay updated on more opportunities and updates for the next book head over to https://consult-a-blindguy.ck.page/wfh100 and sign up to the mailing list and get a FREE copy the 100 work from home ideas list. Good luck on your journey let me know if you have any success I would love to here how things go for you. An if you wouldn't mind please give this book a review it would be greatly appreciated.

Testimonials

Diana Art

Andrew at Consult a Blind Guy has given me a lot of help with the many aspects of content creation as a Youtuber. He often goes above and beyond to help with any question or tech issues our community has. He's very attentive to helping the community he serves. I've gotten help with content creation strategies, tech issues, as well as the business side of Youtube. And when he helps with an issue he is very thorough, most often making a video to answer our questions. I highly recommend his business services!

Lauren Wheatley

Andrew offers a friendly safe place to go to for advice whether it be for the blind/vip community tech problems or starting and growing your brand. It shows that he draws from a lot of experience but will ask for help or research the issue if he's not certain he has the best answer. Great person serving the blind/vip community.

Rodeline Jerome

Thank you so so much Andrew! You've no idea how much you help today! I had only 20 email subscribers on my list and now with your help, I have 780 emails! Great job man! God bless you.

Nicole Wheatley

A good listener and helpful ally. Willing to help even in matters he knows nothing about. His goal is for everyone to succeed ensuring that everyone's voice is heard

www.ingramcontent.com/pod-product-compliance
Lightning Source LLC
Chambersburg PA
CBHW081346280326
41927CB00042B/3075